TAX ASPECTS OF BUYING
AND LEASING BUSINESS
PROPERTY AND EQUIPMENT

TAX ASPECTS OF BUYING AND LEASING BUSINESS PROPERTY AND EQUIPMENT

Thomas F. Cunnanc

PRENTICE-HALL, INC.
Englewood Cliffs, N.J.

PRENTICE-HALL INTERNATIONAL, INC., *London*
PRENTICE-HALL OF AUSTRALIA, PTY. LTD., *Sydney*
PRENTICE-HALL OF CANADA, LTD., *Toronto*
PRENTICE-HALL OF INDIA PRIVATE LTD., *New Delhi*
PRENTICE-HALL OF JAPAN, INC., *Tokyo*

"This publication is designed to provide accurate and authoritative information in regard to the subject matter covered. It is sold with the understanding that the publisher is not engaged in rendering legal, accounting, or other professional service. If legal advice or other expert assistance is required, the services of a competent professional person should be sought."

*—From the Declaration of Principles jointly adopted by a
Committee of the American Bar Association and a Committee
of Publishers and Associations.*

Library of Congress Cataloging in Publication Data

Cunnane, Thomas F
  Tax aspects of buying and leasing business
property and equipment.

  Includes bibliographical references.
  1. Capital investments--United States. 2. Industrial equipment leases. 3. Leases--Taxation--United States. I. Title.
HG4028.C4C85   336.2'424'0973   74-1390
ISBN 0-13-884965-X

To My Wife, Mary

About the Author

Thomas F. Cunnane is a partner in the Philadelphia law firm of White and Williams. He counsels business, industry, and individuals on a wide range of tax matters, including the tax and financial aspects of purchasing and leasing business property and equipment.

The author has spoken before professional groups and is a contributor to tax and financial journals, including *Taxes, Journal of Accountancy* and the *Pennsylvania CPA Spokesman*.

Mr. Cunnane is a member, Section of Taxation, American Bar Association, the Philadelphia Bar Association, the Pennsylvania Institute of Certified Public Accountants and the American Institute of Certified Public Accountants. The author is a cum laude graduate of the University of Pennsylvania Law School.

Getting Full Value
from This Book

The decision to lease or to purchase business property and equipment is a complicated one involving the weighing of many factors. One factor which has become increasingly important is the tax aspect, i.e., would there be any tax advantage in leasing as opposed to purchasing? Determining whether there is a tax advantage to leasing is not an easy task. Basically, it involves a comparison of the writeoffs provided by leasing with those which would result from a purchase. Of critical importance, however, is a determination of whether the proposed rental deductions under the lease will be subject to attack by the Internal Revenue Service. Obviously, a businessman who chooses to lease rather than purchase, because of the faster writeoff resulting from the lease, will be at a serious disadvantage if the faster writeoff fails to materialize.

This book serves as a guide to those businessmen, and their professional advisers, who must make the decision to lease or to purchase. It should help them to understand better the tax aspects of both leasing and purchasing and enable them more intelligently to evaluate possible tax savings. In addition, since the scope of the book is not limited to the problems involved in deciding whether to purchase or lease, but includes problems which occur in the course of leases, or through the ownership of property, it should also be helpful in dealing with those problems which arise after the lease has been entered into or the purchase has been made.

Chapter 1 presents the advantages and disadvantages of leasing and purchasing. Chapters 2 through 7 focus on the tax problems involved in leasing. Chapter 2 (Lease or Purchase —Overcoming Problems of Classification) and Chapter 3 (The Rental Deduction—Solutions to Classification and Timing Problems) are addressed to the basic problem of whether to lease or purchase, and deal with the critical question of whether apparent tax savings resulting from leasing will survive attack by the Internal Revenue Service. In particular, Chapter 2 discusses those factors that might lead the Internal Revenue Service to reclassify an apparent lease as a purchase for tax purposes, with the resulting loss of the rental deduction. Chapter 3 deals with the situation where the Service concedes that the lease is valid but contends that a portion of the rent is nondeductible or is allocable to a later year. Chapter 4 (Costs of Acquiring a Lease—Leasehold Improvements) is directed primarily at leases of real estate and examines the tax rules governing payments to acquire a lease and leasehold improvements, with particular emphasis on the period over which these costs may be written off. Chapter 5 (The Fine Points of Termination, Cancellation, and Assignment of Leases) discusses the tax problems which arise when a lease ends. Chapter 6 (Realizing Tax Savings through Sale and Leaseback) points up the tax advantages of the sale and leaseback technique, illustrates those situations where it would be appropriate, and outlines possible areas of attack by the Internal Revenue Service. Chapter 7 (Trust and Leaseback: Its Advantages—Pitfalls to Avoid) deals with a variation of the sale and leaseback which has become very popular among small businessmen, particularly professional men.

Chapters 8 through 11 are devoted to the tax aspects of purchasing. Chapters 8 and 9 are relevant to the initial decision to lease or purchase. Chapter 8 deals with the tax problems involved in financing purchases and Chapter 9 discusses the methods of depreciation available to a purchaser, including the ADR system. Chapter 10 focuses on the tax consequences of disposing of property.

Chapter 11 discusses industrial development bonds and examines the circumstances under which they can be used to finance either the purchase or lease of property.

While, obviously, no book can answer all the tax problems that may arise in the course of leasing or purchasing, an effort has been made to discuss the basic questions and many of the more unusual as well. In addition, numerous examples have been used to clarify and illustrate the application of various tax rules, and citations have been provided where appropriate. It is hoped that the result will be a book which not only will familiarize the reader with the tax problems to be encountered in leasing or purchasing, but will help in resolving them.

Thomas F. Cunnane

Acknowledgments

The author acknowledges the assistance of Bernard V. Lentz, Esquire; Stephen H. Green, Esquire; and Stephen C. Zivitz, Esquire, with whom he discussed certain of the problems raised in this book. A particular debt of thanks is due to Brian Smith, C.P.A., who was kind enough to review a number of the chapters on leasing and who made a number of very cogent and helpful suggestions.

Special thanks is also due to my secretary, Miss Kathy Garrity, who typed and retyped numerous drafts without complaint.

Finally, the help of my wife, who edited a major portion of the manuscript, is gratefully acknowledged.

Contents

3. The Rental Deduction—Solutions to Classification and Timing Problems (Continued)

4. Determining Costs of Acquiring a Lease— Leasehold Improvements **55**

5. The Fine Points of Termination, Cancellation, and Assignment of Leases **73**

8. Purchasing—the Critical Tax Aspects of Financing the Purchase (Continued)

9. Techniques for Reducing the Tax Bite Through Depreciation, Repairs, and Improvements on Property **131**

TAX ASPECTS OF BUYING
AND LEASING BUSINESS
PROPERTY AND EQUIPMENT

Chapter 1

Leasing vs. Purchasing—Major Tax and Economic Considerations

A businessman faced with a need for additional property or equipment must decide whether to purchase it or lease it. Although this book focuses on the tax aspects of purchasing and leasing there are other considerations which should be taken into account if the right decision is to be made. This chapter is intended to afford some perspective by offering a general discussion of the factors, both tax and nontax, that should be considered in making a decision to lease or purchase.

REASONS FOR LEASING

There are a number of reasons why a businessman might decide to lease rather than purchase. The most obvious is because he is unable to purchase. This was the situation some years ago when certain manufacturers refused to sell their products and a businessman had no alternative but to lease. Today, there are few items that cannot be purchased, and a decision to lease involves other considerations such as financing, taxes, and obsolescence.

Financing Advantages

Leasing is often thought to be more advantageous than purchasing from a financing viewpoint. Whether this is true in individual cases depends to a large extent on the parties and property involved. There are, of course, situations where leasing offers the only method of financing. This would be the case where a business is unable to purchase because it cannot obtain adequate credit. In such situations, the business may still be able to obtain the use of property through leasing because the amount of credit involved is less (e.g., a lease of a $20,000 machine for 3 years at a rent of $2,000 a year involves credit of only $6,000 whereas a conditional sale of the same machine could involve credit of $20,000), and because lessors often are less concerned with credit ratings.

Even where leasing is not the only method of financing available, companies will frequently choose to lease rather than purchase. In some cases, this may be due to particular circumstances such as cumbersome indenture restrictions on additional borrowing which make it more practical to lease than to negotiate with the indenture holders for permission to borrow additional funds. In most cases, it is because the companies recognize that leasing is an alternative, and for them a more desirable, method of financing.

This might be so for a number of reasons. For one thing, leasing generally offers 100 percent financing in the sense that large initial payments are seldom required. The same is not always true of conventional financing arrangements which often require significant down-payments. Thus, a businessman might be able to finance 100 percent of the cost of an asset by leasing it whereas he could finance only 80 percent if he were to purchase it. This factor has become less important in recent years, at least insofar as equipment financing is concerned, because many sellers, in order to meet competition, are now offering financing terms comparable to those offered by lessors, i.e., small, or no, downpayments and liberal payment terms. It is still a very important consideration where real estate is involved.

In addition to the 100 percent financing aspect of leasing, there may also be a cash flow advantage due to the more rapid tax writeoff which can result from leasing. Although, as will be discussed, this is more characteristic of real estate than equipment leasing, it can be an extremely important factor.

Leasing can also be attractive to many corporations because of its off-balance-sheet financing possibilities. A corporation which borrows money to purchase a piece of equipment must reflect both the equipment and the corresponding liability on its balance sheet. If, however, the equipment is merely leased, then normally the company will have to reflect neither the asset cost nor the liability on the balance sheet. Since the latter treatment is much more desirable from the viewpoint of balance-sheet presentation, it is a factor which can be critical to many companies.

It should be noted that the treatment of leases in financial statements has been under study by both the Financial Accounting Standards Board and the SEC and this could result in a change in the above rule.

Tax Advantages

Leasing is frequently thought to be more advantageous from a tax viewpoint than purchasing. The theory is that rent is completely deductible; whereas a purchaser is limited to a depreciation deduction. The validity of this theory depends to a large extent on the nature of the property leased and the terms of the lease.

Insofar as machinery and equipment are concerned, it is true that, prior to the Internal Revenue Code of 1954, leasing tended to produce greater tax deductions in the early years than depreciation. The introduction, however, of the accelerated depreciation methods in the 1954 Code sharply increased the available depreciation writeoffs in the early years and tended to eliminate any advantage leasing might have had in this respect. Thus, today the leasing of machinery and equipment would appear to offer no significant tax advantage from the viewpoint of faster writeoffs.

The result would be different if the payments under the lease were structured in such a manner that the rent in the early years exceeded even accelerated depreciation. This could be done by providing very high rental payments for the first few years and low payments thereafter, or by means of short-term leases with renewal options, where the rent during the initial period approximates the purchase price and the rent for the renewal periods is nominal. Such arrangements, if upheld, would present a situation where leasing is more favorable tax-wise than purchasing. Unfortunately, lease terms such as the ones mentioned are almost certain to be attacked by the Internal Revenue Service, and a businessman presented with a situation where the rental deductions in the early years exceed accelerated depreciation should realize that there is a possibility (and in some cases, such as the ones mentioned, a probability) that what is in form a lease will be treated as a purchase for tax purposes.

The situation is somewhat different where real estate is concerned. The cutback in the availability of accelerated depreciation for nonresidential real estate as a result of the 1969 Tax Reform Act, and the nondepreciable nature of land, present a situation where leasing can be much more advantageous than purchasing. A businessman who leases, rather than purchases, improved real estate may be able to get a faster writeoff for the improvements than depreciation would produce and he can also take a deduction for the use of the land, a deduction not available to a purchaser. The price paid for the tax advantage is the relinquishment of the residual value. Many businessmen feel, however, that the additional cash flow resulting from the greater writeoffs offered by leasing more than offsets the loss of the residual value.

Although leasing may not offer any significant advantages from the viewpoint of faster writeoffs where machinery and equipment are concerned, it can be very helpful in insuring the effective utilization of the investment credit. The problem of utilizing the investment credit arises from the fact that although certain businesses, such as airlines, use tremendous amounts of equipment qualifying for the credit, their taxable incomes are not great enough to allow them to claim all the investment credit that would result from purchasing such equipment. In order to get around this problem, such companies have frequently entered into leasing arrangements whereby third parties, often limited partnerships set up to provide tax shelter, purchased the equipment and leased it to the companies at a rent which was reduced to reflect the shift of the investment credit to the third party. Thus, the companies were able to indirectly get the benefit of the investment credit through the reduced rental.

Such arrangements are still possible with one significant restriction. As a result of the Revenue Act of 1971 (Code section 46(d)(3)) a noncorporate third-party lessor may claim the investment credit only if (1) it manufactured or produced the property, or (2) the term of lease (taking into account options to renew) is less than 50 percent of the useful life of the property and the lessor's business expense deductions (other than rent and reimbursed expenses) related to the property are more than 15 percent of the rental income from the property for the first year of the lease. This provision, which was obviously aimed at the equipment-leasing limited partnerships set up for tax shelter, will not, however, affect leases involving corporate lessors, such as banks. Thus, it is still practical for companies to shift the investment credit by leasing rather than buying equipment.

In addition to the federal income tax aspects of leasing, there are often state and local tax aspects. In states which use formulas to allocate the income of multi-state businesses, leased assets are sometimes not taken into account. As a result, it may be possible for a multi-state business to reduce its overall state tax liability through a program of purchasing assets in some states and leasing in others. Also, in certain states and cities which impose taxes based on total capital or total assets, it may be possible to avoid a tax on equipment or property by leasing rather than purchasing.

Other Advantages

In addition to the possible financing and tax advantages of leasing, there are other advantages which may or may not be relevant in particular situations. For example, where a business is considering the purchase of equipment with a relatively high risk of obsolescence (e.g., computers), it is possible, and often advisable, to avoid the risk by leasing the equipment rather than purchasing it.

Leasing can also be of value to businesses which are interested in trying out equipment, but are not sure whether it can be successfully incorporated into their operations. A business faced with such a problem is far better off leasing rather than purchasing the equipment. The same thing is true of a company which has a temporary need for equipment or property. Leasing is the obvious answer.

One benefit frequently associated with leasing is the elimination of maintenance problems. This is because lessors often provide maintenance as part of the rental arrangement. This can be of value in many cases, but there are other situations where it is not really an advantage because the user already has its own servicing facilities.

In addition to the above, there are other benefits that can result from leasing. These are most commonly associated with the leasing of fleets of trucks and automobiles where the lessor, as part of the leasing arrangement, provides what is known as "complete service." This basically means that he will provide fuel, tires, repair parts, insurance, licensing, etc. Such an arrangement can result in savings in personnel for the lessee, and may in addition result in savings due to the lessor's ability to obtain volume discounts which he will pass along to the lessee.

PURCHASING AS AN ALTERNATIVE TO LEASING

Despite the advantages of leasing, many businesses continue to purchase rather than lease. There are a number of reasons why this is so. In some cases, it is not possible to lease and, therefore, the only alternative is purchasing. This was more true in the past, before the advent of leasing companies, than it is today, but even now there are times when leasing is not possible. For example, a company which wants to acquire a piece of real estate may find that the owner is not interested in leasing the property and that the only way to obtain it is by purchasing it. In some cases, particularly where the real estate is improved, it may be possible to arrange for a group of investors to buy the property and then lease it to the company, thus avoiding the need for the company itself to purchase. Where the property is unimproved, or otherwise unattractive to investors, there may be no alternative to outright purchase.

Even where leasing is possible, a lack of awareness of the advantages of leasing on the part of the prospective buyer, or the complexities of arranging a lease, particularly where third-party investors must be brought into the picture, may result, almost by default, in a decision to purchase.

Finally, it must be recognized that although leasing can, in general, offer significant advantages, these advantages may not be present in every case.

COMPARING THE COST OF LEASING
WITH THE COST OF PURCHASING

Obviously, a critical element in any decision to lease or purchase is a comparison of the relative costs. Cost, unfortunately, is not always easy to determine. One might start off by comparing the total rental payments to be made under the lease with the selling price of the property. For example, a businessman who has the option of buying a machine for $7,500 or renting it for five years at a rental of $1,700 a year will find that the total of the rental payments will exceed the purchase price of the machine by $1,000.

This is only the start, however, because the purchase of an item means either immediate payment in full or a series of payments. Both involve an interest factor which must be added to the purchase price in order to determine the true cost of purchasing.

Where the purchaser plans to borrow the purchase price from a bank or other lending institution, or to purchase under an installment sales contract, the interest cost is generally fairly easy to compute. The situation is a little more complicated when the purchaser must go to the market, i.e., issue bonds or debentures to finance the purchase, since the interest cost will depend on the market at the time the bonds or debentures are issued and thus may be somewhat unpredictable. In addition, the issuance of such securities will involve legal, accounting, and underwriting fees which must be treated as a cost of borrowing. Where a company chooses to purchase an asset without borrowing from outside sources, the interest cost is the amount the company could otherwise have earned with the money. For example, if a company could have earned 10 percent a year with the money it uses to purchase a machine, then the cost of financing the purchase internally is 10 percent a year.

The amount and timing of the depreciation deductions a purchaser would be entitled to, as compared with the rental deductions a lessee would be entitled to, are also important in determining the cost of leasing versus purchasing. Where land and buildings are involved, leasing will often produce tax deductions both earlier and greater in amount than purchasing. The same is generally not true where equipment is concerned.

Where leasing does produce greater and faster tax writeoffs, as in the case of land and buildings, the difference can be a critical one since the amount that can be earned on the increased cash flow resulting from the additional deductions reduces the net cost of leasing. It is this increased cash flow, and the money that can be earned with it, that often makes leasing less expensive than purchasing. The corollary is that a lease which does not produce faster writeoffs than a purchase is often, although not always, a more expensive arrangement than purchasing.

Although the interest charges and the amount and timing of tax deductions are critical factors in evaluating the cost of leasing versus purchasing, there are other factors which may or may not come into play. Maintenance expense is an example. An agreement by the lessor to provide free maintenance will reduce the cost of leasing as will the ability of a lessor to purchase at a discount which he is prepared to pass along in whole or in part to the lessee.

The cost of insurance should also be considered. Where property is leased, the landlord will generally carry adequate fire and liability insurance and pass the cost on to the lessee in the form of rent. Unfortunately, since the landlord, not the lessee, is the insured the lessee may find itself sued by the insurance company should a fire or other liability occur as a result of the lessee's negligence. In order to protect against such a possibility the lessee may want to insure itself against such risks. This, however, means that the lessee is in effect paying for insurance twice.

One factor which should not be overlooked in comparing the cost of leasing with that of purchasing is residual value. Unlike a purchaser, a lessee normally has no interest in the residual value, i.e., the right to the item leased after the lease term has expired. In some cases, this residual value is of dubious worth, particularly with items like machinery and equipment which have a useful life not greatly in excess of the lease term. In other cases, for example, where land is involved, the residual may be quite valuable.

Residual value can often be the critical factor in a decision to purchase rather than lease. Even where the current cost of leasing is considerably less than that of purchasing, many companies choose to purchase because they conclude the residual value of the property is worth more than the current saving that leasing will produce.

Chapter 2

Lease or Purchase—Overcoming
Problems of Classification

As discussed in Chapter 1, leasing can, in certain cases, offer tax advantages. In making a decision to lease based on tax considerations, however, it is important to consider the possibility of the Internal Revenue Service attempting to reclassify the lease as a purchase for tax purposes.

The Service will attempt such reclassification in situations where it feels the lessee is in substance the owner of the property rather than a mere lessee. For example, a lessee who leases equipment with a useful life of only ten years for five years, with an option to renew for an additional five years at a nominal rental, will generally be treated as having purchased rather than leased the property. Similarly, a lessee who leases land for 20 years, but has an option to purchase at a nominal price, will also be treated as a purchaser rather than a lessee. In both cases, the tax advantages of leasing will be denied because the "lease" puts the "lessee" in the economic position of owner rather than that of lessee.

The Service will not, of course, attack leases where the tax advantages are legitimate. For example, a business which leases a piece of used equipment for a term significantly less than its useful life may wind up with a rental deduction which exceeds the deductions it could have claimed had it purchased the equipment, but it has paid for the larger deduction by forfeiting any right to the equipment after the lease term. Similarly, a business which leases land, but which under the lease has no option to purchase, may be getting a deduction for what is a nondepreciable asset, but it has earned that deduction by giving up any right to the land after the lease period.

REVENUE RULING 55–540

The Service has issued a number of revenue rulings that deal with the problem of when a lease will, for tax purposes, be treated as a purchase. The most important of these rulings is Revenue Ruling 55–540 which sets forth guidelines to be used in determining the tax implications of leases of business equipment.

Revenue Ruling 55–540[1] starts out by recognizing that new and unique types of agreements have been developed to meet the needs of users of industrial and business equipment. It further recognizes that whether an agreement, which is in form a lease, is in substance a conditional sales contract depends on the intent of the parties as evidenced by the terms of the agreement, considered in the light of the facts and circumstances existing at the time it was executed. It also acknowledges that in determining the intent of the parties no general rule, applicable to all cases, can be laid down, and that each case must be considered in the light of its own particular facts. It then goes on to state that in the absence of compelling persuasive factors to the contrary, an intent warranting the classification of a transaction for tax purposes as a sale rather than a lease will generally be found where one or more of the following conditions are met:

1. Portions of the periodic payments are made specifically applicable to an equity to be acquired by the lessee.

2. The lessee will acquire title upon the payment of a stated amount of "rentals" which, under the contract, he is required to make.

3. The total amount that the lessee is required to pay for a relatively short period of use constitutes an inordinately large proportion of the total sum required to be paid to secure the transfer of title.

4. The agreed "rental" payments materially exceed the current fair rental value.

5. The property may be acquired under a purchase option at a price which is nominal in relation to the value of the property at the time when the option may be exercised, as determined at the time of entering the original agreement, or which is a relatively small amount when compared with the total payments to be made.

6. Some portion of the periodic payments is specifically designated as interest or is otherwise readily recognizable as the equivalent of interest.

The ruling also points out that the fact that an agreement makes no provision for the transfer of title or specifically precludes transfer of title does not in itself exclude the transaction from being classified as a sale.

After setting forth the guidelines to be used in determining whether a transaction should be treated as a lease or a purchase, Revenue Ruling 55-540 then applies the guidelines to various types of agreements giving the following examples:

A. Short-term agreements which usually concern mobile equipment or relatively small articles of equipment. The "compensation for use" provisions in these agreements are usually expressed in terms of an hourly, daily, or weekly rental, and the

---

[1] 1955-2 C.B. 39.

rental rates are relatively high in relation to the value of the article. There may be an option to purchase the equipment at a price fixed in advance which will approximate the fair market value of the equipment at the time of the election to exercise the option. In this type of agreement, all costs of repairs, maintenance, taxes, insurance, etc., are obligations of the lessor. (Agreements of this type will usually be considered to be "true" leases.)

B. Agreements entered into by taxpayers engaged in the business of leasing personal property to others, either as their principal business activity or incidental thereto. Under the terms of these agreements, the amounts payable, called rental rates, are ordinarily based on normal operations or use, plus a surcharge for operations in excess of the normal stated usage. In some instances, the rental is based on units produced or mileage operated. Termination of the agreement at stated periods is provided upon due notice by either party. If the agreement includes an option to purchase, the option price has no relation to the amounts paid as rentals. (Such arrangements will normally be considered to be "true" leases.)

C. Agreements providing for a "rental" over a comparatively short period of time in relation to the life of the equipment. The agreed "rental" payments fully cover the normal purchase price plus interest. Title usually passes to the lessee upon the payment of a stated amount of "rental" or on termination of the agreement upon the payment of an amount which, when added to the "rental" paid, approximates the normal purchase price of the equipment plus interest. (Such transactions will generally be treated as purchases rather than leases.)

D. Agreements which provide for the payment of "rental" for a short original term in relation to the expected life of the equipment, with provision for continued use over substantially all of the remaining useful life of the equipment. During the initial term of the agreement, the "rental" approximates the normal purchase price of the equipment, plus interest, while the "rentals" during the remaining term or renewal period or periods are insignificant when compared to the initial rental. These agreements may or may not provide for an option to acquire legal title to the equipment upon the termination of the initial period or at any stated time thereafter. (Agreements of this type will generally be treated as purchases.)

E. Agreements similar to the arrangement in D. above, but with the added factor that the manufacturer of the equipment purports to sell it to a credit or finance company, which either takes an assignment of such an existing agreement with the user or itself later enters into such an agreement with the user. In some instances, the lessor may be a trustee acting for or on behalf of the original vendor. (These agreements will also usually be considered to be purchases.)

In addition to the general guidelines set forth in Revenue Ruling 55-540, the Internal Revenue Service has published a number of other Revenue Rulings giving specific examples of situations where an agreement which is in form a lease will be treated as a purchase. There are also numerous court cases dealing with the problem and perhaps the best way of examining the issue is to list and discuss those factors that the Internal Revenue Service and the courts have found relevant in determining whether a transaction is a lease or a purchase.

RIGHT TO OFFSET RENTAL PAYMENTS
AGAINST PURCHASE PRICE

The most obvious case where a lease will be treated as a purchase involves the situation where the agreement provides that the lessee either acquires title or has the right to take title upon completion of all the rental payments.

> *Example:* Taxpayer rents a piece of machinery for eight years at a rental of $3,000 a year. The rental agreement provides that at the end of the eighth year title will pass automatically to the taxpayer.

In such a situation, it is obvious that the lessee, if not in form a purchaser, is certainly in substance a purchaser, and should be treated as such.[2]

The situation is somewhat different where the lessee has a right to purchase the property by crediting rental payments already made against the purchase price.

> *Example:* Taxpayer rents a building for ten years at a rental of $20,000 a year. At any time, taxpayer has the right to buy the building for $250,000 and credit any rent previously paid against the purchase price.

Such an arrangement, while not insuring that title will pass to the lessee, does give him an equity interest of sorts and raises a serious question as to the true nature of the transaction. As a result, it is quite likely that any transaction allowing the lessee to credit rental payments against the purchase price will be carefully scrutinized by the Internal Revenue Service with the disallowance of the rental deduction under Revenue Ruling 55–540 an almost inevitable result.

Whether the Commissioner's disallowance will be upheld by the courts depends to a large extent on the particular facts involved. One writer has suggested that where a lease expressly provides that all or a portion of the rental payments are to be credited against the option price, then the payments will, in all probability, be disallowed as rent to the extent that they can be so applied.[3] While there is considerable truth in such a statement, it should be recognized that not all the cases involving a right to offset rental payments against the purchase price have been decided adversely to the taxpayer. There have been a number of recent cases, primarily in the Tax Court, where lease treatment has been upheld despite the right of the lessee to credit rental payments already made against the option price. For example, the *Norman Baker Smith*[4] case involved a situation where the taxpayer leased a piece of improved real estate for a period of five years at a monthly rental of $350. At any time within the five-year period the lessee had

---

[2] See *Truman Bowen*, 12 T.C. 446 (1949), acq. 1951-2 C.B. 1; *Chicago Stoker Corporation*, 14 T.C. 441 (1950).
[3] Anderson, *Tax Planning of Real Estate, 6th Edition*, page 203.
[4] 51 T.C. 429 (1968).

the option to purchase the property for a price of $75,000 with 25 percent of the rents previously paid being applied against the purchase price.

Although only a portion of the rent paid could be credited against the purchase price, the court did not rely on this as the basis for its decision in favor of the taxpayer. Rather, the court held the arrangement was a lease because the transaction in its entirety had the characteristics of a lease, pointing specifically to the fact that a substantial payment in excess of the credited rental payments was required to exercise the option.

A similar result was reached in the *Estate of Clara Stundun*[5] where the taxpayer had leased an apartment house for a 25-month period at a rental of $2,200 a month with all rental payments to apply against the option price of $240,000. Despite the right of the lessee to credit the rent paid against the purchase price, the court held the transaction to be a lease, again pointing to the fact that a substantial additional payment was required upon exercise of the option. The court also relied heavily on the fact that the seller-lessor had specifically insisted on the lease-option rather than an outright sale in order to protect her security position in the event the lessees-buyers were unable to make the appropriate payments during the first years.

The rule the above cases (and the other cases cited in footnote 5) seem to be following is that a transaction will be upheld as a lease, even where the option price is determined by reference to the price at which the lessee could have originally purchased the property and rental payments are offset against such option price, provided a substantial additional payment is required and the transaction otherwise has the characteristics of a lease.

> *Example;* A leases a building, which he could buy for $150,000, for five years at a rental of $10,000 a year. A has the option at any time during the term of the lease to buy the building for $150,000 with prior rental payments being credited against the purchase price. Assuming the transaction otherwise has the characteristics of a lease, the right to credit prior rental payments against the purchase price will probably not result in the lease being treated as a purchase. If, however, the rental payments were $28,000 a year and A had the right to purchase the property for $150,000 with prior rental payments being credited against the purchase price then the lease might very well be treated as a purchase.

OPTION TO PURCHASE

Even where the lessee does not have a right to offset rental payments against the option price, the very existence of the option itself can result in the transaction being questioned.

Because it is frequently impossible[6] to determine whether an option to purchase will be exercised or not, it has been suggested that for tax purposes the characterization of amounts paid as rent under such leases should be deferred until such time as the lessee has either exercised or not exercised the option. This would mean that the lessee would not be entitled to

---

[5] 1970 P-H T.C. Memo ¶ 70,020. See also, *Kitchin v. Comm.*, 353 F.2d 13 (4th Cir., 1965); *Tomlison v. U.S.*, 6 A.F.T.R.2d 5304 (D.C. Ark., 5-25-60); and *WBSR, Inc.*, 30 T.C. 747 (1958), acq. 1958-2 C.B. 8.

[6] There can, of course, be cases where the option arrangement is so favorable to the lessee that it is obvious that the option will be exercised.

a rental deduction and the lessor would not be taxed on rental income until it became apparent whether or not the option would be exercised at which time the transaction could be characterized as a true lease or a conditional sale. The Fourth Circuit actually adopted such a view for a time in the famous *Kitchin* case.[7] Ultimately, however, because of various problems (e.g., who would be entitled to depreciation), the Fourth Circuit reversed itself[8] and it is now settled that a transaction must be classified initially as either a lease or a conditional sale.

Classifying a lease with an option to purchase as a true lease or as a conditional sale is, unfortunately, not always an easy matter. The clearest cases are those where the option price is obviously nominal.

> *Example:* Taxpayer leases a tract of land for ten years at a rental of $10,000 a year and at the end of the tenth year has the option to purchase the land for a dollar.

A nominal option price will invariably result in the classification of a purported lease as a conditional sale. Thus in *Oesterreich v. Comm'r.*,[9] the Ninth Circuit had no difficulty in classifying a 68-year lease of real estate as a sale where the agreement gave the lessee the right to take title at the end of the term upon the payment of $10. Similarly, the Tax Court had no difficulty in classifying an alleged lease as a conditional sale where the lease term was for one year at a rental of $895 a month with an option to purchase at the end of the year for $1.[10]

How substantial the option price must be before it moves out of the "nominal" class is difficult to say. Furthermore, substantiality of the option price is not in itself conclusive. The real test is whether the parties intended a lease or a conditional sale. If the intent is found to be the latter, the fact that the option price is substantial is irrelevant. This is clearly illustrated by the *Berry*[11] case where an agreement to rent for two years at a total rent of $30,000, with an option to purchase, was held to be a conditional sale despite the fact that the option price was $100,000.

Recognizing that the substantiality of the option price is not in itself sufficient to guarantee lease treatment, what sort of an option price will justify lease treatment? The answer is an option price which represents the expected fair market value of the property. One way to arrive at such a value is to provide for an independent appraisal at the time the option is exercised. An appraisal is not essential, however, and the parties may set the option price at the time of entering into the lease. Such an option price will be upheld provided it reflects the *expected* fair market value of the property at the time when the option becomes exercisable. The fact that subsequent developments alter the fair market value of the property is irrelevant.[12]

---

[7] 340 F.2d 895 (1965).

[8] 353 F.2d 13 (1965).

[9] 226 F.2d 798 (9th Cir., 1955).

[10] *Quartzite Stone Co.*, 30 T.C. 511 (1958), *non. acq.* 1959-1 C.B.6, *aff'd on another issue* 273 F.2d 738 (10th Cir.).

[11] *Marvin Berry*, 1952 P-H T.C. Memo ¶ 52,093.

[12] *Benton v. Comm.*, 197 F.2d 745 (5th Cir., 1952).

Example: A and B negotiate a lease whereby A will lease an office building for ten years at a rental of $10,000 a year. A insists on having an option to purchase the building at the end of the ten years. After consulting with an independent real estate broker who advises them that the anticipated fair market value of the building in ten years will be approximately $100,000, the parties include in the agreement an option for A to purchase the building at the end of the lease term for $100,000. In the seventh year of the lease, an industrial development park is started nearby and it becomes obvious that the building will be worth far more than $100,000 in three years when the lease ends. Despite the fact that the option price no longer represents fair market value, the lease will not be reclassified as a purchase since the option price did represent the expected fair market value when the lease was entered into.

RELATIONSHIP OF LEASE TERM TO USEFUL LIFE OF PROPERTY

Although the presence of an option to purchase may raise a question as to whether a lease is a true lease, the absence of an option to purchase does not guarantee lease treatment. There is also serious danger that a lease will be treated as a purchase where the term of the lease approximates the useful life of the leased property. An example would be the situation where a taxpayer leases for nine years property with an anticipated useful life of only ten years.

Obviously, where the lease term *exceeds* the anticipated useful life of the property, the lessor has for all practical purposes sold the property. Thus, a lease for ten years of property with a useful life of eight years will, and should be, treated as a sale rather than a lease. As one writer put it ". . . it is difficult to conceive of why a 'lease' for a period substantially equal to, or in excess of, the useful life of the property should not be treated as a sale."[13]

It is, of course, not necessary for the lease term clearly to exceed the expected useful life of the property in order for a lease to be treated as a purchase, and a question arises as to just how close the two can be before the Internal Revenue Service will attempt to treat the transaction as a purchase.

The only published ruling on the subject is Revenue Ruling 55–541.[14] Revenue Ruling 55–541 involved the situation where equipment with a 10-to-15-year useful life was leased for a term of 13 years. The Service held that the purported lease was a conditional sale rather than a lease. Although there were other factors in Revenue Ruling 55–541 that would call for the same result,[15] the ruling does suggest that it must be reasonably clear that the useful life is in excess of the lease term if an attack is to be avoided.

---

[13] Zeitlin, *Tax Planning In Equipment—Leasing Shelters,* 21st Tax Institute—University of Southern California, 621 at 641 (1969).

[14] 1955-2 C.B. 19.

[15] E.g., the aggregate rentals for the first three years exceeded the list price of the equipment and the rental for the renewal period of ten years was nominal.

OPTIONS TO RENEW

Even where the lease term does not approximate the useful life of the property, there may be problems where there are options to renew.

If the options to renew are at the same rental as in the original lease, there should be no problem. If, however, the rental for the renewal period is significantly less than the rental for the original period, then there is a possibility the Internal Revenue Service will question the transaction. The problem the Service is concerned with is illustrated by Revenue Ruling 60–122[16] which deals with the following situation:

> Under a "Long-term Rental Contract," corporation C furnished an item of equipment to corporation A for an initial period of 36 months for a total consideration of $462x. The contract provided for indefinite renewal after the 36-month period, in one-year periods at $30x per year which includes what would ordinarily constitute a maintenance charge of $22x per year. The price of such item, if purchased outright, would be $370x.

The Internal Revenue Service held that under these facts the transaction should be treated as a sale rather than a lease. There were two reasons for this conclusion. One, the total amount paid in the first 36 months exceeded the outright purchase price of the equipment. Two, since the rent for the indefinite renewal periods, exclusive of the maintenance charge, was nominal, the lessee as a practical matter had a right to use the property for its useful life. The combination of the two factors led the Service to conclude that the parties had intended a conditional sale rather than a lease.

Although the Service's position has obvious merit, a district court case, *Gem, Inc.*[17] poses a problem in the application of Revenue Ruling 60–122. In the *Gem* case, a taxpayer leased a plant from a county in Mississippi for 20 years with renewal rights for another 79 years at a nominal rental. The rent for the first 20 years was sufficient to pay both principal and interest on the bonds which had been floated to pay for the cost of building the plant. This, coupled with the nominal rent for the renewal periods, resulted in a situation almost identical to that of Revenue Ruling 60–122 (which was not mentioned in the opinion),[18] and the Service attacked the taxpayer's rental deductions on the theory that a portion of the rent represented payment for an equity interest in the property.

Interestingly enough, the court rejected the Commissioner's argument and allowed the taxpayer's rental deductions on the ground that the Internal Revenue Service had not shown that there was a reasonable certainty that the taxpayer would exercise its options to renew. The imposition of the burden of showing a reasonable certainty of renewal on the Service is in sharp contrast with Revenue Ruling 60–122 which assumes that under the circumstances the renewal options will be exercised and would place the burden on the taxpayer to show otherwise.

---

[16] 1960-1 C.B. 56.

[17] 192 F. Supp. 841 (N.D. Miss., 1961).

[18] Presumably Revenue Ruling 60-122 had not as yet been issued when the case was argued.

The *Gem* case aside, it should be noted that it is not necessary for the Commissioner to show that the taxpayer has an equity in the property, that is, that a conditional sale rather than a lease was intended, in order for the Commissioner to attack leases with options to renew. He can also do so on the ground that even though the lease is a true lease, a portion of the rentals paid during the early years constitutes "advance rentals" applicable to later years. This problem will be discussed more fully in a later chapter.[19]

RELATIONSHIP OF RENT TO FAIR RENTAL VALUE

The relationship of the rent to the current fair rental value of the property is certainly one of the most, if not the most, important factors involved in the determination of whether a "lease" is to be considered a true lease or a conditional sale. As one writer has pointed out:

> if it can be established that the amount of the rental payments is equivalent to "fair rental value" or some other rational basis, the government will have considerable difficulty in sustaining a position that the transaction was a conditional sale.[20]

This is true even in the presence of other factors which would normally dictate conditional sale treatment. For example, the *Kitchin* case, cited previously for another point,[21] involved the situation where the lessee had an option to purchase, with previous rentals to be applied against the purchase price. Although such an arrangement will frequently result in conditional sale treatment, the lease was held to be a true lease by the Fourth Circuit because it was clear that the periodic payments represented a fair return for the use of the property.

Of course, the relationship of the rent called for in the lease to the fair rental value of the property does not always work in favor of the taxpayer. Where it is reasonably clear that the rent required under the terms of the lease exceeds the fair rental value, and one of the preceding factors such as an option to purchase is present, a court will invariably conclude that a conditional sale was intended.

If the rent called for under the lease exceeds the fair rental value of the property but none of the other factors discussed in this chapter is present, then the excess rent is either the result of a miscalculation by both parties as to the true rental value of the property, or a bad bargain by the lessee. Whichever the cause, an attempt to reclassify the lease as a conditional sale would, under such circumstances, clearly be unwarranted since the parties intended a true lease.

OTHER FACTORS

Although the items we have discussed are the more significant ones in determining whether a lease is a true lease or a conditional sale, there are other factors that can be important. The fact that a portion of the payments by the lessee is specifically designated as, or

---

[19] Chapter 3.
[20] Katcher, *Bureau of National Affairs Tax Management Portfolio* #12-3rd at A-35.
[21] *Kitchin v. Comm.*, 353 F.2d 13 (9th Cir., 1965).

readily recognized as the equivalent of, interest is obviously relevant in determining whether a conditional sale was intended. For example, in the *Judson Mills* case,[22] a textile manufacturer acquired new machinery under various agreements which required fixed monthly rental payments for approximately five years, after which the taxpayer could purchase the machinery for relatively small amounts. Despite the fact that the agreements purported to be leases, correspondence between the taxpayer and the sellers allocated the total payments between principal and interest, and schedules were included with the seller's letters showing what portion of each monthly payment represented principal and which represented interest. With such background, the Tax Court had no difficulty concluding that the "leases" were really conditional sales agreements.

There is also serious question as to whether the parties intended a true lease where the lessee makes significant improvements which have a useful life in excess of the lease term. For instance, in the *Lensing* case,[23] the taxpayer entered into an agreement whereby he agreed to lease a farm to another party for two years at a rental of $25,000 a year. The lessee was given an option, which he subsequently exercised, to purchase the farm within the lease term at a price of $115,000 with prior rental payments to be applied in full against the purchase price.

The taxpayer treated the rental payments of $50,000 as proceeds from the sale of real estate rather than rent and reported the gain on the installment basis. The Commissioner took the position that the agreement was a true lease and attempted to tax the $50,000 as ordinary income. The taxpayer contested the deficiency and the case ended up in the Tax Court which, in a memorandum decision, decided in favor of the taxpayer. One of the factors which strongly influenced the court's decision was the fact that the lessee upon taking possession of the land had made extensive permanent improvements costing approximately $20,000, and had also removed the fences encircling the property. The Tax Court felt that these were simply not acts of a mere lessee.

The absence of a true reversionary right in the lessor also tends to lead to the conclusion that a purported lease is actually a sale. This is illustrated by the *Starr* case[24] in which the lessee rented a sprinkler system for a period of five years at an annual rental of $1,240 with an option to renew for an additional five years at a rental of $32 a year. If the lessee did not renew the lease, the lessor had six months in which to remove the system from the lessee's premises.

Since sprinkler systems are usually tailor-made for a specific property, and since the cost of removal could be substantial, it was obvious that the lessor's reversionary right was for all practical purposes worthless and this was a strong factor leading to the court's conclusion that the parties intended a sale rather than a lease.

---

[22] *Judson Mills*, 11 T.C. 25 (1948), acq. 1949-1 C.B. 2.
[23] *George S. Lensing*, 1961 P-H T.C. Memo ¶ 61,268.
[24] *Estate of Delano T. Starr v. Comm.*, 274 F.2d 294 (9th Cir., 1959).

CONSEQUENCES OF A LEASE BEING
TREATED AS A PURCHASE

Assuming, because of the presence of one or more of the aforementioned factors, a transaction is determined to be a conditional sale rather than a true lease, what are the consequences of such a characterization?

The most obvious consequence of having a lease treated as a purchase is that the lessee-purchaser is not allowed a deduction for rent but instead is allowed interest and depreciation deductions. This may not be critical in situations where tax advantages were not the reason for choosing to lease rather than purchase, but obviously in those situations where the lease was chosen primarily for tax reasons the result can be quite unfavorable. Presumably in such cases, the lease payments were structured so as to give the lessees faster writeoffs than they would otherwise have received.

> *Example:* Taxpayer leases a tract of land for $50,000 a year for ten years. Under the terms of the lease, the taxpayer has an option to purchase the property at the end of the lease for $100,000. Should the Internal Revenue Service successfully reclassify the lease as a purchase, the taxpayer will lose his rental deduction of $50,000 a year and, since land is a nondepreciable asset, will be entitled to claim a deduction only for the interest element of each $50,000 payment.

Suppose that the property involved is depreciable, and therefore, the taxpayer is entitled to a depreciation as well as an interest deduction, must the depreciation deduction be computed under the straight line method or can an accelerated method be used? In other words, has the taxpayer forfeited the right to elect an accelerated depreciation method by failing to elect it initially?

An analysis of the Regulations would indicate that there is no reason why the depreciation allowance cannot be computed using one of the accelerated methods of depreciation since Reg. 1.167(a)-10 specifically provides that where a taxpayer fails to claim an allowance for depreciation because he erroneously treated a capital item as a deductible expense, he is not precluded from using one of the accelerated methods of depreciation provided in Section 167(b).

The question of the additional 20 percent first year depreciation allowance presents difficulties. It would appear that under the Regulations this election must be made in the initial return, and cannot be made at a later date.[25] Therefore, the failure to claim purchase treatment initially would have the effect of precluding the election of the additional 20 percent first year depreciation.

To the extent that any of the years in which the lessee claimed a rental deduction are barred by the Statute of Limitations, such rental payments cannot, of course, be treated as part

---

[25] Reg. 1.179-4(a).

of the basis of the property for depreciation purposes since to do so would in effect permit a double deduction.[26]

> *Example:* Taxpayer leases a machine for five years at a rental of $20,000 a year with options to renew for an additional ten years at a rental of $1,000 a year. The taxpayer's return is examined in the fifth year of the lease, after the Statute of Limitations has run on the first year, and the rental deductions for the second through the fifth years are disallowed on the ground that the lease is really a purchase. In computing the depreciation deductions for the second through the fifth years, the taxpayer must use a basis for the property of $90,000 ($110,000 total payments less $20,000 first-year payment which the Commissioner could not disallow because the Statute of Limitations had run on it).

In addition to a depreciation deduction, the lessee-purchaser is also entitled to an interest deduction to the extent that a portion of the "rental payments" represents interest. Prior to the enactment of the imputed interest rules of Section 483, the amount of the interest deduction varied depending on the particular facts and circumstances of each case. For example in the *Frenzel* case,[27] the Tax Court allowed an interest deduction at the rate of 5 percent since the lessor had set the rent to provide for repayment of its investment plus a 5 percent return. In the *Estate of Starr*,[28] the Ninth Circuit suggested that the interest deduction might be determined by amortizing over the term of the lease the amount by which the total "rental" payments exceeded the normal selling price of the item in question; or, alternatively by using an interest rate of 6 percent since the fire loss provision of the contract used this as the discount rate.

Subsequently, however, in the *Wilshire* case,[29] the Ninth Circuit modified its suggestion that the interest portion of the payments might be determined by deducting the normal selling price of the asset from the total payments due under the agreement and imposed the further restriction that the interest portion of each payment could not exceed the highest rate allowed under local law (12 percent). The court was forced to this restriction by the facts of the *Wilshire* case which would have resulted in a fantastic rate of interest in the last years of the lease since the total amount due under the 68-year lease was $700,000 and the fair market value of the property was only $75,000. The *Wilshire* case should not, however, be taken as authority for the proposition that the taxpayer *must* be allowed a deduction for the highest rate of interest allowed under local law since it was the government's failure to introduce evidence as to the normal "going" rate that led the court to set the interest at the legal limit of 12 percent, notwithstanding its recognition of the fact that this rate was probably much higher than the going rate.

This disparity between the maximum legal rate of interest and the going rate of interest came back to haunt the Ninth Circuit in the *Hedrick* case[30] in which the lessor who had been dealing with the Wilshire Corporation found that the Commissioner was now imputing interest

---

[26] *Fireman's Insurance Co.*, 30 B.T.A. 1004 (1934); *Kaufman's, Inc.*, 28 T.C. 1179 (1957), acq. 1958-2 C.B. 6.
[27] *Paul W. Frenzel*, 1963 P-H T.C. Memo ¶ 63,276.
[28] 274 F.2d 294 (1959).
[29] *Comm. v. Wilshire Holding Corp.*, 288 F.2d 799 (1961).
[30] 406 F.2d 587 (1969).

income to it at the rate of 12 percent, the same rate that the court had set for the lessee-purchaser in the *Wilshire* case. Since the lessor-seller had never had a chance to produce evidence as to the actual rate of interest in *Wilshire*, the court held that it was not bound to an interest rate of 12 percent, despite the decision in *Wilshire*, and remanded the case to the Tax Court so that the lessor could introduce evidence as to the actual rate of interest. On remand, the Tax Court[31] found the rate of interest to be 7 percent and this was upheld on appeal.[32]

The imputed interest rules, which became effective after December 31, 1963, present somewhat of a problem insofar as the aforementioned cases are concerned. Under Section 483, the Commissioner has provided for an interest rate of 5 percent where none is stated in contracts involving deferred payment sales. Thus, presumably, a lessee will be entitled to a deduction of at least that amount where the Commissioner recasts a lease as a conditional sale.

Whether the imputed interest rules bar deductions in excess of 5 percent is a question which has not as yet been ruled on. Obviously, it is a question of critical importance since in many cases the effective interest rate built into the lease is far in excess of 5 percent. The fact that Section 483 does not actually apply to a particular lessor-seller because the transaction does not involve a capital asset does not help the lessee-buyer since the Regulations specifically provide that the imputed interest rules still apply to the buyer in such cases.[33] Neither the Regulations nor the Code, however, specifically prohibits a deduction for interest in excess of 5 percent, although neither do they authorize it. There is a very troublesome statement in the *Hedrick* case[34] in which the court states that, despite the possibility of inconsistent results in the *Wilshire-Hedrick* situations, in view of the enactment of Section 483 there should be no reason for inconsistent results in the future. While the court's statement is only dicta, it would seem that if the maximum interest that can be imputed to the seller under Section 483 is 5 percent, then under this view the maximum interest that can be deducted by the buyer is also 5 percent.

It is suggested, however, that since Section 483 was intended to prevent sellers from converting interest income into capital gains, it was never intended to limit the interest deduction of a buyer, even where the interest rate has not been stated, and that a buyer should be allowed to establish the actual interest rate and claim a corresponding deduction in any transaction where a lease is recast as a sale. Although this could result in the buyer receiving an interest deduction in an amount greater than the seller is required to report as interest income, it certainly makes more sense to allow this than to limit the buyer to a deduction corresponding to the amount of interest income the seller is required to report.[35]

Finally, in addition to the depreciation and interest deductions, the lessee-purchaser is also entitled to claim the investment credit if the property which he is treated as having purchased is qualifying property.[36]

---

[31] 1969 P-H T.C. Memo ¶ 69,234.

[32] 457 F.2d 501 (9th Cir., 1972).

[33] Reg. 1.483-2(b)(3)(ii).

[34] *Supra* note 30 at page 589.

[35] It should be noted that the imputed interest rules of Section 483 present no problem in the sale-leaseback area since the recasting of a sale-leaseback transaction results in a loan rather than a sale and the imputed interest rules only apply where there has been a sale.

[36] Rev. Rul. 72–408, 1972 P-H ¶ 55,330.

ATTEMPTS BY THE INTERNAL REVENUE SERVICE
TO TREAT A PURCHASE AS A LEASE

Although leases are frequently challenged by the Internal Revenue Service on the theory that they are in reality disguised installment purchases, it is extremely unusual for the Service to attempt to reclassify a purchase as a lease. This is because the tax deductions resulting from a purchase are usually not any greater than under a lease and thus reclassifying a purchase as a lease would not result in the collection of any additional tax.

There are exceptions to every rule, however, and there is at least one case where the Service will try to treat a purchase as a lease. It is where the purchase is financed by a non-recourse mortgage calling for payment of all, or most, of the principal in the form of a "balloon" some years down the road. The situation is best illustrated by the *Mayerson* case.[37]

In the *Mayerson* case, the taxpayer purchased, on December 31, 1959, a building for $332,500, giving a purchase-money note in the face amount of $332,500 secured by a long-term mortgage. The note was non-recourse and required payments of $5,000 on December 31st of 1959 and January 4th of 1960. The balance of the purchase price was not due until 99 years later although it was permissible for the borrower to pay off the note earlier and he could do so with a lower principal payment. Interest was at the rate of $18,000 a year until such time as the principal due dropped below $300,000 in which case an interest charge of 6 percent of unpaid principal was substituted for the flat amount. It was understood that the taxpayer would find the best use for the property and after determining such use try to secure conventional financing for the purpose of liquidating the purchase-money mortgage, although the time period within which this might be accomplished was somewhat indefinite.

In 1964, the taxpayer was able to lease the building for use as a garage and, by using the lease as collateral, secured a conventional mortgage from a lending institution. The taxpayer then negotiated a settlement of the purchase-money mortgage on the property by paying a flat sum of $200,000.

In examining the taxpayer's returns for the years 1960 and 1961, the Internal Revenue disallowed the depreciation deductions which the taxpayer had claimed for the building. The Service's theory was that in view of the fact that the note was non-recourse, and only $10,000 of the purchase price need be paid before the 99th year, the transaction was really a lease rather than a purchase and therefore the taxpayer was not entitled to depreciation but was limited to amortizing the $10,000 down payment (treated as a cost of acquiring the lease) over the 99-year period. As an alternative, the Service claimed that in effect the taxpayer had nothing more than an option to purchase, with the $10,000 down payment being the cost of the option.

The Tax Court rejected both of the Commissioner's theories and held for the taxpayer concluding that the parties had intended a sale and mortgage and that the form of the transaction was consistent with this intent. Subsequently, the Service acquiesced in the

---

[37] *Manuel D. Mayerson*, 47 T.C. 340 (1966).

result[38] but pointed out in Rev. Rul. 69–77[39] that its acquiescence was based on the particular facts in the case and would not be relied on in other cases except where it was clear that the property had been acquired at its fair market value in an arm's length transaction involving a *bona fide* purchase and debt obligation. Thus, the Service will continue to challenge situations designed to improperly create or inflate depreciation deductions.

---

[38] 1969-2 C.B. XXIV.
[39] 1969-1 C.B. 59.

Chapter 3

The Rental Deduction—Solutions to Classification and Timing Problems

In Chapter 2, we discussed the possibility of the Internal Revenue Service attempting to treat a lease as a conditional sale, with the resulting disallowance of the rental deduction. Even where the Internal Revenue Service concedes that an arrangement is not a conditional sale, however, it may still contest the deductibility of the rental payment, attempting to deny a deduction altogether or to defer the deduction to a future period or periods.

Before analyzing the possible lines of attack by the Internal Revenue Service, it might be well to consider what the term rent means.

WHAT IS RENT?

Perhaps the simplest way to describe rent is to say that it is a payment made by one party, the lessee, for the right to use or occupy property of another party, the lessor. It is usually payable in monthly or other periodical installments, but it can be paid in a lump sum and can be based on a percentage of the lessee's sales or income.

Although rent is usually paid directly to the lessor or his agent, it can include payments to third parties. For example, a lease might require the lessee to pay real estate taxes on the leased property. The payment of such taxes would be considered rent just the same as a direct payment to the lessor.[1] As a matter of fact, it is not at all uncommon today for a lease of real estate to require the lessee to pay not only real estate taxes, but also other expenses connected with the property such as insurance and maintenance costs. Such leases are referred to as net leases and are customary where the lessor is holding the property as an investment and wants to be assured of a fixed return unaffected by increases in real estate taxes, insurance, or other expenses connected with the property.

In addition to payments made to the lessor, or to third parties on the lessor's behalf, rent may also consist of improvements to the leased property.

---

[1] Reg. 1.162-11(a).

Example: A wants to lease a piece of unimproved land from B for five years. B agrees to lease the land to A at a rental of $20,000 a year and to credit the cost of any improvements made by A against the rent for the year in which the improvements are made. Since A receives a direct credit against the rent for the cost of improvements, any improvements made by him will be considered as having been made by the lessor and A may deduct the full rent due even though, as a result of improvements, only a portion of the rent is actually paid in cash.[2]

Not all improvements by a lessee to leased property are considered as rent, of course, and, unless there is provision for crediting the cost of the improvements against the rent, or other facts indicating that it was the intent of the parties that they be rent, improvements will normally not be considered rent.[3]

The question of whether rent is deductible depends on whether the leased property is used in a trade or business or is held for the production of income. If the property is not used in a trade or business or held for the production of income then the rent is a nonbusiness expense and cannot be claimed as a deduction.

Example: A rents a three-story building for $600 a month. It contains first-floor offices and two apartments (one on the second floor and one on the third). A uses the first floor offices for his insurance agency, uses the second floor for his living quarters, and rents the third floor to a retired couple for $100 a month. A fair allocation of the rent A pays for the building would be $400 for the first floor offices, $120 for the second-floor apartment which A uses as living quarters and $80 for the third-floor apartment which he rents.

Of the $600-a-month rent which A pays for the building, the $400 allocable to the first-floor offices is deductible because the offices are used in A's insurance business. The $80 allocable to the third floor is also deductible since the third-floor apartment is used for the production of income. The $120 allocable to the second-floor apartment, which A uses as his residence, is not deductible since it is neither used in A's business nor used for the production of income.

CLASSIFICATION PROBLEMS—DISGUISED DIVIDENDS, ETC.

An attempt by the Service to deny a deduction for rental payments (other than by treating the lease as a conditional sale) will often involve a contention that the rental payments are in reality something other than rental payments. Such a claim will frequently be made where the lessor and lessee are related, e.g., the lessor owns stock in the lessee or the lessor and lessee are affiliates. In such cases, the Internal Revenue Service may suspect that a portion of the rental payment involves a disguised dividend or an arbitrary shifting of income rather than true rent.

---

[2] *Your Health Club, Inc.,* 4 T.C. 385 (1944), *acq.* 1945 C.B. 7.
[3] See Chapter 4 for a more extensive discussion of this point.

> *Example 1:* A, the sole shareholder of a corporation, leases a building, which he owns, to the corporation for use as a warehouse. The lease calls for rent of $20,000 a year, although the normal rent for a building of this type would be only $10,000 a year. Absent other facts, it would appear that a portion of the rental payment is a disguised dividend rather than true rent.
>
> *Example 2:* A and B corporations are brother-sister corporations owned by X, an individual. A is very profitable and has been paying heavy taxes. B has not been profitable and has substantial net operating losses. A leases machinery from B at a rental of $150,000 a year when the normal rental would be $70,000. Absent other facts, it would appear that A is arbitrarily shifting income to B in order to take advantage of B's net operating losses.

The fact that the lessor and lessee are related does not, of course, mean that the rent is automatically nondeductible. It is only where the rent is excessive that there will be a disallowance, and the disallowance will be only for that portion of the rent which is excessive. Thus, in example 1 above, the disallowance would be $10,000, not $20,000, and in example 2, $80,000, not $150,000.

Whether rent is excessive or not is a question of fact that frequently involves expert opinion. Related taxpayers who are trying to determine a fair and reasonable rent for leased property would do well to consult a broker or other expert. Consulting the expert in advance, and following his advice, not only reduces the likelihood of an attack by the Commissioner, but also provides the taxpayer with evidence of reasonableness should the Commissioner contest the deduction.[4]

It is important to realize that when the Internal Revenue Service contends that rent paid to a related taxpayer is unreasonably high, the taxpayer bears the burden of proving that the rental charge is reasonable.[5] This burden can be met by expert opinion, by comparison with rentals paid in transactions with nonrelated parties, or by any other type of evidence that tends to support the arms-length nature of the rental charge. Failure to produce evidence as to the reasonableness of a rental arrangement challenged by the Internal Revenue Service will result in the loss of a deduction for the excessive portion of the rental payment.

Lease of Property to Controlled Corporation

Rental deductions are particularly vulnerable to attack where the lessor owns a controlling interest in the lessee. For example, in the *Utter-McKinley Mortuaries* case,[6] a controlling shareholder of a corporation leased property from a third party for less than $3,000 a year. He then subleased it to the corporation at a rental of $12,000. The inability of the corporation to give an adequate reason for the difference in rent resulted in a disallowance of $9,000 a year of

---

[4] *American Metal Products Corp.*, 34 T.C. 89 (1960) acq., 1963-2 C.B. 3 *aff'd on another issue* 287 F.2d 860.

[5] E.g., *International Color Gravure, Inc.*, 1961 P-H T.C. Memo ¶ 61,015.

[6] *Utter-McKinley Mortuaries v. Comm.*, 225 F.2d 870, (9th Cir., 1955).

the rental payment. Similarly, a disallowance was upheld in the *Kirk* case[7] where a corporation which had been renting a property from its president and controlling shareholder for $3,600 a year entered into a new lease with the stockholder that provided for a rent based on a percentage of the corporation's sales. The new lease was entered into after the stockholder had retired as president and resulted in an increase in rent approximately equal to his former salary as president of $20,000. The Tax Court concluded that the fair rental value of the property was only $12,000 a year and disallowed a rental deduction for the excess of the revised rent over $12,000. It also denied a compensation deduction for the excess since the shareholder had retired and there was no evidence that the excess was intended as compensation for services.

Lease of Property from Controlled Corporation

The Commissioner's attacks are not limited to situations where a corporation leases property from a shareholder at an excessive rent. The Internal Revenue Service is also interested in arrangements where a shareholder leases property from a corporation at a lower-than-normal rent.

> *Example:* A owns all the stock of X corporation. X corporation owns a building which it has been renting to a tenant on a long-term lease for $15,000 a year. Upon expiration of the lease term, and at a time when leases are generally being renewed at high rentals, X leases the property to A for $15,000. A then turns around and leases the property for $18,000 a year. Absent other facts, it would appear that the sole purpose of the lease to A was to shift income from X to A.

The Service's readiness to attack such arrangements is illustrated by the *58th Street Plaza Theatre*[8] case. In the *58th Street Plaza* case, a corporation which had been profitably operating a theatre leased from a third party sublet the theatre to the wife of the controlling shareholder. The wife then operated the theatre employing her husband as manager. The maximum profit which the corporation could obtain under the sublease was approximately $8,500 a year, which was considerably less than it had netted in prior years from the operation of the theatre.

In the first year of the sublease, the wife realized a net profit of $40,000 (before payment of rental) from the operation of the theatre and reported it as income on her tax return. The Internal Revenue Service took the position that the sublease was not *bona fide* and taxed the $40,000 to the corporation. The Service also taxed the $40,000 to the wife as a dividend.

Both the Tax Court and the Second Circuit upheld the Commissioner concluding that there was no business purpose for the sublease and that it had been entered into solely for tax avoidance purposes. In reaching this conclusion, the courts relied on the fact that the corporation had been profitably operating the theatre and could anticipate that the execution of the sublease would result in the loss of a large part of the profit which could be reasonably

---

[7] *J. J. Kirk, Inc.*, 34 T.C. 130 (1960), *aff'd* 289 F.2d 935 (6th Cir.).
[8] *58th Street Plaza Theatre, Inc. v. Comm.*, 195 F.2d 724 (2d Cir. 1952).

expected from future operations. In addition, both the Tax Court and the Second Circuit concluded that the corporation and its shareholders knew that profits of the corporation would be subject to excess profits tax, whereas the income of the wife would not be. The courts thought that the prospective tax saving in the arrangement was too obvious to have been overlooked.

Disguised Capital Contribution

As the foregoing cases illustrate, the Internal Revenue Service is on the lookout for disguised dividends to shareholders, either in the form of excessive rent on property leased to the corporation by the shareholder or in unreasonably low rentals on property leased by the shareholder from the corporation. The Service's concern with rental arrangements between corporations and their shareholders is not restricted, however, to the disguised dividend situation. The Service is also interested in situations where a shareholder pays an unreasonably high rent to a corporation in which he owns all or most of the stock. Since a lessee does not pay excessive rent without reason, the Commissioner could argue that the excess is a contribution to capital rather than a deductible expense.[9]

> *Example:* A owns all the stock of a corporation from which he rents a building at a yearly rental of $40,000. The corporation is badly in need of additional capital. If, under these circumstances, the rent on the building is increased to $60,000 a year, the Internal Revenue Service could argue that the increase represents a disguised capital contribution rather than true rent.

As a matter of fact, the Commissioner made this argument in *Estate of Sullivan*,[10] a Tax Court case. In the Sullivan case, a partnership rented land and buildings from a related corporation. Initially, the rent was set at 1½ percent of gross sales, but it was raised to 2 percent on the advice of a firm of consultants who pointed out that since the corporation was losing money each year it could never repay a debt owed to one of the partners unless the rents were raised to a point at which the corporation could make a profit. In making the recommendation, it was also pointed out the increased rental would result in certain tax savings, principally to the partners. Based on the recommendation the rent was increased from 1½ percent to 2 percent of gross sales.

In contesting the deduction, the Internal Revenue Service argued that a portion of the rent constituted a contribution to capital rather than true rent. The court, however, ruled against the Commissioner pointing to expert testimony of Realtors that the 2 percent rate was reasonable and also emphasizing the fact that there was not a complete identity of interests between the partners and the corporation. The case, nevertheless, does demonstrate the willingness of the Commissioner to raise the "disguised capital contribution" argument.

---

[9] RESEARCH INSTITUTE TAX COORDINATOR L-4609.
[10] *Estate of Frederick W. Sullivan, Sr.*, 10 T.C.M. 729.

Leases Between Other Related Parties

Although the preceding discussion dealt with the problem of leases between shareholders and corporations which they own or control, the same principles apply to other related lessors and lessees. For instance in the *Davis* case,[11] a retail liquor dealer leased a building from his father at a rental of 5 percent of gross sales with a minimum guarantee of $200 a month. The building had previously rented for $140 a month and the father had purchased it, at the son's suggestion, for only $9,800. The father received over $20,000 in rents in each of the years in question. On these facts, the Tax Court allowed a deduction for only $3,600, holding the excess to be unreasonable rent. Similarly, in the *Midland Ford* case,[12] rent was found to be excessive where the lessor and lessee were controlled by the same interests and the rental permitted the landlord to recover virtually double its investment in the property in less than three years.

Percentage Rentals

Although leases between related parties are always subject to question, leases calling for percentage rentals tend to be particularly suspect.

This is not to say that related parties should not enter into percentage leases. There are situations where percentage leases are quite appropriate, and the fact that the parties are related should not deter them from entering into such leases.

> *Example:* Retail stores located in shopping centers often pay as rent a base amount plus a percentage of sales in excess of a set figure. The fact that one of the lessees in a shopping center is related to the lessor should not preclude their entering into a percentage lease where such a lease would otherwise be appropriate.

At the same time, it should be recognized that the opportunities for shifting income can be much greater where percentage rentals are involved and therefore one entering into such a lease should be prepared to justify its reasonableness.

The reasonableness of such leases frequently cannot be demonstrated. For example, in the *Davis* case,[13] mentioned previously, the taxpayer was unable to convince the Tax Court that a percentage lease with his father, which produced rents ranging as high as $23,500 a year, was reasonable where the property had been leased to third parties at fixed rentals of less than $1,700 a year.

Similarly, in *Tube Processing Co. v. U. S.*,[14] a corporate manufacturer of tubing for airplane engines entered into a percentage lease with the guardian of two children who controlled the corporation's stock. The guardian of the children, their father, was also the

---

[11] *Herbert Davis,* 26 T.C. 49 (1956).
[12] *Midland Ford Tractor Co. v. Comm.,* 277 F.2d 111 (8th Cir. 1960).
[13] *Supra.* note 11.
[14] 15 A.F.T.R.2d 179, Dist. Ct. Ind. 12/24/64.

president of the corporation. The lease, which was for a manufacturing building, provided for an annual rental of $10,000 or 1¾ percent of the annual net sales of the lessee, whichever was greater. In addition, the lessee was to pay state and local taxes, insurance, and utilities. The lease was subsequently amended to provide that the maximum net rental was not to exceed $50,000 a year.

On examining the corporation's books, the Service concluded that the rent paid under the lease was unreasonably high and disallowed portions of the rental deductions for the years in question. The taxpayer paid the deficiencies and sued for refunds but the District Court upheld the Commissioner. In so doing, the court stressed a number of factors which supported the Commissioner's contention that the rent was unreasonably high. Among these was the fact that percentage leases are preferably used only for the rental of prime retail property, where the value of the property is in its location, and are rarely used for industrial property. As a matter of fact, the taxpayer's percentage lease was apparently the only percentage lease for industrial property in the Indianapolis area, the area in which the taxpayer was located.

In addition, the court found that the fair rental value of the leased property at the beginning of the lease was not more than $6,000 a year even though the minimum rent called for under the lease was $10,000 a year. The court was of the opinion that the minimum rent payable under a percentage lease should be less than, not exceed, the fair rental value of the property.

The court felt, also, that the lease had not been negotiated at arm's length since the guardian, who was also the chief officer of the corporation, had merely approved the terms of the leases that had been prepared by an attorney who specialized in tax work and was the attorney for both the guardianship and the corporation.

REIMBURSEMENT AGREEMENTS BY SHAREHOLDER-LESSORS

The fact that a corporation is not allowed to deduct rent paid to a shareholder-lessor because it is excessive does not mean that the payment is not income to the shareholder. On the contrary, the shareholder will still be required to report the payment as income, notwithstanding the loss of the deduction at the corporate level.

> *Example:* Taxpayer leases a building to his wholly-owned corporation at a rental of $20,000 a year. The Internal Revenue successfully contests the corporation's rental deduction on the ground that the fair rental value of the property is only $15,000 a year. The disallowance of $5,000 of the rental deduction at the corporate level does not reduce the lessor's income. He will still be taxed on $20,000, i.e., $15,000 in rental income and $5,000 in dividends.

In order to avoid this result, it has been suggested[15] that the corporation and shareholder enter into an agreement whereby the shareholder will agree to repay to the corporation any portion of the rent which is later determined to be nondeductible. Such agreements have been

---

[15] RESEARCH INSTITUTE TAX COORDINATOR L-4606.

used successfully in cases involving repayment by shareholder-employees of disallowed salary, with the shareholder-employees receiving deductions for the amount repaid.[16] Presumably, the same rule would apply to agreements covering disallowed rental payments.

It is important to realize that if such an agreement is to be utilized it should be entered into initially rather than after the disallowance. In the *Simon* case,[17] the Sixth Circuit rejected a shareholder's claim of a deduction for rent repaid to a corporation where the repayment agreement was entered into retroactively after the disallowance.

TIMING PROBLEMS

Until this point, we have been concerned primarily with classification problems, i.e., the possibility that the Internal Revenue Service and the courts might treat a "rental" payment as something else, e.g., a dividend. In the following discussion, we will concentrate on those situations where the Internal Revenue Service disallows a deduction for what is admittedly a rental payment.

Although a successful attempt by the Service to reclassify a "rental" payment will normally result in a permanent loss of the deduction, the same is generally not true where the problem is one of timing, i.e., the Commissioner admits that the item is rent but contends that it is not currently deductible. In such cases, it is usually conceded that the taxpayer will eventually be entitled to deduct the payment.

Section 267

There is one exception to this general rule and it involves payments by an accrual basis tenant to a related cash basis landlord. Under Section 267 of the Code, payments by an accrual basis tenant to a related cash basis landlord are not deductible unless payment is made within two and one-half months after the close of the tenant's taxable year.

> *Example:* X corporation leases property from its sole shareholder, A, at a yearly rental of $10,000. Both X and A are on a calendar year, but X uses the accrual method of accounting and A the cash method. X accrues the rental payment for 1972 but does not actually pay it until June of the next year. Since the payment is not made within 2½ months after the close of X's taxable year, X may not deduct its accrual for rent expense.

The regulations, however, go beyond the initial disallowance and take the position that Section 267 results in a permanent loss of the deduction, even for the year in which payment is made. The theory is that an accrual is deductible only in the taxable year for which it is properly accruable, and, therefore, there can be no deduction for the payment itself. Thus, in

---

[16] *Vincent E. Oswald,* 49 T.C. 645 (1968) *acq.* 1968-2 C.B. 2; Rev. Rul. 69-115, 1969-1 C.B. 50.
[17] *U. S. v. Ruben Simon,* 281 F.2d 520 (6th Cir., 1960).

the example set forth above X will, under the regulations, never get a deduction for its 1972 rent.[18]

The parties who are considered "related" within the meaning of Section 267 include:[19]

1. Members of a family (brothers and sisters, spouse, ancestors, and lineal descendants);

2. An individual and a corporation more than 50 percent in value of the outstanding stock of which is owned, directly or indirectly, by or for such individual;

3. Two corporations more than 50 percent in value of the outstanding stock of each of which is owned, directly or indirectly, by, or for, the same individual, if either one of such corporations, with respect to the taxable year of the corporation preceding the year in which the interest is accrued was, under the law applicable to such taxable year, a personal holding company or a foreign personal holding company;

4. A grantor and a fiduciary of any trust;

5. A fiduciary of a trust and a fiduciary of another trust, if the same person is a grantor of both trusts;

6. A fiduciary of a trust and a beneficiary of such trust;

7. A fiduciary of a trust and a beneficiary of another trust, if the same person is a grantor of both trusts;

8. A fiduciary of a trust and a corporation more than 50 percent in value of the outstanding stock of which is owned, directly or indirectly, by or for the trust or by or for a person who is a grantor of the trust; or

9. A person and an organization to which Section 501 (relating to certain educational and charitable organizations that are exempt from tax) applies and which is controlled directly or indirectly by such person or (if such person is an individual) by members of the family of such individual.

The Advance Rental Problem

In timing cases not falling under Section 267, the eventual deductibility of rental payments is generally conceded, and the Commissioner is concerned only with the denial of a current deduction. What the Service is really contending is that, although the payment in question is rent, it is a payment not for current use, but for future use, and is therefore not

---

[18] Reg. 1.267(a)-1(b)(2). See, however, *W. C. Leonard & Co.*, 324 F. Supp. 422 (1971, D.C. Miss.) which allowed a corporate lessee to deduct an accrual for rent due its controlling shareholder under the theory of constructive receipt. The Service announced it would follow the *Leonard* decision, in cases involving similar facts (Rev. Rul. 72-317, 1972 P-H ¶ 55,197).

[19] Sec. 267(b) and Reg. 1.267(b)-1(a)(2).

currently deductible. In essence, the Commissioner is arguing that the payment represents the payment of rent in advance.

The question of whether a rental payment is for current or future use is a factual question and a difficult one at that. Where rental payments are level throughout the lease term, including renewal periods, it is extremely unlikely that the question of advance rents will arise. It is only where the lease agreement provides for declining payments that the problem of advance rentals comes into play.

> *Example 1:* Taxpayer rents a tract of land for ten years. The rent is $30,000 a year for the first five years and $10,000 a year thereafter. Since one would normally not expect the rental value of land to decrease, the decline in rent after the first five years suggests that a portion of the payments for the first five years may constitute advance rent.

> *Example 2:* Taxpayer leases a truck for six years. The rent for the first year is $1,000 and it decreases by $100 each year thereafter. Taxpayer is responsible for maintenance. Since one would normally expect equipment to decrease in value as time goes on, and since taxpayer, not the lessor, will be responsible for maintenance expense, which will increase as time goes on, the decreasing rental probably reflects an anticipated decline in the usefulness of the truck rather than an advance rental situation.

The Service's attitude toward declining rental payments is best illustrated by Revenue Ruling 60–122.[20] In Revenue Ruling 60–122, the lessor furnished the lessee with an item of equipment for a period of 36 months at a rent of $16x per *month*. The agreement was renewable for three one-year periods (an additional 36 months) on payment of $16x per *year*. At the end of the three-year renewal period, the equipment had to be returned to the lessor. The net result of the arrangement was that the lessee had the use of the equipment for 72 months by making 39 equal payments of $16x each.

Since the useful life of the equipment was substantially longer than 72 months, the Service did not attempt to treat the lease as a purchase. However, it did limit the monthly rental deduction to $1/72$ of the total payments to be made. The Service's theory was that since the rent during the renewal periods was nominal, and the useful life of the property in excess of 72 months, it had to be assumed that the lease would be renewed. Therefore, a portion of the payments made during the basic lease term of 36 months constituted an advance payment of rent applicable to the renewal periods of 36 months, and the total rent had to be prorated over the 72 month period.

Revenue Ruling 60–122 is troublesome since many leases provide for declining rentals. Where there is no economic justification for declining payments, it is hard to dispute its applicability. Where, however, there is economic justification, then the Treasury should not attempt to reallocate the rental payments. An example of the latter situation is the *Riss* case.[21]

---

[20] 1960-1 C.B. 56.
[21] *Riss & Co., Inc.*, 1964 P-H T.C. Memo 64,190, *aff'd in part, rev'd in part and rem'd on another issue* (C.A. 8) 374 F.2d 161.

In the *Riss* case, a corporation leased tractors and trailers to a related corporation. The rentals were set so as to correspond with the 200 percent declining balance depreciation deductions of the lessor. As a result, the monthly rentals on trailers started at $181 and dropped to $54 in the sixth year. Tractor rents started at $595 a month and dropped to $26 by the fifth year. Because of the declining rents, the Treasury took the position that a portion of the rent in the early years constituted advance rent not deductible until later years.

The Tax Court rejected the Treasury's argument since it found no evidence that the parties intended rental prepayments. The court concluded that the desire to match the rent with the lessor's depreciation deductions was a legitimate one and suggested that the fact that the lessee had to bear the cost of maintaining the equipment also justified declining rental payments since such maintenance cost would presumably increase with age and usage.

The approach of the Tax Court to the declining-rent situation seems correct. There is little justification for the Internal Revenue Service attacking a declining-rent arrangement where the purpose is to match the depreciation deductions of the lessor or to compensate for increased maintenance costs of the lessee. Declining rents would also seem to be justified where the usefulness or efficiency of the item leased decreases with time due to obsolescence. For example, declining rents would seem to be justified in the computer-leasing industry where technological developments are rapid and equipment tends to become outdated in a relatively short time.

By the same token, however, a true advance rental situation should be treated as such. For instance, in *Main & McKinney Bldg. Co. v. Commissioner*,[22] a taxpayer purchased a lease with 98 years to run. The taxpayer agreed to pay, in addition to the rent stipulated in the lease, additional rent of $10,000 a year for the first 25 years. Since the taxpayer was unable to show any reason why the rent for the first 25 years should be higher, the court held the additional payments were to be amortized over the remaining 98 years of the lease rather than deducted in the years paid.

Other Timing Problems

Although the time at which a taxpayer can deduct a rental payment will depend on whether the payment can be classified as "advance rent," it will also depend on the taxpayer's method of accounting and the effective date of the lease. Taxpayers on the cash method of accounting are generally allowed to deduct rental payments in the year paid. Taxpayers who are on the accrual basis are entitled to the deduction in the year in which the rent accrues regardless of the date of actual payment.[23] For example, a calendar-year taxpayer on the accrual basis who pays the first year's rent in May on a lease that does not start until September is allowed to deduct in the first year only $4/12$ of the payment,[24] although a cash-basis taxpayer would be entitled to deduct the whole amount. It should be noted, however, that the fact that a

---

[22] 113 F.2d 81 (5th Cir. 1940).

[23] *Grand Ave. Motor Co. v. U. S.*, 124 F. Supp. 423 (D.C. Minn. 1954).

[24] *Bloedel's Jewelry, Inc.*, 2 BTA 611 (1925).

taxpayer is on the cash basis does not mean that he can deduct advance rentals in the year paid. Apportionment of advance rentals is required even in the case of a cash-basis taxpayer.[25]

> *Example:* A, a cash-basis taxpayer, rents a building for ten years at a rental of $10,000 a year. In the first year of the lease, A pays $30,000 which represents the rent for the first three years of the lease. Even though A is on the cash basis, only $10,000 of the payment may be deducted in the first year. The balance must be deducted in the years to which it applies.

---

[25] *Henry Cartan,* 30 T.C. 308, *acq.* 1958-2 C.B. 4.

Chapter 4

Determining Costs of Acquiring a Lease— Leasehold Improvements

A lessee will not infrequently find himself obligated to make payments in addition to rent. Such payments, which are in a broad sense costs of acquiring the lease, include security deposits, advance rentals, brokerage commissions, and payments to prior lessees.

SECURITY DEPOSITS

A lessee will usually be required under the terms of a lease to deposit a sum of money with the lessor, to be forfeited in the event the lessee damages the leased property or otherwise breaches his obligations under the lease. Such a sum is generally referred to as a security deposit, and it must be returned to the lessee at the end of the lease provided the forfeiture conditions have not occurred.

Because a lessee has a right to recover his security deposit he is not entitled to deduct it until such time as it is clear that it will not be returned to him.[1] Thus, a security deposit may not be deducted either initially or through amortization over the life of the lease.

> *Example:* A rents a building for a term of five years at a rental of $10,000 a year. As a condition of the lease he is required to make a security deposit in the amount of $10,000. Since the $10,000 is a deposit, A may neither deduct it initially nor amortize it over the life of the lease.
>
> At the end of the lease, it is agreed that $4,000 of the security deposit is forfeited because of damage to the property. A is entitled to take a deduction for the $4,000 in the year it is forfeited.

Recognizing that a security deposit may not be deducted initially, can it be deducted in the year the damage occurs, even though actual forfeiture does not take place until a later year?

---

[1] *Minneapolis Security Building Corp.*, 38 B.T.A. 1220 (1938).

The problem is complicated by the fact that the lessee could, if he chose, avoid forfeiture by repairing the damage, in which case he would presumably be entitled to an immediate deduction for the cost of the repairs.

> *Example:* X rents a business office and as a condition of the lease makes a security deposit of $5,000. The term of the lease is ten years. In the eighth year of the lease, one of X's employees accidentally damages a rear wall in the building. The cost of repairing the damage is estimated at $1,000. X chooses not to repair the damage and at the end of the lease $1,000 of the security deposit is forfeited. Must X wait until the security deposit is actually forfeited to claim the deduction or can he claim a deduction in the eighth year of the lease, the year in which the damage occurs?

It would seem that if the amount of the damage can be ascertained with reasonable certainty then an accrual-basis taxpayer should be entitled to deduct, in the year the damage occurs, the amount of the security deposit that will be forfeited, even though actual forfeiture will not occur until a later year.[2] On the other hand, where the amount of the damage cannot be ascertained with reasonable certainty, then obviously a deduction must await the year of actual forfeiture.

A cash-basis taxpayer is probably not entitled to a deduction until the actual year of forfeiture unless he chooses to repair the damage in lieu of forfeiting the security deposit, in which case a deduction should be allowed in the year in which he pays for the cost of such repairs.

ADVANCE RENTALS

Contrasted with a security deposit is the payment by a lessee of all or a portion of his rent in advance. For example, a lease will frequently require not only a security deposit, but also the payment of a month's, or in some cases, a year's rent in advance.

Unlike security deposits, advance rental payments are deductible since they are normally not recoverable by the lessee. That they are deductible does not, of course, mean that they are currently deductible and, in fact, advance rentals are not deductible immediately but must normally be amortized over the life of the lease even by a cash-basis taxpayer.[3]

> *Example:* A leases a building for 20 years at a rental of $4,000 a year. Instead of paying the rental at the rate of $4,000 a year, A pays the entire rent of $80,000 the first year. A will be allowed to deduct only $4,000 the first year and the other $76,000 will have to be deducted at the rate of $4,000 a year over the remaining 19 years.

The one exception to this rule would be in the situation where the advance rentals are specifically applicable to a particular year or years. In such cases, the advance rent must be deducted over the years to which it applies.[4]

---

[2] But see, *Sunset Color Works,* 21 B.T.A. 304 (1930), and *Empire Printing & Box Co.,* 5 B.T.A. 203 (1926).
[3] *N. B. Smith,* 51 T.C. 429 (1968).
[4] *Lola Cunningham,* 39 T.C. 186, 190 (1962), acq. 1963-2 C.B. 4.

> *Example:* Taxpayer leases a piece of equipment for ten years at a yearly rental of $1,000 and pays the rent for the first five years ($5,000) in advance. In such a case, the advance rent should be amortized over the first five years of the lease rather than over the life of the lease.

Sometimes, of course, a payment may have certain of the characteristics of both a security deposit and an advance rental. This would be the case where the lessor has the option of returning a security deposit or applying it to the last year's rent. In such a situation, the payment will be treated as an advance payment of rent rather than a security deposit.[5] As a practical matter, it doesn't make any difference to the lessee since the payment won't be deductible until the final year of the lease anyway.[6]

There are, unfortunately, many situations where it is extremely difficult to determine whether or not a lease involves advance rentals. This is particularly true where the lease calls for declining rentals.

> *Example:* A leases a piece of equipment for ten years. The rental is $3,000 a year for the first year, but thereafter drops by $200 a year so that the schedule of rent is as follows:
>
> | | |
> |---|---|
> | First year | $3,000 |
> | Second year | 2,800 |
> | Third year | 2,600 |
> | Fourth year | 2,400 |
> | Fifth year | 2,200 |
> | Sixth year | 2,000 |
> | Seventh year | 1,800 |
> | Eighth year | 1,600 |
> | Ninth year | 1,400 |
> | Tenth year | 1,200 |

In such cases, the key question is whether the higher payments in the early years are because the property is more valuable during those years (i.e., the property tends to become less useful with the passage of time) or are simply advance rentals (payments for the future use of property). The problem is discussed more fully in Chapter 3, but the basic point to be noted is that there must be economic justification for the declining rental schedule if the lessee is to receive current deductions for the higher earlier payments. Revenue Ruling 60–122[7] illustrates the problem.

In Revenue Ruling 60–122, a lessee rented a piece of equipment for a period of 36 months at a rent of $16x per *month*. The agreement provided for three one-year extensions at a rental of $16x per *year* so that the lessee could have the use of the property (which had a useful life in excess of 72 months) for 72 months by making 39 payments of $16x each.

Instead of allowing the lessee a deduction of $16x a month for the first three years and $16x a year for the following three years, the Service limited the monthly rental deduction to

---

[5] *J. and E. Enterprises, Inc.*, 1967 P-H Memo T.C. ¶ 67,191.
[6] *Supra* note 4.
[7] 1960-1 C.B. 56.

$^1/_{72}$ of the total payments to be made. This was based on the theory that since the rental during the renewal periods was nominal, and the useful life of the property was in excess of 72 months, it had to be assumed that the lease would be renewed. Since there was no reason why the rental payments during the renewal periods should be less than the rental payments during the original lease period, it was concluded that a portion of the payments during the first 36 months of the lease constituted advance rent and were properly allocable to the last 36 months.

BONUSES

Distinguished from the situation where the lessee pays all or a portion of the rent in advance is the case where the lessee, in order to obtain the lease, agrees to pay not only the designated rental, but also an additional sum, frequently designated a "bonus," in order to induce the lessor to enter into the lease.

> *Example:* A wants to rent a tract of land for 20 years and offers to pay a rental of $10,000 a year. The owner of the tract finds the proposed rental attractive but is reluctant to enter into such a long-term lease. In order to induce the owner to enter into the lease, A agrees to pay him, in addition to the rent of $10,000 a year, a bonus of $30,000 on execution of the lease.

Because the benefit of a bonus payment extends over the life of the lease it may not be deducted immediately but must be amortized over the term of the lease.[8] Thus, in the preceding example, the bonus of $30,000 will have to be amortized at the rate of $1,500 a year over the 20-year life of the lease.

This is true even where the bonus payment is not a fixed sum. For example, in *Galatorie Bros. v. Lines,*[9] where the lessee agreed to pay a fixed monthly rental plus 50 percent of the first year's profits, the Fifth Circuit held that the amount of profits paid to the lessor was not deductible in full in the year paid, but had to be prorated over the term of the lease.

It is also true where the bonus is in the form of annual payments rather than a lump sum.

> *Example:* B enters into a 25-year lease at a rental of $10,000 a year. He is also required to pay as a bonus an additional $5,000 a year for the first ten years of the lease.

Despite the fact that the $5,000 payments are to be made only for the first ten years, B will be required to amortize them over the full term of the lease for tax purposes.[10] Thus, B's deduction for the bonus payments will be at the rate of $2,000 a year for 25 years rather than $5,000 a year for the first ten years.

This is not to say, of course, that in every case in which the payments in the early years

---

[8] *Baton Coal Co. v. Comm.,* 51 F.2d 469 (3rd Cir., 1931), cert. denied 284 U.S. 674.

[9] 23 F.2d 676 (5th Cir. 1928).

[10] *Main and McKinney Building of Houston, Texas v. Comm.,* 113 F.2d 81 (5th Cir. 1940); *University Properties, Inc. v. Comm.,* 378 F.2d 83 (9th Cir., 1967).

exceed the payments in the later years the excess will have to be amortized over the term of the lease. In the prior example, the $5,000 payments were designated as a bonus and were separate from the rental payments. If, instead, the rental payments had simply been set at $15,000 a year for the first ten years and $10,000 a year thereafter, the taxpayer would have a better chance of a current writeoff, although even under these circumstances the Internal Revenue Service might try to characterize a portion of the early payments as advance rentals. This problem was mentioned earlier in this chapter and is discussed more fully in Chapter 3.

OTHER COSTS OF ACQUIRING A LEASE

Bonuses are not the only cost a lessee may incur in obtaining a lease. Additional costs would include brokerage commissions, legal fees, and other expenses involved in the negotiation and preparation of the lease. Since all these items are costs of acquiring the lease, they must be amortized over its term.[11]

> *Example:* X corporation is interested in securing a lease on an office building. It engages the services of a real estate agent who locates a suitable building and helps negotiate a favorable 30-year lease. X pays the real estate agent a commission of $6,000 for locating the property and negotiating the lease. The $6,000 may not be deducted currently but must be amortized over the term of the lease at the rate of $200 a year.

The same rule applies to any item which is a cost of acquiring a lease even though it may not be a conventional cost such as the aforementioned brokerage commissions or legal fees. For example, in the *King Amusement* case,[12] a corporation wanted to renew its lease on a building. The lessor was willing provided the lessee secured responsible parties to guarantee the payment of the rent. The corporation requested its shareholders to act as guarantors but only two of them would agree to do so, and then only if they received a fee of $25,000 each. The corporation agreed to pay the requested fees and claimed a deduction for the $50,000 in the year that it was paid. The Commissioner contested the immediate writeoff of the $50,000 contending it had to be written off over the term of the lease.

Although the taxpayer argued that the rules governing the writeoff of expenditures incurred in the acquisition of a lease were not applicable since the payments were made to a third party, and not the lessor, the court found this distinction unpersuasive and held the payments had to be written off over the term of the lease.

An example of an even more unconventional cost of acquiring a lease is contained in Revenue Ruling 68–260.[13] In the situation presented in Revenue Ruling 68–260, a taxpayer, wanting to expand his business, purchased the stock in trade and fixtures of a store in order to obtain an assignment of the store's lease. The stock in trade and fixtures were then sold at a

---

[11] Regs. 1.162-11(a); *D.N. & E. Walter & Co.*, 4 B.T.A. 142 (1926), *acq.* VI-2 C.B. 7.
[12] *King Amusement Co. v. Comm.*, 44 F.2d 709 (6th Cir., 1930), *cert. denied* 282 U.S. 900.
[13] 1968-1 C.B. 86.

loss. Although such a loss would normally be deductible immediately, the ruling, focusing on the fact that the goods and fixtures were purchased solely for the purpose of acquiring an assignment of the lease, takes the position that the loss is not deductible currently, but must be treated as a cost of acquiring the lease, to be amortized over its remaining term.

PURCHASE OF LEASEHOLD INTEREST FROM ANOTHER LESSEE

Occasionally, a businessman seeking to lease a piece of property will find that the property is already leased to someone else. In such cases, the prospective lessee will usually negotiate with the current lessee with a view towards assignment or cancellation of the existing lease.

Whether the prospective lessee seeks an assignment or a cancellation of the existing lease will depend on its terms and the willingness of the lessor to allow assignment. Where the prospective lessee considers the terms of the existing lease unfavorable, he may want to negotiate a new lease with the landlord, in which event, he will try to persuade the existing lessee to consent to a cancellation of his lease. However, if the terms are favorable, the prospective lessee will try to arrange for an assignment rather than a cancellation of the lease.

In any event, it is clear that whether the prospective lessee takes an assignment of the existing lease or pays the present lessee to cancel its lease, the payment is a cost of acquiring a lease and must be amortized over the remaining term of the old lease, in the case of an assignment, or over the life of the new lease, where the old one is cancelled and a new one negotiated.[14]

> *Example:* A is interested in leasing a property on which B holds a lease with eight years remaining. If A pays B $10,000 for assigning his rights under the lease to A, then A can amortize the $10,000 over the remaining eight years of the lease. If, instead of paying B $10,000 to assign his rights under the lease, A pays B $10,000 to agree to a cancellation of the remaining term of his lease and then negotiates a new ten-year lease with the lessor, the $10,000 will have to be written off over the ten-year term of the new lease.

The situation is complicated somewhat where the lease which is purchased gives the lessee the right to use certain improvements (e.g., a building) already on the property. If the life of the improvements is less than the term of the lease, there would be an advantage to the lessee if he could depreciate all or a portion of the price paid for the lease over the remaining useful life of the improvements rather than over the term of the lease.

> *Example:* A has a lease on a tract of land on which he has erected a building. The lease has a remaining term of 40 years and the building a remaining useful life of 20 years. A assigns his interest in the lease and building to B for $100,000. If B could allocate all or a portion of

---

[14] Reg. 1.162-11(a).

the $100,000 to the building, he could write it off over 20 years rather than over the 40-year remaining term of the lease.

1. Improvements Made by Prior Lessee

Unfortunately, the law in this area is not altogether clear. Where the improvements were made by a prior lessee, Revenue Ruling 61–217[15] allows the purchaser to depreciate that portion of the price paid for the lease which is applicable to the improvements over the remaining useful life of such improvements.

> *Example:* A leases a tract of land for 60 years at a rental of $10,000 a year. A then erects a building with a useful life of 40 years at a cost of $200,000. Ten years later, A assigns his interest in the property to B for $200,000. The fair rental value of the tract absent the building is still $10,000 a year. Under these circumstances, B may depreciate the cost of the lease ($200,000) over the remaining useful life of the building (30 years) rather than over the remaining term of the lease (50 years).

The determination of whether all or a portion of the price paid for a lease is allocable to improvements is a difficult one. In the example above, the fair rental value of the land at the time of the assignment was still $10,000 a year and, therefore, when B assumed A's rental obligation under the lease of $10,000 a year, and also agreed to pay A $200,000, it was obvious that the $200,000 was a cost of acquiring the building and should be so treated. This is not always the case and, as Revenue Ruling 61–217 indicates, there can be situations where the price paid to the prior lessee reflects not only the value of the improvements placed on the property by such prior lessee, but also the increased rental value of the underlying land. In such cases, the price paid the prior lessee must be apportioned between the improvements (to be depreciated over the remaining useful life of such improvements if it is shorter than the remaining term of the lease) and the underlying lease (to be amortized over the remaining life of the lease).

> *Example:* Assume the facts are the same as in the preceding example except that at the time A assigns its interest in the lease to B the fair rental value of the land, absent the building, is $15,000 a year, and the value of the leasehold (the right to rent the land at a rental of $10,000 a year) absent the building is $100,000. Under these facts, the $200,000 payment by B will have to be allocated, $100,000 to the building (to be depreciated over 30 years) and $100,000 to the leasehold (to be amortized over 50 years).

Suppose, however, that in a situation like the above the fair rental value of the land absent the building is less than the rental called for in the lease. This means that the price really being paid for the building is the payment to the present lessee plus the discounted value of the excess rental payments.

---

[15] 1961-2 C.B. 49.

> *Example:* Assume the facts are the same as in the preceding example except that the fair rental value of the land absent the building is only $5,000 a year, even though the rent required under the lease is $10,000 a year. On these facts, the price B is paying for the building is $200,000 plus the present (discounted) value of $5,000 a year extra rent for the next 50 years.

In such circumstances, is B entitled to write off the present value of the excess rent over the 30-year life of the building or must it deduct the rent as paid over the 50-year remaining term of the lease?

The logical answer would seem to be that since the discounted cost of the additional rent is really being paid for the right to use the building it should be written off over the life of such building.

The difficulty this approach causes is that one must then characterize the excess of the extra rental payments over their discounted value and decide what should be done with it. For example, assume that in the above illustration the present value of the extra rental (the excess of the rental payments over the fair rental value of the land alone) is $90,000. If the full (undiscounted) amount of the extra rent to be paid is $250,000 ($5,000 a year × 50 years), then using the present-value approach forces us to clarify the $160,000 difference. Unfortunately, it is difficult to say just what it represents. In a sense it is interest and yet it really is not.

Our inability to characterize the difference between the total extra rent due under the lease and the present value of such payments raises a question as to whether the discounting approach is correct. What has really happened economically is that A has purchased the building for $200,000 in cash plus payments of $5,000 a year (the excess of the yearly rental payment under the lease over the yearly fair rental value of the land) for the next 50 years, or a total of $450,000. Thus, A should be allowed a basis of $450,000 for the building which he can then depreciate over its useful life of 30 years, and his rental deduction will be $5,000 a year, the fair rental value of the land absent the building, rather than the rent of $10,000 a year called for under the lease. Although this result might seem somewhat strange, it bears out if we realize that we must separate the purchase of the building from the lease of the underlying land and that $5,000 of each $10,000 payment that A makes under the lease is not rent but is a payment on the purchase price of the building.[16]

The above conclusion must be modified, of course, to the extent that the imputed interest rules of Section 483 come into play. Since Section 483 applies to the buyer as well as the seller, the effect of its application to our situation would be to reduce the basis of the building by the amount of interest imputed to the transaction. This interest would be deducted over the term of the payments (50 years) rather than the life of the building (30 years).

2. Improvements Made by Lessor

Although the Internal Revenue Service will allow a subsequent lessee to depreciate that portion of the cost of a lease which is allocable to improvements made by a prior lessee over the

---

[16] See *Oxford Paper Co. v. Comm.*, 194 F.2d 190 (2nd Cir., 1952); Rev. Rul. 55-675, 1955-2 C.B. 567.

life of such improvements, the same is not true as to improvements made by the lessor. In such situations, the Service takes the position that the entire cost of the lease must be amortized over the remaining term of the lease since neither the original lessee nor the subsequent lessee has made any investment of capital in the improvements.[17]

> *Example:* A holds a lease with a remaining term of 90 years on a tract of land on which the lessor erected a building with a remaining useful life of 30 years. B needs a building and purchases A's interest in the lease for $100,000. It is conceded that the $100,000 was paid solely because of the building and that it would not have been paid if the building were not on the tract.
>
> Despite the fact that the $100,000 was paid solely for the use of the building, the Internal Revenue Service takes the position that it must be written off over the remaining term of the lease (90 years) rather than over the useful life of the building (30 years) even though it is conceded by the Service that a writeoff over the life of the building would be proper if the building had been erected by A, the prior lessee.

The difficulty with the Service's argument is that an assignee who pays extra for a leasehold interest because of improvements, such as a building, obviously has invested capital in the building whether the leasehold improvements were made by the lessor or a prior lessee. This was recognized by the Sixth Circuit in *The 1220 Realty Company* case[18] where the taxpayers acquired certain leases in order to use the buildings on the leaseholds. The remaining life of the buildings (which had been erected by the lessor) was 20 years and the remaining terms of the leases from 64 to 68 years.

The taxpayer, after introducing evidence to the effect that the leasehold estates would have no value absent the buildings, contended that it was entitled to depreciate the cost of the leases over the remaining life of the buildings. The Commissioner objected, but the court upheld the taxpayer, taking issue only with the taxpayer's failure to allocate a portion of the cost to the land. Although the case was remanded to the Tax Court for a finding as to the proper allocation of cost between the buildings and land, the court clearly recognized the right of a lessee who has purchased an improved leasehold to write off the cost allocable to the improvements over the life of such improvements, whether constructed by a prior lessee or the lessor. There is also reason to believe that the Second Circuit would apply the same rule. Although the *Dab* case[19] was decided against the taxpayer, the opinion indicates that the Second Circuit would probably have allowed the lessee to write off a portion of the cost of acquiring the leasehold over the life of the improvements (which had been made by a predecessor of the lessor) if the lessee had been able to show that a portion of the price paid for the leasehold was really applicable to such improvements.

---

[17] Rev. Rul. 61-217, 1961-2 C.B. 49.

[18] *The 1220 Realty Company v. Comm.*, 322 F.2d 495 (6th Cir., 1963).

[19] *Dab v. Comm.*, 255 F.2d 788 (2nd Cir., 1958).

OPTIONS TO RENEW

Up to this point, we have assumed that there were no options to renew under the lease and, therefore, there was no problem in determining the period over which the costs of acquiring the lease had to be amortized. The existence of an option or options to renew complicates the problem. Obviously, the lessee would be better off if he could amortize the costs of acquiring the lease over its initial term and ignore the possibility of renewal.

> *Example:* A acquires a ten-year lease on a building with an option to renew for two additional ten-year periods. The costs of acquiring the lease are $12,000. A's deduction for amortization of the cost of acquiring the lease will be $1,200 a year if only the initial term of the lease has to be taken into account. If the option periods are taken into account, the deduction will be reduced to $400 a year.

The Internal Revenue Code sets forth a strict mathematical rule for determining whether renewal periods are to be taken into consideration. Section 178[20] of the Code provides that, where a lessee has incurred costs in acquiring a lease, renewal periods must be included in determining the period over which such costs are to be amortized if less than 75 percent of the cost is attributed to the portion of the original lease term remaining at the date of acquisition, unless the lessee can show that it is more probable that the lease will not be renewed than it will be renewed. The following example illustrates how the rule works:

> *Example:* Lessee pays $20,000 for a ten-year lease with a ten-year renewal option. If $14,000 is attributable to the original ten-year lease, then less than 75 percent of the cost is attributable to the original lease term and the $20,000 cost must be amortized over the entire 20-year period. If, on the other hand, the portion of the cost attributable to the original ten-year period is $16,000, then over 75 percent of the cost would be attributable to the original lease and the entire cost could be amortized over the ten-year initial term of the lease.

Obviously, the problem of allocating cost between the original lease and possible renewal periods is a difficult one. The Regulations provide that the allocation shall be made on the basis of facts and circumstances of each case and suggest that in some cases an allocation might be based on the principles used to measure the present value of an annuity, giving the following example.[21]

> *Example:* Lessee A acquires a lease with respect to unimproved property at a cost of $100,000 at which time there are 21 years remaining in the original term of the lease with two renewal options of 21 years each. The lease provides for a uniform annual rental for the

---

[20] Sec. 178(a)(2).
[21] Reg. 1.178-1(b)(5)(ii).

remaining term of the lease and the renewal periods. It has been determined that this is an appropriate case for the application of the principles used to measure the present value of an annuity. Assume that in this case appropriate rate of interest is 5 percent. By applying the tables (Inwood) used to measure the present value of an annuity of $1 per year, the factor representing the present value of $1 per annum for 21 years at 5 percent is ascertained to be 12.821, and the factor representing the present value of $1 per annum for 63 years at 5 percent is 19.075. The portion of the cost of the lease ($100,000) attributable to the remaining term of the original lease (21 years) is 67.21 percent or $67,210 determined as follows: $\frac{12.821}{19.075}$ or 67.21 percent.

Although the statute does allow a lessee, even where the 75 percent test is not met, to amortize the cost of acquiring a lease over its original term, if he can show that it is more probable than not that the lease will not be renewed, it is extremely unlikely that such a burden can be met in the average case. It is also important to note that even in the case where the cost allocable to the initial term of the lease is 75 percent or more, the renewal period or periods may be taken into account if a reasonable certainty of renewal exists.[22]

LEASEHOLD IMPROVEMENTS

Leasehold Improvements by Lessor

When a lessor makes improvements to leased property, he is normally entitled to depreciate the cost of such improvements. A tenant, of course, cannot claim depreciation with respect to improvements made by his landlord unless he has contributed to their cost.[23]

> *Example:* A erects a $100,000-building on land which he leases to B. B is not entitled to claim depreciation with respect to the building. If A had agreed to erect the building only if B contributed half the cost, then B would be entitled to depreciate his contribution over the life of the building or amortize it over the remaining term of the lease, whichever is shorter.

Improvements by Lessee

Improvements by the lessee can be grouped into two general classes, permanent and non-permanent. Non-permanent improvements are those which either are not attached to the property or, if attached, can be removed without significant damage to the remaining property. Permanent improvements are those which either become part of the leased property or are attached to it in such a manner that they cannot be removed without significant damage.

> *Example:* A leases a tract of land from B and erects a factory building on it. He then installs various machines which have to be bolted to the walls or floor of the building. Although the

---

[22] Sec. 178(c).
[23] *Weiss v. Weiner,* 279 U.S. 333 (1929).

building would be a permanent improvement, the machines would be considered non-permanent improvements.

Since a tenant normally has the right to remove non-permanent improvements, he must depreciate them over their useful life and cannot amortize their cost over the remaining term of the lease where that is shorter.

> *Example:* Taxpayer installs a machine with a useful life of 15 years in a building on which he holds a lease with eight years remaining. The machine can be removed without significant damage to the building. On these facts, the taxpayer must depreciate the machine over its 15-year useful life and may not amortize it over the remaining lease term of eight years.

The situation with respect to permanent improvements is quite different. Since permanent improvements cannot be removed from the property, their cost is recoverable by the lessee either through an amortization allowance over the remaining period of the lease or by way of an allowance for depreciation based on the useful life of the property, whichever is shorter.[24]

> *Example:* Assume the facts are the same as in the preceding example except that the machine is permanently affixed to the property. The taxpayer should amortize the cost over the remaining useful life of the lease (eight years) rather than the machine's useful life (15 years).

Prior to the introduction of accelerated depreciation, lessees sometimes tried to make the lease term shorter than the life of permanent improvements in order to get a quicker writeoff for the improvements. With the advent of accelerated depreciation, much of the incentive to do this disappeared. The use of accelerated depreciation methods, even with a longer life, often produces deductions comparable to those that would result from straight line amortization over a shorter period.

Leases for Indefinite Terms—Options to Renew

Where a lease involves options to renew, or is for an indefinite term, the normal rule allowing depreciation over the useful life of the property or amortization over the remaining term of the lease, whichever is shorter, no longer applies.

If a lease is for an indefinite period, or the lessee is a tenant at will, or on a month-to-month or year-to-year basis, there can be no amortization and the costs of leasehold improvements may be recovered only through an allowance for depreciation based on their useful life.[25]

---

[24] Regs. 1.162-11(b)(1); 1.167(a)-4.

[25] *Simons Brick Co.,* 14 B.T.A. 878 (1928), *acq.,* VIII-2 C.B. 48, N.A. VIII-2 C.B. 71, *affirmed on another issue* 45 F.2d 57; *Standard Tube Co.,* 6 T.C. 950 (1946).

> *Example:* Taxpayer permanently attaches a machine costing $6,000 with a ten-year life to the floor of a building which he leases on a year-to-year basis. Because the lease term is year-to-year the cost of the machine must be depreciated over its useful life.

Of course, if the lease should be cancelled and the tenant has to give up the improvements before recovering their cost, he is entitled to deduct the remaining undepreciated cost in the year of cancellation.[26]

> *Example:* Assume the same facts as in the preceding example except that after six years the taxpayer decides not to extend the lease any longer, and title to the machine passes to the lessor. The remaining undepreciated cost of the machine is $4,000. This $4,000 should be written off in full in the year the lease is not renewed.

The situation is somewhat different where the lessee has an option to renew. In such cases, Section 178 permits amortization, but provides that the renewal periods must be taken into consideration in determining the period of amortization if the term of the original lease remaining after the completion of the improvement is less than 60 percent of the useful life of the improvement. The following example illustrates how the rule works:

> *Example:* Lessee completes an improvement with an estimated useful life of 15 years at a time when the lease has ten years to run with the right to renew for an additional ten years. Since the remaining term of the lease (ten years) is more than 60 percent of the useful life of the improvements (15 years), the improvement may be amortized over the remaining portion of the original lease and the renewal period ignored. Had the useful life of the improvement been 17 years, the tenant would have been forced to depreciate the building over its useful life of 17 years since the 60 percent test would not have been met and therefore the period for amortization would have been 20 years (remaining lease term of ten years plus 10-year renewal period).

It should be recognized, that even where the 60 percent rule is not met (i.e., the term of the original lease remaining after completion of the improvement is less than 60 percent of the useful life of the improvement), the renewal period will not be included if the lessee can prove that nonrenewal is more probable than renewal.[27] Conversely, even where the 60 percent test is met, the renewal period will be included if a reasonable certainty of renewal exists.[28]

Section 178 sets forth a special exception where the lessor and lessee are related persons. The exception[29] provides that where the parties are related within the meaning of Section 178(b)(2)

> . . . then, in determining the amount allowable to the lessee as a deduction for such taxable year for exhaustion, wear and tear, obsolescence, or amortization in respect

---

[26] *Cassatt v. Comm.*, 137 F.2d 745, (3rd Cir., 1963); *Robert C. Coffey*, 21 B.T.A. 1242 (1931), *acq.* X-2 C.B. 14.
[27] Sec. 178(a).
[28] Sec. 178(c).
[29] Sec. 178(b)(1).

of any building erected (or other improvement made) on the leased property, the lease shall be treated as including a period of not less duration than the remaining useful life of such improvement.

A lessor and lessee are considered to be related persons if they are members of an affiliated group within the meaning of Section 1504 or are, with certain modification, related persons within the meaning of Section 267(b).[30]

Leasehold Improvements As Additional Rent

Occasionally, the terms of a lease will require a lessee to make improvements to the leased property.

> *Example:* A agrees to rent a tract of land to B for $10,000 a year plus B's promise to erect a suitable fence around the property.

In such cases, a question arises as to whether the improvements are intended to be a substitute for rent. If they are, then the lessee is entitled to a rental rather than a depreciation or amortization deduction. This does not necessarily mean, however, that the lessee will be entitled to write off the cost of the improvements in one year.

Where the improvements are in lieu of a particular year's rent, their cost can be written off in such year.[31]

> *Example:* X rents a tract of land to A at a rental of $20,000 a year. The agreement provides that in lieu of paying the first year's rent A shall make improvements to the tract costing $20,000. The cost of the improvements is deductible by A in full in the first year of the lease.

Where the improvements are intended as rent but are not in lieu of a particular year's rent, the Internal Revenue Service may try to classify them as advance rent to be amortized over the term of the lease. This could result in a considerable disadvantage to the lessee where the useful life of the improvements is less than the term of the lease.

> *Example:* A leases property for a term of ten years at a rental of $5,000 a year. Under the terms of the lease, he is required to make certain improvements to the property. Such improvements have an estimated useful life of five years and cost $30,000. If the improvements constitute rent, then the Internal Revenue Service may require that their cost be amortized over the ten-year term of the lease. If the improvements are not considered rent, they can be depreciated over their useful life of five years.

Whether improvements required of a lessee under the terms of a lease will be treated as rent depends on the facts and circumstances of each case. The key case on the question is the

---

[30] Sec. 178(b)(2)(B).
[31] *Your Health Club, Inc.*, 4 T.C. 385 (1944), *acq.* 1945 C.B. 7.

Blatt case,[32] a 1938 Supreme Court case, which deals with the question of whether improvements required under the terms of a lease are income to the lessor. In the *Blatt* case, a lessor entered into an agreement to lease a building for ten years for use as a motion picture theatre. The lease required the lessee to install theatre seats and other items necessary to the operation of a motion picture theatre. The improvements were to become the property of the lessor on termination of the lease.

In holding that the improvements did not constitute additional rent, the Supreme Court relied on the fact that although the lease required improvements, it did not specify individual items or the time or amount of any expenditure. The Court then quoted from its prior opinion in *Duffy v. Central R. R.* to the effect that "Rent is a fixed sum, or property amounting to a fixed sum, to be paid at stated times for the use of property . . .; it does not include payments, uncertain both as to time and amount made for improvements. . . ."[33] The Court elaborated on this by commenting that "Even when required, improvements by the lessee will not be deemed rent unless the intention that they shall be is plainly disclosed."[34]

As a general rule then, improvements by a lessee, even though required under the terms of the lease, will not be regarded as rent unless it is clear that they are so intended. Cases where such an intent will be found are those where the lease recites that the cost of the improvements constitutes additional rent[35] or where the lease provides that the cost of improvements can be credited against the rent.[36] It is also possible that leasehold improvements will be treated as rent where the terms of the lease require such improvements but call for no other rent.[37]

Fee Purchased by Lessee

As we discussed, a lessee who makes permanent improvements will generally amortize their cost over the remaining term of the lease or depreciate them over their useful life, whichever is shorter.

Assuming that in a particular case the remaining term of the lease is shorter than the useful life of the improvements, what happens where the lessee purchases the fee interest? May he continue to amortize the cost of such improvements over the remaining period of the extinguished lease?

The question is answered in the negative in Revenue Ruling 60–180.[38] In this ruling, the Internal Revenue Service takes the position that a lessee who purchases the fee interest must depreciate the remaining cost of improvements which he made to the property over their useful life rather than over the remaining term of the extinguished lease.

---

[32] 305 U.S. 267 (1938).

[33] 268 U.S. 55 at 63.

[34] *Supra* note 32 at 277.

[35] *Frank T. B. Martin*, 11 B.T.A. 850 (1928).

[36] *Your Health Club, Inc.*, 4 T.C. 385 (1944), *acq.* 1945 C.B. 7; *Isidore Brown*, 22 T.C. 147, *aff'd* 220 F.2d 12 (7th Cir., 1955).

[37] See I.T. 4009, 1950-1 C.B. 13, declared obsolete by Rev. Rul. 67-123, 1967-1 C.B. 383. *Contra Comm. v. Cunningham*, 258 F.2d 231 (9th Cir., 1958).

[38] 1960-1 C.B. 114.

> *Example:* A leases a property for 20 years and erects a building with a useful life of 30 years on it. Since the term of the lease is less than the useful life of the property, he amortizes the cost of the building over the 20-year term of the lease rather than its 30-year useful life. Should A purchase the fee interest in the fifth year of the lease, he will be required to depreciate the balance of the cost of the building over its remaining useful life (25 years) rather than continue to amortize it over the remaining term of the extinguished lease (15 years).

The same principle applies to that portion of the price paid for the fee which represents the value of improvements on the property. In *Millinery Center Building Corp. v. Commissioner,*[39] the lessee of a tract of land had already fully amortized the cost of improvements when it purchased the fee interest. Since the price paid exceeded the value of the land, and there was no evidence that the excess was paid to cancel a burdensome lease, the Court held that the excess represented the value of the improvements and was to be depreciated over the remaining life of such improvements and not over the remaining term of the extinguished lease.

> *Example:* Taxpayer leases land for 25 years and erects a building with a useful life of 40 years on it. Since the term of the lease is less than the useful life of the property, he amortizes the cost of the building over the 25-year term of the lease. In the 24th year, he purchases the fee for $200,000, the land having a value of $150,000. Since the $50,000 excess of the purchase price of the fee over the value of the land must represent the value of the building, it must be depreciated over the remaining 15-year useful life of the building, rather than over the remaining term of the extinguished lease.

OBLIGATION OF LESSEE TO REPAIR AND MAINTAIN LEASED PROPERTY

Suppose a lease obligates the lessee to repair, replace, and otherwise maintain the leased property. Can the taxpayer set up a tax-deductible reserve or claim depreciation for the estimated cost of repair and replacement?

It would appear fairly clear that a taxpayer cannot claim depreciation for the estimated costs of repair and maintenance nor can he set up a deductible reserve.[40] The actual cost of repairs and maintenance, however, is deductible in the year in which incurred, the same as it would be if the lessee owned the leased property outright.[41]

> *Example:* X corporation leases a building for a 20-year term. Under the terms of the lease, X must maintain and keep the building in good repair. It is estimated that the cost of maintaining and repairing the building will be approximately $40,000 over the 20-year term

---

[39] 350 U.S. 456 (1956).
[40] *Weiss v. Weiner,* 279 U.S. 333 (1929); *Harris v. Emery,* 10 B.T.A. 297 (1928).
[41] *Rose v. Haverty Furniture Co.,* 15 F.2d 345 (5th Cir., 1926).

of the lease even though repairs and maintenance for the first year run only $500. X may not set up a deductible reserve nor depreciate the $40,000 estimated cost of maintenance and repair, but may deduct maintenance and repair costs only as actually incurred. Thus X's deduction for repair and maintenance expense for the building for the first year is limited to $500, the actual cost of repairs and maintenance.

The situation is somewhat different where replacements are involved. Since replacements normally extend the useful life of property, they generally cannot be expensed in the year made but must be capitalized and written off over the life of the property or the remaining term of the lease whichever is shorter.

> *Example:* A leases various items of construction equipment from B under a ten-year lease. The lease obligates A to keep the equipment in good repair and replace any equipment that wears out. In the fifth year of the lease, one of the pieces of equipment wears out and A replaces it at a cost of $10,000. The new piece of equipment has a useful life of eight years. A may not expense the cost of the replacement but must amortize it over the remaining term of the lease.

Despite the general rule that replacements must be capitalized and written off over their useful life or the remaining term of the lease, whichever is shorter, the Seventh Circuit has allowed a taxpayer to deduct the cost of such replacements as a current expense where the replacements had a fairly short useful life and similar expenditures of substantially the same amount could be expected on a fairly regular basis. The case in question, *Illinois Central R. R. v. Commissioner*,[42] involved the lease of some 2,300 railroad cars and locomotives. Under the terms of the lease, the lessee was required to retire and replace a certain number of units each year in order to preserve the going-concern value of the operation. Since the replacements had a relatively short useful life and occurred in substantial amounts on a regular basis, the court allowed the lessee to expense the costs of replacement.

The *Illinois Central* case involved railroad equipment and therefore could be distinguished by the Commissioner on the ground that the case really involved the retirement system of accounting, a system which is generally used only by railroads. At times, though, the Commissioner has taken a broader view of the matter as evidenced by the *Manger Hotel Corp.* case.[43] In the *Manger* case, the taxpayer leased a furnished hotel. Under the lease, he was obligated to replace unserviceable furnishings, fixtures, and equipment. On replacing cash registers, a calculating machine, carpets, rugs, and draperies, the taxpayer charged them to expense rather than capitalizing them. The Commissioner conceded that these items were deductible indicating that he may be taking an expanded view of the *Illinois Central* case.

Where the items in question have a significant useful life and there is no fixed program for replacement, there is no doubt as to the Service's position. As to such items, both the Commissioner and the Tax Court take the view that capitalization is required. Thus, in the

---

[42] 90 F.2d 458 (1937).
[43] 1950 P-H T.C. Memo ¶ 50,238.

Journal-Tribune Publishing Co. case,[44] a lessee of a newspaper plant and equipment agreed to replace and repair worn equipment and tried to write off the cost of replacement as an expense. The Commissioner objected and the Tax Court upheld him on the ground that since the items in question all had a useful life in excess of a year their cost could be recovered only by way of depreciation over their remaining useful life or the remaining term of the lease, whichever was less. Interestingly enough, the Tax Court was reversed by the Eighth Circuit which laid down a very broad general rule that any expenditures made in compliance with a lessee's obligation to maintain leased machinery by replacing worn-out items are ordinary and necessary business expenses. The Court of Appeals, of course, placed its principal reliance upon the railroad cases which the Tax Court had distinguished. The Court of Appeals for the Tenth Circuit agrees with the Tax Court rather than the Eighth Circuit and in the *Hotel Kingkade* case,[45] disallowed the deduction of expenditures for various items of the hotel equipment such as pipes, dishwashers, fire hoses, etc. on the ground that the expenditures were not customary and frequent enough to justify an immediate writeoff.

Despite the conflict between the Eighth Circuit and the Tenth Circuit, both courts are in agreement that where the replacements represent additional properties, and not replacements of property covered under the lease, that such additions must be depreciated over their useful life and cannot be written off in one year unless their useful life is one year or less.

------

[44] 216 F.2d 138 (1954).
[45] *Hotel Kingkade v. Comm.*, 180 F.2d 310 (1950).

Chapter 5

The Fine Points of Termination, Cancellation, and Assignment of Leases

Chapter 4 discussed the tax problems involved in entering into a lease. This chapter deals with the tax consequences of terminating a lease.

There are a number of ways in which a lease might terminate. First, it may simply terminate through expiration of the lease term. We might refer to this as normal termination. Second, it may terminate because the lessee purchases the underlying fee interest. Third, the lessee or the lessor may cancel the lease before the end of its term. Finally, the lessee may assign all or a part of his interest to another party.

NORMAL TERMINATION

Termination of a lease upon the expiration of the lease term generally presents no problems. Any costs of acquiring the lease not previously written off may be written off[1] and the same is true of leasehold improvements[2] except as to improvements which the lessee has the right to, and does, remove.

> *Example:* A enters into a ten-year lease for a tract of land with an option to renew for an additional ten years. The cost of acquiring the lease is $10,000 of which less than 75 percent is attributable to the initial ten-year term. A also erects a small building for $15,000 with a useful life of 25 years. Pursuant to the requirement of Section 178, A amortizes the cost of acquiring the lease and the cost of the building over 20 years (the original lease term plus the ten-year renewal period).

---

[1] *Oliver Iron Mining Co.,* 13 T.C. 416 (1949), *acq.* 1950-1 C.B. 4.
[2] *Bowman v. Comm.,* 32 F.2d 404 (C.A. Dist. Col. 1929).

If the lease terminates at the end of its initial term of ten years, A will be entitled to write off in such year the unamortized cost of acquiring the lease and the remaining cost of the building.

In addition, should the lessee be obligated to restore the leased property, then the costs of restoration are also deductible in the year of termination.

> *Example:* Under the terms of a ten-year lease, A is obligated to restore the leased premises to their original condition on termination. When the lease terminates in the tenth year, A incurs costs of $3,000 in effecting such restoration. Such costs are deductible in the year of termination.

PURCHASE OF THE FEE INTEREST

The situation is somewhat different where a lessee terminates a lease by purchasing the underlying fee interest. In such cases, the lessee may not write off his unamortized lease costs as in the case of normal termination. Rather, these costs must be added to the purchase price and treated as part of the cost of the property.[3]

> *Example:* Taxpayer leases a tract of land for ten years. The cost of acquiring the lease is $10,000. At the end of the sixth year, having amortized $6,000 of the cost of acquiring the lease, the taxpayer purchases the fee interest for $40,000. The taxpayer may not continue to amortize the cost of acquiring the lease, but must take the unamortized cost ($4,000) and add it to the basis of the land.

A similar rule applies to leasehold improvements, i.e., they must be depreciated over their remaining useful life.[4]

The question of whether the price paid for the fee itself can be written off was considered by the Supreme Court in the *Millinery Center Building Corporation* case.[5] The *Millinery* case involved the situation where a lessee leased a tract of land for 21 years, with options to renew for two additional 21-year periods, and erected a $3,000,000 building on it. The lease provided that on termination the building would vest in the lessor at the lessor's option.

During the first 21-year period of the lease, the lessee fully depreciated the entire $3,000,000 cost of the building. Subsequently, it exercised its option to renew the lease and the lease was renewed for an additional 21 years. Shortly thereafter, the lessee entered into an agreement with the owner of the property whereby it purchased the fee and was released from its obligations under the new lease. The price paid was $2,100,000.

The value of the land, as unimproved, was $660,000 and the lessee attempted to deduct the difference between the value of the unimproved land and the price paid as an ordinary or

---

[3] *Henry Boos*, 30 B.T.A. 882 (1934).
[4] Rev. Rul. 60-180, 1960-1 C.B. 114.
[5] 350 U.S. 456 (1956).

necessary expense of doing business, or in the alternative, to amortize it over the remaining term of the cancelled lease as a payment for cancellation of a burdensome lease.

The Supreme Court, however, concluded that the excess of the price paid over the value of the unimproved land was attributable to the building, and therefore, the taxpayer was neither entitled to deduct the difference immediately as a business expense nor to amortize it over the remaining period of the lease. Instead, the court held, the difference of $1,440,000 should be depreciated over the remaining useful life of the building.

It should be noted that the *Millinery Center* case specifically reserves the question of what happens where the price paid for the fee exceeds the value of the improvements and the underlying land. In such a case, it would seem that the excess must be payment for cancellation of a burdensome lease and the lessee should be allowed to write it off over the remaining period of the cancelled lease.

> *Example:* If in the *Millinery Center* case the price paid for the fee had been $3,000,000, the value of the unimproved land $660,000 and the value of the building $1,440,000, then the purchase price would exceed the value of the land and building by $900,000. Presumably, this represents a payment for cancellation of a burdensome lease and the taxpayer should be allowed to amortize it over the remaining period of the cancelled lease.

CANCELLATION BY LESSEE

A lessee who cancels a lease is normally entitled to deduct in the year of cancellation the unamortized cost of acquiring the lease[6] as well as the remaining cost of non-removable leasehold improvements.[7] In addition, payments to the lessor as damages for cancellation of the lease are also deductible.[8]

> *Example:* A enters into a ten-year lease for a tract of land. The cost of acquiring the lease is $5,000 and A has the property graded at a cost of $3,000. At the end of six years, having amortized 60 percent of the cost of acquiring the lease and the leasehold improvements, A cancels the lease and pays the lessor $2,000 in damages. A is entitled to write off in the year of cancellation not only the $2,000, but also the unamortized portion of the costs of acquiring the lease and leasehold improvements.

The above rules do not apply where the lessee cancels the old lease and enters into a new lease on the same premises. In such cases, the unamortized cost of the original lease is considered part of the cost of the new lease to be amortized over the term of the new lease.[9] The same rule would seem to apply to leasehold improvements, i.e., the unamortized cost of such

---

[6] *Supra* note 1.
[7] *Peerless Steel Equipment Co.*, 1967 P-H T.C. Memo ¶67,181; *Bowman v. Comm.*, *supra* note 2.
[8] Rev. Rul. 69-511, 1969-2 C.B. 24.
[9] *Pig & Whistle Co.*, 9 B.T.A. 668 (1927); *Phil Gluckstern's, Inc.*, 1956 P-H T.C. Memo ¶56,009.

improvements will have to be written off over the term of the new lease or their remaining useful life, whichever is shorter.

> *Example:* Taxpayer enters into a ten-year lease of a factory building which has a useful life of 40 years. The cost of acquiring the lease is $10,000 and the taxpayer makes structural improvements to the building costing another $20,000. At the end of the seventh year of the lease, after the taxpayer has amortized $7,000 of the costs of acquiring the lease and $14,000 of the cost of the improvements, the lease is cancelled and the taxpayer and the lessor enter into a new 20-year lease. The taxpayer may not write off the remaining costs of acquiring the old lease and the leasehold improvements in the year the old lease is cancelled, but instead must amortize them over the 20-year period of the new lease.

Suppose, however, the new lease is not for a definite term, but is month-to-month or at will. There is one old case, *Washington Catering Co.*[10] which allowed a writeoff of the unamortized costs of leasehold improvements in the year of cancellation of a lease even though the lessee continued to occupy the premises on a month-to-month basis. Although the Commissioner acquiesced in the case, the decision is somewhat open to question, particularly where it appears fairly certain that the lessee will continue to occupy the premises indefinitely, notwithstanding the fact that it only has a month-to-month lease.

This was brought out rather clearly in the *Standard Tube Co.* case.[11] The taxpayer in the *Standard Tube* case had been renting premises from the Ford Motor Company since 1928. In 1936, a written lease was executed which expired on December 31, 1938. During 1936 and 1937, the taxpayer expended $98,000 for the installation of a seamless tube mill and related equipment, and almost $19,000 for foundations and installation costs for other machinery and equipment. Although the term of the written lease expired on December 31, 1938, the taxpayer continued to occupy the property on a year-to-year basis and continued to depreciate the cost of the assets over their useful life.

In 1939, the taxpayer sold the seamless tube mill and auxiliary equipment and claimed a loss for its undepreciated cost. This loss was ultimately utilized on the taxpayer's 1941 return under the then carryover provisions of the Internal Revenue Code.

The Internal Revenue Service examined the taxpayer's 1941 tax return and disallowed the loss on the sale of the tube mill and also the depreciation claimed for the year with respect to the $19,000 of foundation and installation costs relating to the other machinery and equipment. The Service took the position that the cost of the tube mill and the foundation and installation costs of the other machinery and equipment should have been written off in 1938, the year in which the lease terminated.

Despite the formal termination of the lease, the Tax Court concluded that it was apparent that both the lessor and the lessee were agreed that the tenancy would be continued indefinitely, and that the expenditure of over $100,000 in 1936 and 1937 would not have been made if the lessee had not anticipated some sort of extension of its occupancy. Accordingly, the

---

[10] 9 B.T.A. 743 (1927), *acq.* VII-2 C.B. 41.
[11] 6 T.C. 950 (1946).

court held that a writeoff of the unamortized cost of the mill and equipment in the year the lease formally terminated would have been improper and that the taxpayer was correct in depreciating the cost of such assets over their remaining useful life.

What the case illustrates is that the termination of a tenant's legal right to occupy premises will not justify the writeoff of unamortized leasehold improvements if, as a practical matter, it is reasonably clear that the tenant will remain in possession.

LIQUIDATION OF A CORPORATE LESSEE

The writeoff of unamortized leasehold costs and leasehold improvements where a corporate lessee is liquidated has been the subject of considerable litigation over the years, particularly where the lessor owns stock of the liquidating corporation. This was the situation in the *Cooper Foundation* case.[12] In the *Cooper* case the lessee, a corporation, paid a premium in order to enter into a 25-year lease. Shortly thereafter, the lessor acquired all the stock of the lessee, the lease was cancelled, and the lessee liquidated. In the lessee's final tax return a loss was claimed for the unamortized portion of the premium paid to acquire the lease.

The Commissioner challenged the writeoff and argued that the unamortized premium was not deductible by the corporation in the year of dissolution since the cancellation of the lease was in substance a distribution in liquidation and a transfer of the leasehold interest to the corporation's shareholder. The Fifth Circuit accepted the Commissioner's theory and refused to allow a writeoff of the unamortized portion of the premium in the year of dissolution.

The *Cooper* case is to be contrasted with the *Strauss* case.[13] In the *Strauss* case, a wholesale beer and liquor distributor entered into a 15-year lease with lessors owning 60 percent of its stock. After six years, the corporation lost its liquor franchise which accounted for 75 percent of its business. After trying unsuccessfully to obtain another franchise, the corporation cancelled its lease and subsequently dissolved. It claimed a loss in the year of dissolution for the unamortized cost of its leasehold improvements on the theory that, since the lease had been cancelled and title to the improvements passed to the lessor, the year of dissolution was the proper year for the writeoff. The Service contested the deduction, relying on the *Cooper* case and *Tom L. Burnett Cattle Co.*,[14] a case involving facts and a result similar to the *Cooper* case.

The District Court distinguished these cases, however, and allowed the writeoff in the year of dissolution, placing great emphasis on the fact that there was a valid business reason for the cancellation and liquidation, i.e., the loss of 75 percent of the lessee's business, and also relying heavily on the fact that the taxpayer was not wholly-owned by the lessor and the lease appeared to be an arms-length lease. Thus, if the rationale of the *Strauss* case prevails, a corporation will be allowed to write off the unamortized costs of acquiring a lease or the unamortized costs of leasehold improvements in the year in which the lease is cancelled

---

[12] *Cooper Foundation v. O'Malley*, 221 F.2d 279 (8th Cir., 1955).
[13] *Strauss v. U. S.*, 199 F. Supp. 845 (W. D. La. 1961).
[14] *Tom L. Burnett Cattle Co.*, 1960 P-H T.C. Memo ¶60, 015.

preparatory to dissolution, even where the lessor is a shareholder of the lessee corporation, provided there is a *bona fide* business reason for the cancellation.

This should be true even where the lessor is the sole shareholder of the corporate lessee although it must be admitted that the *Strauss* case did not go quite this far.

Assuming that there is a lack of business motive for the cancellation as in the *Cooper* case, so that the lease is deemed to be distributed to the stockholder lessor, what happens to the unamortized costs of acquiring the lease or the unamortized cost of leasehold improvements?

The *Wolan* case[15] takes the position that the proper treatment in such circumstances is for the shareholder to continue to amortize the cost of acquiring the lease over the remaining term of the cancelled lease.

> *Example:* X corporation, the stock of which is wholly owned by Y, enters into a ten-year lease for a building. The costs of acquiring the lease are $40,000. Two years after X enters into the lease, Y purchases the building. Six months later, the lease is cancelled and X is liquidated. Assuming there was no valid business reason for the cancellation of the lease and liquidation, X would not be entitled to write off the unamortized costs of acquiring the lease in the year of dissolution, but Y will be allowed to amortize them over the remaining period of the cancelled lease.

Arguably, although the *Wolan* case does not reach the point where leasehold improvements are involved, their unamortized cost should be depreciated over their remaining useful life or amortized over the remaining term of the cancelled lease, whichever is shorter.

The situation is somewhat different where a liquidating corporation cancels a lease and the shareholders of the corporation are not related to the lessor. In such a case, it cannot be argued that the lease has been distributed to the shareholders and, in fact, all rights relating to the lease are extinguished at the time it is cancelled. It would, therefore, seem that the corporation should be allowed to deduct the unamortized cost of acquiring the lease, and the unamortized cost of leasehold improvements, in the year of cancellation. The *Strauss* case mentioned above would surely support this conclusion.

> *Example:* Taxpayer, a corporation, leases a tract of land from an unrelated lessor for 20 years. The cost of acquiring the lease is $20,000 and the cost of non-removable leasehold improvements is $40,000. In the 17th year of the lease, after $17,000 of the cost of acquiring the lease and $34,000 of the cost of the leasehold improvements have been amortized, the lease is cancelled. The taxpayer is entitled to write off in the year of cancellation the unamortized cost of acquiring the lease ($3,000) and the unamortized cost of leasehold improvements ($6,000).

Suppose, however, that the lease in question is assignable and that the corporation which is liquidating assigns the lease to its shareholders. For example, assume that a corporation which paid $10,000 to acquire a lease subsequently liquidates, assigning the lease to its

---

[15] *Wolan v. Comm.*, 184 F.2d 101 (10th Cir., 1950). The *Cooper* case, *supra* footnote 12, suggests the same result.

shareholders who are unrelated to the lessor. In such circumstances, it would seem clear that the corporation will not be entitled to claim a deduction in the year of dissolution for the unamortized costs of acquiring the lease. The shareholders will, of course, under the *Wolan* case be entitled to write off the unamortized portion of acquiring the lease over its remaining term.

CANCELLATION BY LESSOR

Cancellation by the lessor will normally result in a payment to the lessee as damages for cancellation.

> *Example:* A leases a building from B for 20 years at a rental of $10,000 a year. In the 11th year of the lease, B decides he needs the building for his own use and wishes to cancel A's lease. It is recognized that should A agree to the cancellation he will be forced to rent another building at a higher rent, plus he will incur certain moving expenses. These additional costs will approximate $15,000. B therefore agrees to pay A $15,000 as damages for cancellation of the lease.

Section 1241 of the Internal Revenue Code provides that such payments are to be considered as amounts received in exchange for the lease. Since leases of business property and equipment are either real property or property of a character subject to depreciation,[16] the result of Section 1241 is to allow payments received for cancellation of a lease used in the taxpayer's trade or business to qualify for Section 1231 treatment. This is usually a favorable result[17] since under Section 1231 if a taxpayer's Section 1231 transactions for the taxable year result in a net gain, then the gain is treated as a capital gain, and if they result in a net loss, the loss is treated as an ordinary loss.

> *Example 1:* A leases a property for a 15-year term. At the end of five years, the lessor requests cancellation of the lease and offers to pay $8,000 as damages for cancellation. Assuming A has no other Section 1231 transactions during the year, the $8,000 gain will be taxed as a long-term capital gain.

> *Example 2:* Assume the same facts as in the above example except that A had another Section 1231 transaction during the year which resulted in a $50,000 loss. In this case, since the Section 1231 transactions for the year will result in a net loss ($50,000 loss + $8,000 gain = $42,000 net loss), the $8,000 will not be treated as a capital gain but will offset the ordinary loss from the other Section 1231 transaction.

Any investment by the lessee in the lease must be taken into consideration in computing the amount of the gain or loss. For example, a lessee who has paid a premium to acquire a lease

---

[16] Reg. 1.162-11(a); Rev. Rul. 72-85, 1972 P-H ¶54,912.

[17] This assumes, of course, that the leasehold interest has been held for more than six months.

should offset the unamortized cost of such premium against the amount he receives as damages for cancellation of the lease in determining his gain or loss on the transaction.[18]

> *Example:* A paid a premium of $20,000 to acquire a ten-year lease. In the sixth year of the lease, having amortized $10,000 of the cost of acquiring it, he accepts $7,000 as damages for cancellation by the lessor. A has incurred a loss of $3,000 on the cancellation ($10,000 unamortized cost of acquiring the lease − $7,000 damages).

The same thing is true as to leasehold improvements, i.e., their unamortized cost must also be offset against the amounts received as damages for cancellation of the lease in order to determine the gain or loss on cancellation.

> *Example:* Taxpayer enters into a 20-year lease for a tract of land and erects a building with a 25-year life on it at a cost of $100,000. At the end of the tenth year, the lessor cancels the lease and the taxpayer accepts $60,000 in damages. The taxpayer's gain from the cancellation is $10,000 ($60,000 damages less $50,000 unamortized cost of leasehold improvements).

As a result of the Revenue Acts of 1962 and 1964, depreciation recapture must also be taken into consideration if the cancellation results in a gain to the lessee. Where the property leased is machinery or other Section 1245 property, the Regulations take the position there is recapture, to the extent of the gain, of the post-1962 amortization or depreciation of the cost of acquiring the lease and of leasehold improvements.[19]

> *Example:* A holds a favorable five-year lease on a cargo ship. The lease is assignable and A assigns it to B for $25,000. After two years, when B has amortized $10,000 of the cost of acquiring the lease, the lessor offers B $30,000 to cancel the lease. B will have a gain from the cancellation of $15,000 ($30,000 payment for cancellation less unamortized cost of acquiring the lease, $15,000) of which $10,000 (amortization claimed by B while he held the lease) will be treated as ordinary income under the depreciation recapture rules.

A similar problem exists with respect to leases of land or buildings since the House Committee Report to the '64 Act makes it clear that ". . . a leasehold of land or of section 1250 property is intangible real property, and accordingly such a leasehold is section 1250 property.[20]

As a practical matter, where real property is concerned, depreciation recapture is generally a problem only as to leasehold improvements and even then only where their useful life is less than the term of the lease. The reason for this is that there can be depreciation recapture under Section 1250, after the first year of the lease,[21] only to the extent that

---

[18] *Cassatt v. Comm.*, 137 F.2d 745 (3rd Cir., 1943).

[19] Reg. 1.1245-3(a)(2). It should be noted that there is a question as to whether the regulation is a valid interpretation of the statute. See, *Horvitz*, 129-2nd T.M., *Depreciation Recapture*—Section 1245—General, at A-43.

[20] H. Rept. No. 749, 88th Congress, 1964-1 C.B. (Part 2) 125 at 401.

[21] Where property is held for one year or less all depreciation or amortization claimed is subject to recapture.

post-1964 depreciation exceeds straight line depreciation.[22] Since the costs of acquiring a lease must be amortized, i.e., deducted in equal amounts over the life of the lease, there can obviously be no excess depreciation with respect to such costs after the first year. The same is true as to leasehold improvements which have a useful life greater than the term of the lease. Their cost must also be amortized in equal amounts over the term of the lease and, therefore, there can be no excess depreciation. Where, however, the useful life of the improvements is less than the term of the lease, then the lessee would depreciate rather than amortize their cost and Section 1250 could apply.

> *Example:* A leases a tract of land for 50 years and erects a warehouse with a useful life of 40 years at a cost of $100,000. A depreciates the building using double declining balance depreciation. Three years later, the lessor cancels the lease and A accepts $125,000 as damages. Depreciation for the three years has been $14,263. Straight line depreciation for the three years would be $7,500. The gain to A from the cancellation is $39,263 ($125,000 damages less $85,737 adjusted basis for building) of which $6,763 is treated as ordinary income because of depreciation recapture.

Partial Cancellation

Section 1241 will apply even where the payment is for partial cancellation. Thus, a payment to a lessee by a lessor for a reduction in the term of the lease or a cancellation as to a portion of the leased premises will also qualify for Section 1241 treatment.[23]

> *Example 1:* Taxpayer leases a building for a term of 20 years. In the fifth year of the lease, the lessor cancels the last ten years of the lease and pays the taxpayer $15,000 in damages. The $15,000 payment is covered by Section 1241.

> *Example 2:* Taxpayer leases a 4-acre tract of land for 50 years. In the tenth year of the lease, the lessor cancels the lease as to two of the four acres and pays the taxpayer $50,000 in damages. The $50,000 payment qualifies for Section 1241 treatment.

Lease Subject to Sublease

The fact that a lease is subject to a sublease may affect the treatment of payments received by the lessee to compensate for the lessor's cancellation of the lease. In Revenue Ruling 129,[24] the Internal Revenue Service took the position that where a lease with less than two years to run and subject to subleases was surrendered, the proceeds received by the lessee were ordinary income to the extent that they were attributable to the rents that would have been received from the sublessee.

> *Example:* Taxpayer leases a property for five years. After a year, he subleases the property for the balance of the lease term to B at a rental of $4,000 a year. When the lease has only a

---

[22] Sec. 1250(b)(1).
[23] Reg. 1.1241-1(b).
[24] 1953-2 C.B. 97, *reaffirmed* Rev. Rul. 56-531, 1956-2 C.B. 983, *clarified* Rev. Rul. 72-85, 1972 P-H ¶54,912.

year and a half remaining, the lessor cancels it and pays $6,000 to the taxpayer as damages. Under Revenue Ruling 129, the $6,000 would be treated as ordinary income rather than as Section 1231 gain.

Lessor and Lessee Related

The treatment of payments received by the lessee as damages for cancellation of a lease will also be affected if the lessor and lessee are related. For example, in the *McEnery* case,[25] a lessee relinquished the remaining term of his lease to the lessor for $11,000. The lessor was a corporation, almost 90 percent of whose stock was owned by the lessee, his spouse, and his minor children. Despite the lessee's contention that the $11,000 constituted a long-term capital gain, the Tax Court in a memorandum decision held that the relinquishment of the leasehold was a sale or exchange of depreciable property and therefore the amount received by the lessee was ordinary income under Section 1239 of the Code rather than capital gain.

Payment from Sublessee

Occasionally the payment to cancel a lease will come from a sublessee rather than the lessor.

> *Example:* A leases a property from B for five years. A then subleases the property to C for three years. Two years later C decides it wants the property for more than 3 years and offers A $20,000 if it will surrender its lease to the lessor, thus allowing C and B to negotiate a longer term lease.

If A accepts the payment it will qualify as a payment in exchange for A's leasehold interest[26] since there is no requirement under Section 1241 that the payment be received only from the lessor.

ASSIGNMENT OF A LEASE

Where a lease does not prohibit assignment, or the lessor is willing to consent to assignment notwithstanding the terms of the lease, a lessee may sell his interest in the lease by assigning it to a third party who agrees to pay the rent stipulated in the lease and perform all other obligations of the lessee under the lease. The assignment of a leasehold interest is to be distinguished from a sublease since in a sublease the lessee retains an interest in the property; whereas in an assignment, he relinquishes his entire interest in the leased property, even though he may remain contingently liable on the lease.

> *Example:* Taxpayer leases a property for 20 years. In the fifth year of the lease, he transfers his remaining interest in the lease to B in exchange for $10,000 and B's promise to pay the

---

[25] *J. P. McEnery,* 1967 P-H T.C. Memo ¶67,213.
[26] *Metropolitan Building Co.,* 282 F.2d 592, (9th Cir., 1960).

rent due under the lease. Taxpayer has made an assignment of his interest in the lease. If he had given B the right to occupy the property for only ten of the remaining 15 years of the lease, he would have effected a sublease rather than an assignment since he retained an interest in the property.

Whether a transaction results in an assignment or a sublease is important from a tax viewpoint because the assignment of a lease used in the taxpayer's trade or business is treated as the sale of a Section 1231 asset, with the normal result being capital gains treatment if the Section 1231 transactions for the year result in a net gain. Amounts received from a sublessee, on the other hand, are treated as ordinary income.

Despite the advantages of assigning a lease as opposed to subleasing, many transactions fall into the latter category because the lessee chooses, or is forced, to retain an interest in the property. For example, a lessee who assigns a lease but is unable to get the lessor to release him from liability on the lease may be forced to retain a right to reenter in the event of a breach of the assignee's obligations. Although the lessee has, as a practical matter, relinquished all interest in the lease, the retention of the technical right to reenter in the event of the assignee's default will cause the assignment to be treated as a sublease.[27] Similarly, the retention of a renewal option[28] or the reservation of the right to exercise a purchase option[29] will also cause an assignment to be treated as a sublease. Thus, if a lessee is seeking the favorable tax treatment that results from having a transaction classified as an assignment rather than a sublease, he must be sure to relinquish his entire interest in the property.[30]

---

[27] *Voloudakis v. Comm.*, 274 F.2d 209 (9th Cir., 1960).

[28] *Fairmount Park Raceway, Inc.*, 1962 P-H T.C. Memo ¶62,014 (the taxpayer also retained a right of re-entry).

[29] Rev. Rul. 57-537, 1957-2 C.B. 52.

[30] The fact that the lessee may remain contingently liable on the lease does not render the transaction a sublease so long as the lessee has not retained the right to reenter on default. Rev. Rul. 72-85, 1972 P-H ¶54,770.

Chapter 6

Realizing Tax Savings Through
Sale and Leaseback

The sale and leaseback has become increasingly popular in recent years, both as a means of raising working capital and because of the tax advantages it can offer.

A sale and leaseback is essentially a financing device. It enables the owner of business property to convert the property into working capital while at the same time retaining its use. It more commonly involves real estate, rather than equipment, for reasons which will be discussed later.

The alternative to the sale-leaseback is conventional financing, e.g., a mortgage. A mortgage produces no particular tax advantages but does generate working capital. Frequently, however, the sale and leaseback technique will produce a greater amount of working capital than the conventional mortgage. This is because a purchaser, assured of a profitable long-term lease, may be willing to pay more for the property than a mortgagor would lend.[1] In addition, a sale and leaseback can offer certain tax advantages not available through conventional financing.

TAX ADVANTAGES OF A SALE AND LEASEBACK

Perhaps the best way to illustrate the tax savings possible through a sale-leaseback is by discussing the *May Dept. Store Co.* case,[2] one of the more famous cases in the sale-leaseback area.

In the *May Dept. Store* case, the taxpayer was interested in generating working capital. It owned a parking lot with a cost of approximately $2,500,000 and a fair market value of $460,000. Whether the company could have mortgaged the parking lot and for what amount

---

[1] As discussed in Chapter 1, it is often impossible to get a mortgage representing 100 percent of the value of a property. Leasing frequently offers an opportunity for 100 percent financing and thus can produce a greater amount of working capital. In addition, leasing offers the not inconsequential advantage, also discussed in Chapter 1, of off-balance sheet financing.

[2] 16 T.C. 547 (1951) *acq.*, 1951-2 C.B. 3.

was not discussed. Presumably, it could not have mortgaged the property for more than its fair market value.

Rather than mortgage the property, the company entered into a sale-and-leaseback transaction which provided for the sale of the parking lot to a group of investors at a price of $460,000 ($100,000 down and the balance payable over 20 years at 4 percent) and a leaseback for 20 years at an annual rental of $32,000 plus real estate taxes and certain other charges. The sale produced immediate working capital of $100,000, and a tax loss of over $2,000,000, which saved almost $1,500,000 in excess-profits taxes. The result of the transaction was that the department store was able to increase its working capital by $1,600,000 (the down payment on the purchase price plus the tax saving). This increase in working capital far exceeded the amount (a maximum of $460,000) which would have been produced had the company tried to borrow against the property.

The *May Dept. Store Co.* case is a classic case in illustrating the usefulness of the sale-leaseback technique. It should be noted that although the sale and leaseback itself produced some working capital, what really made the transaction a financial success was the tax loss. Since the parking lot was essentially a nondepreciable asset, the taxpayer never would have realized this loss had it continued to hold the property.

It is not essential, of course, that a property have a high cost in relation to its fair market value in order to make a sale and leaseback advantageous. A taxpayer who owns a piece of land with a fair market value comparable to its cost could also benefit from a sale and leaseback since the leaseback would enable him to claim a rental deduction for use of the land; whereas, previously, because land is not depreciable, he had no deduction at all. Whether such a transaction will produce an *initial* infusion of working capital depends on the terms of the sales agreement. Many such agreements provide for payment of the purchase price on the installment basis in which case there would not be any significant initial increase in working capital. To the extent the sale is for cash, of course, the taxpayer would experience an immediate increase in working capital. In any event, gaining a tax deduction for the use of the land will produce a significant increase in working capital over a period of years whether the sale is on the installment basis or not.

> *Example:* A company sells a piece of land for what it paid for it, i.e., $360,000, payable $20,000 a year for 18 years. It then leases it back for 20 years at a rental of $20,000 a year thereby reducing its income taxes and increasing its working capital by approximately $10,000 a year. Over the 20-year period its total working capital will have been increased by $152,000, computed as follows:
>
> | | |
> |---|---|
> | $360,000 | sales price |
> | –400,000 | rental payments |
> | 192,000 | tax saving at 48 percent |
> | $152,000 | net increase in working capital |

The sale and leaseback can also be attractive in a situation where depreciable property with a high fair market value has a low depreciable base, either because it was purchased some time ago and the base has been substantially reduced through depreciation or because the initial cost was low. In such a situation, the owner could sell it, recognize a capital gain, and then take ordinary deductions for the amount of the rental payments. If the taxpayer is a corporation, it has in effect traded a capital gain taxed at a 30 percent rate for deductions which offset income otherwise taxable at 48 percent.

> *Example:* A, a corporation, owns a building which cost $200,000 and which has been fully depreciated for many years. It has a fair market value of $500,000. If A were to sell the building and then rent it back at its fair rental value of $20,000 a year for 25 years, A would have a capital gains tax of $150,000 to pay in connection with the sale (30 percent of $500,000) but would save $240,000 in taxes as a result of the rental deductions (48 percent of $500,000).

The usefulness of the sale and leaseback in the above situation has to some extent been reduced by the depreciation recapture rules in cases where the low basis is the result of depreciation. The recapture rules do not, however, provide for complete recapture since only the excess of accelerated over straight line depreciation is subject to recapture, and even the excess may not be subject to recapture to the extent it is attributable to pre-1970 depreciation.[3] Thus, the technique can still be quite profitable even where the low basis is the result of depreciation.

> *Example:* A corporation owns a factory which cost $500,000 and on which $400,000 of depreciation has been claimed. The factory has a fair market value of $1,000,000. Excess depreciation since 1970 was $50,000. If the corporation should sell the building and then rent it back for 25 years at a rental of $40,000 a year, it will pay $279,000[4] in tax as the result of the sale but will save $480,000 in taxes due to the rental deduction (48 percent of $40,000 a year × 25 years).

The recapture rules, of course, have no application where the low basis is the result of a low initial purchase price.

LOSS OF REVERSION

It should be noted that despite the advantages of the sale and leaseback, particularly from a tax viewpoint, there is one basic disadvantage. The disadvantage is that the seller-lessee

---

[3] Sec. 1250.

[4]

$1,000,000	selling price	
− 100,000	basis	
$ 900,000	gain	
$ 850,000	capital gain taxed at 30%	($255,000)
50,000	ordinary gain taxed at 48%	(24,000)
		$279,000

must relinquish the reversionary right to the property. This means that the lessee will normally have no further right to the property once the lease term has expired. Thus, he gives up not only the right to use the property after the lease term, but also the right to any future appreciation in value.

> *Example:* X corporation owns a tract of land which it has been using in its business. The land cost $300,000 and has a fair market value of $400,000. Its fair rental value under a 20-year lease would be $20,000 a year. If X sells the land for cash and then as part of the transaction rents it back at its fair rental value, it will initially increase its working capital by $370,000 ($400,000 sales price less $30,000 capital gains tax). Over the next 20 years, it will pay $400,000 in rent with an after tax cost of approximately $200,000. Thus, at the end of the 20-year period, X would seem to be ahead in terms of cash flow by $170,000 ($370,000 − $200,000). X will, however, have lost any right to the property, and should it have appreciated during the term of the lease by say $100,000, X will have lost this appreciation also. Thus the cost to X of increasing its working capital by $170,000 would seem to be $500,000, the value of the land at the end of the 20-year lease term.

Despite the obvious disadvantage of losing the reversionary interest, businesses continue to enter into sale-and-leaseback transactions. They do so because they are convinced that the working capital advantages outweigh the loss of the reversionary interest. The theory is that the amount that can be earned with the working capital produced by the transaction will justify the loss of the reversion.

Determining whether a sale-leaseback would be advisable in a particular case is not easy since it involves, among other things, predicting what the company will be earning on its money a number of years into the future. Computing the value of the reversion at the end of the lease term is also difficult since it requires projecting the property's rate of appreciation (or depreciation) over a significant period of time.

The problem is even more complicated where the property could be mortgaged. In such cases, the immediate infusion of working capital resulting from a sale of the property can be matched to a large extent by mortgaging the property. Thus, the additional cash flow resulting from a sale-leaseback will largely result from the rental deductions exceeding the interest and depreciation deductions available to a mortgagee.

It is also important to realize that the effective interest rate in a sale-and-leaseback transaction (since the purchaser in a sale-leaseback usually looks on the transaction as a financing arrangement, the rent charged will reflect an appropriate interest rate) is usually higher than would be paid on a mortgage. This additional interest cost further reduces the benefit to be derived from a sale-leaseback as opposed to a mortgage.

SALE AND LEASEBACK OF EQUIPMENT

Although the sale and leaseback can be used with machinery and equipment, it is not as commonly used as it is in situations involving real estate. The reason is that the tax advantages generally associated with the sale and leaseback of real estate are not present to the same degree in the sale and leaseback of equipment. First of all, equipment is depreciable and, therefore, one does not normally have the situation, as is frequently true of real estate, of a high-cost, nondepreciable asset. In addition, appreciation in the value of equipment tends to be somewhat limited and again we usually do not have the situation, as is often the case in real estate, of a value substantially in excess of cost. Finally, the depreciation recapture rules are much more restrictive with respect to equipment, thus reducing the possibility of trading a capital gain for ordinary deductions.

> *Example:* A taxpayer sells a building, with an undepreciated cost of $10,000, in a sale-leaseback transaction for its original cost of $30,000. The excess of accelerated over straight line depreciation since 1969 is $5,000. Only $5,000 of the $20,000 gain on the building will be taxed as ordinary income and the balance ($15,000) will be taxed at capital gains rates. If, however, the taxpayer sells a machine purchased in 1964, with an undepreciated cost of $10,000, for its original cost of $30,000, then the entire $20,000 gain will be subject to depreciation recapture and taxed at ordinary income rates.

This is not to say that there are no advantages to the sale and leaseback of equipment. Although the sale and leaseback of equipment does not offer the opportunities for tax savings that the sale and leaseback of real estate does, there still can be tax savings resulting from accelerated writeoffs through rental deductions. In addition, there may be significant non-tax advantages such as elimination of the risk of obsolescence. These were discussed more fully in Chapter 1.

POSSIBLE ATTACKS BY THE INTERNAL REVENUE SERVICE

Obviously, any device which offers significant tax advantages, such as the sale and leaseback of real estate, is going to be subject to close scrutiny by the Internal Revenue Service. One can expect the Service to attack such transactions on a number of grounds. First, where the taxpayer is trying to claim a loss, the Service might take the position that the sale constitutes a "like kind exchange" on which, under the Internal Revenue Code, no loss can be recognized.[5] For example in *Century Electric Co. v. Commissioner,*[6] a taxpayer sold its foundry to a college at a loss of almost $400,000, leasing the property back for a term of 95 years, subject to termination by the taxpayer at ten-year intervals starting with the 25th year. The Commissioner argued, and the court agreed, that a leasehold for such a term was "like kind" property and, therefore, the loss could not be deducted initially but had to be written off over the term of the lease.

The question of when a leasehold becomes "like kind" property is one that unfortunately cannot be answered with absolute certainty. The Internal Revenue Service Regulations take

---

[5] Section 1031 of the Internal Revenue Code provides that if a taxpayer exchanges property held for productive use in trade or business or for investment (but not including stock in trade, securities or certain other items) for property of a "like kind" to be held for productive use in a trade or business or for investment, then no gain or loss will be recognized on the transaction.

[6] 15 T.C. 581 (1950), *affirmed* 192 F.2d 155 (8th Cir., 1951).

the position that a leasehold of real estate for a term of 30 years or more is the equivalent of a fee interest. Therefore, a sale and leaseback of real estate for a term of 30 years or more would be an exchange of "like kind" property.[7] The courts have not always followed this rule, as illustrated by the *Jordan Marsh*[8] case.

In the *Jordan Marsh* case, a taxpayer sold a piece of real estate at a substantial loss, and as part of the transaction took back a lease for a term of 30 years and 3 days. The Service attacked the transaction on the ground that a lease for such a period was essentially equivalent to the fee interest and, therefore, a like-kind exchange within the meaning of Section 1031. The Second Circuit, however, upheld the taxpayer and ruled that the like-kind exchange provisions of the Internal Revenue Code did not apply. It found that a sale for cash, at fair market value, together with a leaseback at fair rental value was not an "exchange" within the meaning of Section 1031, and, therefore, the taxpayer was entitled to deduct the loss.

As a result of the *Jordan Marsh*[9] case, the question of whether a lease for 30 years or more will be treated as like kind property remains somewhat unresolved. Most tax practitioners take the view that the term of the lease should not exceed 30 years[10] if the like kind problem is to be avoided.

As an alternative to an attack under Section 1031, the Commissioner may take the view that the lease is a valuable one in the sense that the rent under it is lower than it normally should be and, therefore, the value of the lease itself should be taken into consideration in computing the loss on the transaction. The Commissioner was successful with this approach in the *Steinway*[11] case, where the taxpayer sold a property for a cash price that was less than fair market value, plus the right to occupy the property rent-free for a period of years. The court held that the value of the right to occupy the property rent-free was part of the sales price.

One apparent way to avoid the *Steinway* problem would be to "carve out" the lease prior to the sale. The seller would then be able to argue that it had not received the lease as part of the sales price and, therefore, its value should not be taken into consideration in determining the loss on the sale.

> *Example:* Instead of selling a property for $400,000 plus the right to occupy the property rent-free, or at a favorable rent, the taxpayer transfers the property *subject to* its right to continue to occupy the property rent-free, or at a favorable rental, for X years.

The difficulty with this approach is that the Commissioner might argue that an allocable part of the property's basis should be allocated to the retained lease. If the Commissioner's argument is accepted, the result could be worse than if the value of the lease had been included in the sales price.

---

[7] Regs. 1.1031(a)-1(c).

[8] *Jordan Marsh Co. v. Commissioner*, 269 F.2d 453 (2nd Cir., 1959).

[9] See also, *City Investing Co.*, 38 T.C. 1 (1962), *nonacq.* 1963-1 C.B. 5.

[10] Leases with an original term of less than 30 years, but with options that may extend the term beyond thirty years, may be treated as leases for more than 30 years, and therefore should, if possible, be avoided.

[11] 46 T.C. 375 (1966), *acq.* 1967-1 C.B. 3.

> *Example:* A sells a tract of land, with a basis of $600,000 and a fair market value of $400,000, for $300,000 subject to A's right to continue to occupy the building at a rental of $5,000 a year for 15 years. On such facts, the Service may take the position that A is not entitled to claim an immediate loss of $300,000 ($600,000 cost less $300,000 selling price) but rather must allocate part of the cost of the land (presumably one-fourth or $150,000) to the reserved leasehold and amortize it over the life of the lease. The effect will be to reduce A's immediate loss by $150,000 even though the inclusion of the value of the leasehold in the purchase price would have reduced the loss by only $100,000.

Even if the Commissioner fails in the above attacks, there is still the basic question of whether the taxpayer has effected a leaseback or has really just borrowed the purchase price of the property. In a situation where the useful life of the property is substantially in excess of the lease term, and there are no renewal options or options to purchase, there will be no problem. Should, however, there be renewal options which approximate the useful life of the property, or options to repurchase, the Commissioner may take the position that the net effect of the transaction is not a sale and leaseback but really the borrowing of money using the property as security.

> *Example:* A sells a building for $500,000 and then leases it back at a rental of $15,000 a year for 20 years, with an option to renew for another 20 years at the same rent. The building has a useful life of less than 40 years. On these facts, the Service might contend that A has mortgaged rather than sold the property.

It should be recognized that the problem here is basically the same as that discussed in Chapter 2, except that in the normal lease situation the question is whether the taxpayer has leased the property or purchased it and here the question is whether the taxpayer has sold the property or borrowed against it.

The consequences of having a transaction treated as a loan rather than a sale and leaseback could be disastrous. Any initial loss will be disallowed and rental deductions, except to the extent that they represent interest charges, will also be disallowed. The taxpayer will be entitled to a depreciation deduction if the property is depreciable. In effect, the taxpayer will be put in the same position as if he had mortgaged the property.[12] Although this may not be a particular problem to one who entered into the transaction for other than tax savings, it will be a serious blow to those whose primary motive for the sale and leaseback was to save taxes.

SALE AND LEASEBACK WITH A CHARITABLE INSTITUTION— THE CLAY BROWN PROBLEM

Until the advent of the Tax Reform Act of 1969, one of the more ingenious uses of the sale-leaseback involved a sale to, and a leaseback from, a charitable organization.

The technique was designed to take advantage of the charity's exemption from income

---

[12] Rev. Rul. 72–543, 1972 P-H ¶55,523.

tax and had been upheld by the Supreme Court in the famous *Clay Brown* case.[13] In that case, the shareholders of a corporation sold its stock to a tax-exempt charity for a nominal down payment with the balance of the purchase price to be paid only out of the profits of the business. The charity liquidated the corporation and leased its assets for five years to a new corporation managed by the former shareholders of the liquidated corporation. The new corporation paid 80 percent of its profits to the charity as rent and the charity passed on 90 percent of the rent to the former shareholders of the liquidated corporation to be applied against the purchase price. Because the charity was exempt from tax on the rental income it received, it was able to pay substantially more for the business than a normal buyer could have paid. In effect, Uncle Sam was paying part of the purchase price.

The Treasury tried to attack the transaction by denying capital gains treatment to the shareholders of the corporation on the sale of their stock to the charity. Initially, the Commissioner took the position that the transaction was a sham. On appeal to the Supreme Court, he abandoned this argument and contended instead that the transaction was not really a sale within the meaning of Section 1222(3) since the entire risk for the transaction rested with the seller, the charity having invested only a nominal amount and having assumed no independent liability for the purchase price.

Despite the Commissioner's contention, the Supreme Court held that the transaction was a valid sale and the proceeds qualified for capital gains treatment.

Having lost its attack on the sellers, the Treasury then concentrated its energies on the charities, trying to classify the rentals received by the charities as unrelated business income. This presented some difficulty since the rules which treated rental income as unrelated business income excluded rental income from a lease of five years or less. Also, as the Committee Reports to the 1969 Act[14] pointed out, there was some question as to whether the tax on unrelated income applied to income from the leasing by a tax-exempt organization of assets constituting a going business.

Nevertheless, the Treasury pressed its attack in a case involving a particularly blatant use of the *Clay Brown* technique. The case in question involved the University Hill Foundation,[15] which had been organized to raise funds for Loyola University of Los Angeles.

During the period 1945 to 1954, the foundation acquired 24 businesses. As in the *Clay Brown* case, the businesses, usually corporations, were liquidated and their assets leased to newly-formed operating companies in which the former owners of the businesses had only minority interests. Under the terms of the leases, the operators retained 20 percent of the profits, the foundation received 8 percent, and the former owners of the business 72 percent.

The Commissioner's attack involved two contentions. One, that by engaging in such transactions, the foundation had really been engaged in business and therefore did not meet the requirements for exemption as a charitable institution within the meaning of Section 101(6) of the 1939 Code and Section 501(c)(3) of the 1954 Code; and, two, the rental received from the

---

[13] *Comm. v. Clay B. Brown*, 380 U.S. 563 (1965).
[14] P. L. 91–172, Senate Committee Report, page 62.
[15] *University Hill Foundation*, 51 T.C. 548 (1969).

leases constituted unrelated business taxable income within the meaning of Section 422(a) of the 1939 Code[16] and Sections 512(a) and (b)(3) of the 1954 Code.

Unfortunately for the Service, the Tax Court, after extensively reviewing the relevant legislative history, concluded that the foundation's activities had not been such as to cause it to lose its exemption under Sections 101(6) and 501(c)(3) and further concluded that the income from the leases was not unrelated business taxable income.

Having been thwarted in the courts, the Commissioner finally turned to Congress and Congress responded in the 1969 Tax Reform Act by adding Section 514 to the Internal Revenue Code.

Section 514, which is specifically aimed at *Clay Brown*-type transactions, handles the problem by providing that the charitable purchaser of a business must include as unrelated business income (taxable at regular rates) the income of the purchased business to the extent the purchase is financed.

The percentage of *gross* income which must be taken into account is the same percentage (but not more than 100 percent) as the "average acquisition indebtedness" for the taxable year in question is of the "average amount of the adjusted basis" of the property during the period it is held by the charitable purchaser during such taxable year.[17]

The purchaser is also allowed to take into account deductions directly connected with the debt-financed property, or the income derived therefrom, by applying the same percentage as is applied to gross income to the total of such deductions,[18] except if the debt-financed property is of a character subject to the allowance for depreciation provided in Section 167 only straight line depreciation may be used in computing the deductions allowable.[19]

> *Example:* Assume that during a given year average acquisition indebtedness on a property is $800,000 and the average adjusted basis $1,000,000. Further assume that the gross income from the property is $200,000 and that deductions directly connected with the property or the income derived from it total $100,000 and that of this $100,000 total $10,000 represents depreciation in excess of the straight line allowance. Unrelated business taxable income for the year would be $88,000 computed as follows:
>
> $$\frac{\text{Average acquisition indebtedness} \quad - \quad \$800,000}{\text{Average adjusted basis of property} \quad -1,000,000} = 80\%$$
>
> | | | |
> |---|---|---|
> | $200,000 gross income | × 80% = | $160,000 |
> | 90,000 deductions (taking into account only straight line depreciation) | × 80% = | 72,000 |
> | Unrelated business taxable income from property | | $ 88,000 |

---

[16] Added by section 301(b) of the Revenue Act of 1950.
[17] Sec. 514(a)(1).
[18] Sec. 514(a)(2).
[19] Sec. 514(a)(3).

Acquisition indebtedness is the unpaid amount of any indebtedness:[20]

1. Incurred by the purchaser in acquiring or improving the property;

2. Incurred before the acquisition or improvement of such property if such indebtedness would not have been incurred but for such acquisition or improvement;

3. Incurred after the acquisition or improvement of such property if such indebtedness would not have been incurred but for such acquisition or improvement, and the incurrence of such indebtedness was reasonably foreseeable at the time of such acquisition or improvement.

Where property is acquired subject to a mortgage, the amount of the mortgage is considered acquisition indebtedness incurred in acquiring the property even though the charity neither assumes nor agrees to pay such indebtedness.[21] One exception to this rule is where the mortgaged property is acquired by devise or bequest.[22] In such cases, the mortgage is not treated as acquisition indebtedness for ten years from the date of acquisition. The same exception applies to property acquired by gift if the mortgage was placed on the property more than five years before the date of the gift and the donor held the property for more than five years before the gift. The exception does not apply, however, if an organization in order to acquire an equity in the property by bequest, devise, or gift, assumes and agrees to pay the indebtedness secured by the mortgage, or where the charity makes a payment for the equity in the property owned by the decedent or donor.

Although Section 514 contains exclusions for certain types of property, such as property substantially all the use of which is substantially related to the exercise or performance of the organization's exempt function,[23] and real property located in the neighborhood of other property owned and used for exempt purposes by the organization,[24] the exclusions are quite limited, and in general, Section 514 now precludes the *Clay Brown*-type of sale and leaseback.

SALES AND LEASEBACKS WITH PENSION AND PROFIT-SHARING TRUSTS

Rather than enter into sale and leaseback transactions with third parties, some companies choose to deal with the retirement trusts they have set up for their own employees. Such transactions, while offering the employer most of the benefits normally associated with a sale to, and leaseback from, a third party, offer the pension or profit sharing trust the higher yield normally associated with sale and leasebacks, plus the residual value of the property at the end of the lease term.

---

[20] Sec. 514(c)(1).
[21] Sec. 514(c)(2)(A).
[22] Sec. 514(c)(2)(B).
[23] Sec. 514(b)(1).
[24] Sec. 514(b)(3).

Despite the advantages of a company entering into a sale-leaseback arrangement with a pension or profit-sharing trust for its employees, there are certain problems that should be taken into consideration by anyone contemplating such a move. First and foremost is the fact that pension and profit-sharing trusts, because of their exemption from income tax, must be run exclusively for the benefit of the participants.[25] Thus the Internal Revenue Service will carefully scrutinize sale and leaseback transactions with such organizations to make sure that the dealings have been arms-length and that the sales price is not too high or the rental too low.

In addition, a loss incurred on a sale of property by an employer to a pension or profit-sharing trust which it has set up is not deductible.[26] Thus, a sale leaseback with a pension or profit-sharing trust set up by the taxpayer would not be available in the *May Dept. Store* situation discussed previously, where the critical factor was the recognition of the loss on the sale.

Also, the arrangement should be handled in such a way as not to create "unrelated business taxable income" to the trust if it can be avoided.[27] Thus, although a lease of personal property alone will probably create "unrelated business taxable income,"[28] leasing personal property along with land will not, provided the rent attributable to the personal property is an incidental amount of the total rents received or accrued under the lease (as determined at the time the personal property is first placed in service by the lessee).[29]

Financing the purchase of the leased property can also create difficulties since Section 514 applies not only to charities, but also to pension and profit-sharing trusts. Therefore, to the extent the purchase of the property is financed, the net income from the lease will be unrelated business income taxable at ordinary rates.

Finally, it should be noted that it is not actually necessary for an employer to sell property to a pension or profit-sharing trust in order to gain the benefits of a sale-leaseback. Rather than sell the property to the trust, an employer might contribute it in satisfaction of its annual contribution to the trust and then lease it back.

> *Example:* In lieu of making its normal cash contribution of $100,000 to its pension plan, a corporation might deed to the pension trust a tract of land worth $100,000 which it has been using in its business. It could then lease the land back from the trust at its fair rental value.

A taxpayer should avoid contributing appreciated property to such trusts since the *General Shoe* case[30] holds that an employer realizes gain on the transfer of appreciated property to a pension or profit-sharing trust even where there is no legal obligation on the part of the employer to make such a contribution.

---

[25] Sec. 401(a)(2).

[26] Sec. 267 disallows losses between certain related parties including the grantor and a fiduciary of a trust (Sec. 267(b)(4)).

[27] Although pension and profit sharing trusts are generally not subject to tax, they are taxed on certain business income unrelated to their exempt function. Sec. 511.

[28] Rev. Rul. 60–206, 1960-1 C.B. 201; Rev. Rul. 69–278, 1969-1 C.B. 148.

[29] Sec. 512(b)(3).

[30] *U. S. v. General Shoe Corp.*, 282 F.2d 9 (6th Cir., 1960).

Example: A contributes property worth $400,000, but with a basis of $100,000, to a profit-sharing trust for A's employees. A realizes a gain of $300,000 on the transaction even though it was not obligated to make the contribution.

RELATED PARTIES

Transactions between related parties are always suspect and this is as true in the sale-and-leaseback area as any other. As pointed out in the previous discussion, losses on sales by employers to pension and profit-sharing trusts which they set up are not recognized because of the relationship of the parties. The same is true where the sale is to a shareholder who owns, directly or indirectly, more than 50 percent in value of the outstanding stock of the seller.[31]

Even where the transaction does not involve a loss so there is no automatic disallowance problem, sale and leasebacks between related corporations or between corporations and their shareholders will be carefully examined to see if income has been improperly shifted.

For example, in Revenue Ruling 68–430,[32] the Internal Revenue Service took the position that a sale and leaseback of mineral properties between a corporation and its wholly-owned subsidiary was to be disregarded for tax purposes where the subsidiary was dormant and the sole purpose of the transaction was to create deductions for both cost and percentage depletion. The plan was that the subsidiary, as owner of the property, would claim cost depletion and the parent, as lessee-operator, would claim percentage depletion. Since the parent continued to control the property, stood in basically the same economic position as it did before the sale, and the sole purpose of the transaction was to avoid taxes, the Service concluded that the sale should be disregarded citing, among other cases, *Gregory v. Helvering.*[33]

Similarly, in Southeastern *Canteen Co. v. Commissioner,*[34] deductions for rental payments under sale and leaseback agreements between related corporations were disallowed, to the extent they exceeded fair rental values for such assets, where the transaction was intended to benefit the controlling shareholder of the corporations, and served no meaningful business purpose insofar as the corporations themselves were concerned.

MORE SOPHISTICATED SALE-LEASEBACK TRANSACTIONS

Until this point, we have confined ourselves to the typical sale-leaseback situation where the owner of a building sells the building, including the land on which it is located, and then leases it back.

Not all sale-leaseback transactions are so simple and there are cases where the owner of a building may wish to sell the land but not the building; or, conversely, the building, but not the land.

---

[31] Sec. 267(b)(2).
[32] 1968-2 C.B. 44.
[33] 293 U.S. 465 (1935).
[34] 410 F.2d 615 (6th Cir., 1969).

Sale and Leaseback of Land Only

There are a number of reasons why the owner of a building might choose to enter into a sale-leaseback as to the land on which the building is located but not the building. First, he may not be able to find an investor who is interested in buying both the land and the building. This would be the case where the investor has no need for the depreciation the building would throw off and considers its appreciation potential limited. Second, even where the purchaser of the land is willing to buy the building, the owner may feel that the additional tax writeoff resulting from a sale and leaseback of the building would not be great enough to justify the additional financing cost which such a sale and leaseback might involve. Third, the immediate depreciation recapture resulting from a sale of the building might more than offset the eventual tax advantage to be derived from rental deductions.

The fact that it might not be desirable to sell the building does not, of course, mean that a sale and leaseback of the underlying land would not be advantageous. Assuming the owner can find an investor who is willing to buy the land, he can convert his nondepreciable investment in the land into a rental deduction. The resulting increase in working capital will hopefully compensate for the loss of the residual value of the land.

Even though a taxpayer sells only land and keeps the building, the sale of the land and the resulting leaseback can have an effect on future depreciation deductions for the building. This would be the case where the leaseback of the land is for a shorter period than the remaining useful life of the building. In such a situation, the taxpayer would amortize the remaining cost of the building over the period for which the land is leased rather than depreciate it over the remaining useful life of the building.

> *Example:* X corporation owns land with a factory on it. The factory has a remaining useful life of 35 years. X decides to sell the land, but not the building, and then lease it back for 25 years with no option to renew. Since the term of the lease is less than the remaining useful life of the factory, X will amortize the undepreciated cost of the factory over the 25-year lease term rather than depreciate it over its remaining useful life of 35 years.

Of course, if the lease on the land is for a greater period than the remaining useful life of the building, the sale and leaseback of the land will have no effect on the depreciation deductions for the building.

> *Example:* If, in the preceding example, X leased the land back for 40 years, then he would continue to depreciate the factory over its 35-year useful life as he had been doing prior to the sale and leaseback.

Sale and Leaseback of Building Only

Contrasted with the situation where the taxpayer sells the land and retains the building is the situation where he retains the land and sells only the building.

There can be several reasons for such a decision. From the taxpayer's viewpoint, he may feel that the land is, or will be, extremely valuable and does not wish to relinquish its residual value even though it would generate additional working capital. Alternatively, the investor who is buying the building may be interested in maximizing his depreciation deductions and is not interested in the land because it is nondepreciable.

Even though the taxpayer may not be interested in selling the land, he may still want to sell and leaseback the building either because he is not interested in its residual value or because he needs working capital and, although interested in the residual value of the building, considers it less important than the residual value of the land. In such a situation, a sale and leaseback as to the building only will be arranged.

Since the investor will be buying only the building and not the land, the taxpayer, as part of the transaction, has to lease the underlying land to the investor. This ground lease must be carefully drawn so that its term is not identical with that of the leaseback of the building. The reason for this is that if the term of the ground lease and the term of the leaseback of the building are identical then the taxpayer will still have the residual value of the building and the sale-leaseback may be treated for tax purposes as a loan, eliminating any tax advantage to either the seller or the investor.

> *Example:* X corporation owns a tract of land on which it has erected an office building. It agrees to sell the building which has a useful life of 40 years to Y and then lease it back for 30 years. Since X corporation will still own the land on which the building is situated, it will be necessary for X to lease the ground to Y. X gives Y a 30-year lease on the underlying ground. Since Y has only a 30-year lease on the ground and X has a 30-year lease on the building, it would appear that Y has no residuary interest in the building and the Internal Revenue Service may contend that the transaction is in reality a loan from Y to X rather than a sale-leaseback.

Even where the term of the underlying ground lease is greater than the term of the building leaseback this does not necessarily mean that the leaseback will be treated as a true lease. In order to be treated as a true lease the residual value can remain with the investor only where the useful life of the building is greater than the term of the leaseback. Thus, if the term of the leaseback is the same or greater than the useful life of the building, the transaction will probably still be treated as a loan.

> *Example:* X corporation, which owns a tract of land with a factory on it, sells the building to A and then leases it back for 50 years. X also gives A a ground lease on the underlying land for 99 years. The building has a useful life of 40 years. Notwithstanding the fact that the term of the ground lease (99 years) is considerably in excess of the term of the leaseback of the building (50 years), since the life of the building is only 40 years, it is obvious that X will have the use of it for its remaining useful life and therefore the transaction should be treated as a loan rather than a sale and leaseback.

Chapter 7

Trust and Leaseback: the Advantages—
Pitfalls to Avoid

A variation of the sale and leaseback which has become increasingly popular in recent years is the trust and leaseback.

The trust-leaseback is designed to shift income from a high-bracket to a low-bracket taxpayer, and involves the transfer of business property in trust for the low-bracket taxpayer with the transferor then renting the property back from the trust and claiming a tax deduction for the rent. It is especially popular among professional men, particularly members of the medical profession, as a means of shifting income from themselves to their children.

> *Example:* A, a radiologist in the 50 percent bracket, thinks he is paying too much in income taxes. His tax adviser suggests a trust-leaseback as one method of reducing taxes and proposes that A transfer some of the fully depreciated equipment he has been using in his practice to a trust for his children (who have no other income) with a view to leasing the equipment back from the trust. A transfers $50,000 worth of equipment to the trust and then enters into a lease which allows him to use the equipment at a rental of $5,000 a year.

Although the trust leaseback can offer significant tax savings, there are a number of pitfalls involved in its use and careful planning is required if it is to survive attack by the Internal Revenue Service. Before looking into the problem areas, however, it might be wise to consider the circumstances in which a trust-leaseback would be appropriate.

SITUATIONS IN WHICH A TRUST AND
LEASEBACK WOULD BE APPROPRIATE

We might start out by observing that in order for the trust-leaseback to work, the rental deductions which the transferor receives as a result of the leaseback must be substantially in excess of the depreciation deductions he would otherwise have been entitled to claim as owner of the property.

> *Example:* A owns a medical building, which cost $200,000 and has a useful life of 40 years and which he is depreciating at the rate of $5,000 a year. If he transfers the building to a trust for his children and then rents it back at a rental of $5,000 a year, he has accomplished nothing since he has merely substituted a $5,000 a year rental deduction for a $5,000 a year depreciation deduction. If, however, the rent is set at $10,000 a year then A will have shifted taxable income of $5,000 a year from himself to the trust.

It should also be recognized that there are some situations where the fair rental value of property cannot be substantially in excess of the depreciation allowance, and therefore, a trust-leaseback is not feasible. This will normally be the case where the asset involved is new, has a relatively short life, and a readily ascertainable rental value. In such situations, although there can be a tax saving from a trust and leaseback, it is usually not significant enough to justify the problems involved in setting up the trust and arranging the leaseback.

> *Example:* A purchases a piece of equipment for $20,000. The equipment has a useful life of four years and can be rented for $5,500 a year. Since A could rent the equipment for $5,500 a year, the rent he can pay if he transfers it to a trust and rents it back is limited to $5,500 a year. This means that the total rental deductions will exceed the depreciation deductions by only $2,000 over a four-year period. Such a difference is not sufficient to justify a trust-leaseback.

There are other cases where a trust-leaseback can be highly advantageous. This would generally be true where the property in question, although still valuable, has been substantially depreciated or where it has significantly appreciated in value. In both situations, the fair rental value of the property will normally exceed the depreciation allowance otherwise allowable.

> *Example 1:* Taxpayer, a dentist, owns a building which he uses in his practice. The building is 40 years old and has been fully depreciated. Its fair rental value is $3,000 a year. If the taxpayer were to transfer the building to a trust for his children, and lease it back at its fair rental value, he would be able to shift $3,000 a year of taxable income to the trust.

> *Example 2:* X, an attorney, owns a small building which he uses for his law offices. The building, which is ten years old, cost $40,000 and he has been taking depreciation at the rate of $1,000 a year. Up until three or four years ago the fair rental value of the building was $2,000 a year. Recently, an acute shortage of office space in the community has caused the fair rental value of the building to increase to $4,000 a year. If X were to transfer the property in trust, and then lease it back, he could shift $3,000 a year of taxable income to the trust ($4,000 rent − $1,000 loss of depreciation).

COMPUTING THE TAX SAVING

In order to determine the tax saving which will result from a trust-leaseback it is important to consider both the transferor's and transferee's tax brackets, since any tax saving which the transferor becomes entitled to as a result of the transfer must be reduced by the tax that the trust and/or the beneficiary will have to pay on the transferred income.

Computing the tax saving to the transferor is quite easy since it involves nothing more than applying the transferor's tax rate to the income shifted each year to the trust. The income shifted to the trust is, of course, the excess of the rental deduction the transferor is entitled to under the lease over the depreciation deduction which he relinquished when he transferred the property to the trust.

> *Example:* A, a dentist, transfers a medical building which he has been using in his practice to a trust for his children and then leases the building back at a rental of $8,000 a year. He has been claiming a depreciation allowance of $2,000 a year with respect to the building. If A is in the 40 percent bracket, the tax saving to him as the result of the transfer and leaseback is computed as follows:

$8,000 rental deduction
–2,000 depreciation deduction

$6,000 taxable income shifted to trust
  40% A's tax bracket

$2,400 annual tax saving to A

Although the tax saving to the transferor will vary from case to case, depending upon the transferor's tax bracket and the amount of taxable income shifted, it is important to realize that with the advent of the maximum tax and its top rate of 50 percent on earned income,[1] the tax saving to the transferor will generally not exceed 50 percent. This is to be contrasted with the situation prior to the maximum tax where the tax saving to the transferor on a trust-leaseback could be as high as 70 percent.

Computing the tax that the trust or its beneficiaries will have to pay on the income shifted from the transferor is a bit more complicated as a result of the Revenue Act of 1969, which introduced the unlimited throwback rule with respect to "accumulation distributions" and eliminated the benefits of accumulation trusts for spouses, and the Revenue Act of 1971, which limited the use of the standard deduction by a person claimed as the dependent of another.

The Unlimited Throwback Rule

Looking first at the impact of the 1969 Act, we find that whereas formerly it was possible, subject to rather limited throwback rules, for a trust to accumulate income and have it taxed at the trust's bracket (which was frequently lower than the beneficiary's), even though the accumulated income was to be eventually distributed to the beneficiary, now, as a result of the 1969 Act, a beneficiary will be subject to tax on accumulation distributions.[2] This does not

---

[1] Sec. 1348.
[2] Sec. 668(a).

mean that there will be a double tax on the accumulated income since the beneficiary will be allowed a credit for the tax paid by the trust.[3] What it does mean is that as a general rule it will no longer be possible to split income between the trust and the beneficiary so as to produce a lower tax than if the income were all taxed to the beneficiary.

> *Example:* A, a pediatrician, sets up a trust for his son, B, and transfers the medical building in which he practices to the trust. He then leases back the building at a rental of $12,000 a year. He had been claiming depreciation of $2,000 a year on the building so the taxable income shifted to the trust is $10,000 a year.
>
> Prior to the unlimited throwback rules introduced by the Revenue Act of 1969, A would have given the trustee the power to accumulate or distribute the income and the trustee would have accumulated sufficient income at the trust level ($4,000) to keep the overall tax at the lowest level possible, in this case, assuming no other taxable income to the trust or the beneficiary, $1,621. As a result of the 1969 Act, the income accumulated at the trust level will eventually be taxed to the beneficiary so that the tax saving resulting from the accumulation ($282 a year) will no longer be possible.

The actual computation of the tax to the beneficiary on accumulation distributions is somewhat complicated. The beneficiary may elect to have the accumulated income taxed under the "exact" method or a "short-cut" method. Under the exact method the tax on the accumulation distributions cannot exceed the aggregate of the taxes that would have been paid if the income in question had actually been distributed in the prior years.[4] The short-cut method is an averaging device which eliminates many of the computations required in the exact method.[5]

It should be noted that even though the unlimited throwback rule has eliminated the income-splitting opportunities of accumulation trusts, they still offer the advantage of tax deferral, i.e., payment of the extra tax is deferred until the accumulated income is distributed, and this can be a significant advantage.

Accumulation Trusts for Spouses

The 1969 Revenue Act not only introduced the unlimited throwback rule but also put an end to another tax-saving device which had achieved a certain degree of popularity, i.e., the accumulation trust for one's spouse.

Prior to the Act, it was permissible to provide that the trust income be accumulated for the benefit of the transferor's wife, to be eventually distributed to her. This usually produced a significant tax saving since the accumulated income was taxed at the trust's bracket, rather than the wife's, even though it was being held for eventual distribution to her.

Unfortunately, the Tax Reform Act provided that income distributed to or accumulated

---

[3] Sec. 668(b)(1).
[4] Sec. 668(b)(1)(A).
[5] Sec. 668(b)(1)(B).

for future distribution to the transferor's spouse is taxable to the transferor[6] and thus it is no longer practical to make one's wife the beneficiary in a trust-leaseback situation.

Limitation on the Standard Deduction

In addition to the changes introduced by the 1969 Revenue Act, Congress further limited the advantages of trusts for dependents when it provided in the Revenue Act of 1971 that where a taxpayer is claimed as a dependent of another, the standard deduction can be used only with respect to the dependent's earned income.[7] What this means as a practical matter is that whereas, previously, a beneficiary of a trust could receive as much as $2,250 ($1,500 minimum standard deduction plus $750 personal exemption) from the trust tax-free, this is no longer possible. Under the new rules, no more than $750 ($750 personal exemption) of the trust's income can be distributed tax free to the beneficiary.

> *Example:* X sets up a trust for his minor son and transfers a fully depreciated building to it. He then leases back the building at a rental of $10,000 a year. The terms of the trust provide for current distribution of income. The son has no other income.
>
> Prior to the Revenue Act of 1971, the son would have been taxed on only $7,750 of the trust income since he would have been entitled to a $1,500 standard deduction and a $750 personal exemption. As a result of the 1971 Act, he is now subject to tax on $9,250 of income ($10,000 − $750 personal exemption). He is not entitled to the standard deduction because he has no earned income.

It is important to realize that the new rule limiting the use of the standard deduction applies only where the taxpayer who would be entitled to the deduction is claimed as a dependent by another. Thus, the limitation would not apply if the beneficiary of the trust were someone for whom the taxpayer was not claiming a dependency exemption, e.g., a parent with more than $750 of other gross income.

> *Example:* A, a dentist, has been giving his widowed 66-year-old mother, who has an income of only $1,000 a year aside from Social Security, $10,000 a year to cover her living expenses. His accountant suggests that A set up a trust to provide her with the $10,000 a year which A has been giving her. A sets up the trust and transfers the building in which he has been conducting his practice, and which is fully depreciated, to the trust. He then leases it back at its fair rental value of $10,000 a year and the trust distributes the $10,000 to his mother. Since A does not claim his mother as a dependent she is entitled to claim a standard deduction of $1,500. She can also offset the unused portion ($500) of her two personal exemptions against her income from the trust so that $2,000 ($1,500 standard deduction and $500 the unused portion of her personal exemptions) of the $10,000 will be received by her tax free and the tax on the balance will be at a much lower rate than if it were taxed to A.

---

[6] Sec. 677(a).
[7] Sec. 141(e).

GIFT TAX IMPLICATIONS

In computing the tax savings which will result from a trust-leaseback, it is important not to overlook any gift tax which may be due as a result of the transfer in trust. While the gift tax is a non-recurring item, it is an out-of-pocket cost which must be paid and therefore should be taken into consideration.

Although the average layman may be surprised to learn that there can be a gift tax in connection with a trust-leaseback, it is quite clear that the first part of the transaction, i.e., the transfer in trust, constitutes a gift to the beneficiaries on which, subject to certain exclusions and exemptions, gift tax must be paid. The amount of the gift tax will, of course, vary depending on the amount of the gift, the nature of the interest given, the availability of gift splitting with one's spouse, and the extent to which the $30,000 lifetime exemption is still available.

Example 1: A, a doctor, decides to make use of the trust-leaseback and transfers a building which he has been using in his practice to a trust for his two children, ages 4 and 5, the income to be distributed currently. The building has a fair market value of $100,000. A is married and neither he nor his wife has made any previous taxable gifts nor have they used any of their lifetime exemptions. On these facts, A's gift tax liability would be $705 and his wife's liability would be the same for a total tax on the transaction of $1,410, computed as follows:

$100,000	value of gift
− 50,000	less one-half treated as made by spouse
− 6,000	exclusions for present interests to children
− 30,000	lifetime exemption
$14,000	taxable gift by A
$705	tax due

Example 2: B, a lawyer, is considering entering into a trust-leaseback arrangement and transferring a building which he has been using in his practice, and which is worth $100,000, to a trust for his children, ages 8 and 10, the income to be distributed currently. B is a widower and therefore gift splitting with his spouse is not available. Also, he has previously used up his $30,000 lifetime exemption and, in fact, has in the past made taxable gifts totalling $20,000. On these facts, B's gift tax liability would be $17,475 computed as follows:

$100,000	value of gift
− 6,000	exclusions for present interests to children
$94,000	taxable gift by A
$17,475	tax due

It should be recognized that even where the gift tax is substantial as in the immediately preceding example, it may (assuming the transferor has not retained the power to amend or revoke the trust, or to appoint the remainder or reversion on death, or to designate the person or persons, who shall enjoy the income)[8] be offset to some extent by the removal of the property transferred from the transferor's estate, with a resulting estate tax saving. Although this saving may be some years in the future it can be quite substantial. For instance, in the aforementioned example we computed B's gift tax liability, if he were to make the transfer in trust, to be approximately $17,000. Depending on the size of B's taxable estate, this tax could be more than offset by the estate tax saving which would result from not having the property included in B's estate. Thus, if we were to assume that B's taxable estate,[9] aside from this property, would be $100,000, then the estate tax saving resulting from the transfer would be at least $35,000[10] or double the gift tax.

OTHER COSTS INVOLVED IN TRUST-LEASEBACKS

Although the gift tax is perhaps the most significant cost of entering into a trust-leaseback arrangement, there are other costs which must be taken into account. These would include items such as the legal fees for setting up the trust and preparing the lease, trustees' commissions, and the cost of preparing tax returns.[11] Generally speaking, no.. of these costs is significant when compared with the overall tax savings that can be achieved through a trust-leaseback; nevertheless, they do reduce the benefits somewhat and should be taken into consideration.

PROBLEM AREAS

Although the trust-leaseback can offer significant tax-saving opportunities, taxpayers who attempt to take advantage of it frequently find themselves under attack by the Internal Revenue Service. Should the Service be successful in its attack, the transferor will be denied a deduction for his rental payments. Thus, not only will the trust and leaseback not have saved taxes, but it may actually increase the overall tax burden since a denial of a rental deduction to the transferor does not eliminate any gift tax paid in connection with the transfer, nor does it necessarily eliminate the income tax at the trust or beneficiary level.

> *Example:* A doctor transfers a fully depreciated building which he has been using in his practice to a trust for his parents and then leases it back at a rental of $6,000 a year. The doctor is in the 50 percent bracket. His parents are in a much lower bracket having taxable income, aside from the $6,000 a year distributed from the trust, of only $4,000. The gift tax on the transfer in trust is $1,500. Based on these facts, the overall tax saving from the transaction, ignoring the gift tax, should be $2,085 a year ($3,000 saved by doctor less $915 additional paid by parents). If the Internal Revenue Service successfully attacks the

---

[8] Sec. 2036–2041.

[9] After the $60,000 exemption.

[10] 30 percent of $117,000 ($100,000 placed in trust plus $17,000 gift tax paid).

[11] In addition, where the property involved is real estate there may also be a real estate transfer tax.

transaction and denies a rental deduction to the doctor, then not only will the son not realize his $3,000-a-year tax saving but the parents may still be liable for the additional $915 in taxes on the trust income. Thus, on an overall basis, the doctor and his parents could end up paying $915 a year more in income taxes than they would otherwise have paid.

Since it is essential that a trust and leaseback be able successfully to withstand attack by the Internal Revenue Service, it should be set up in such a way as to avoid those attributes which have led the courts to uphold the Commissioner's attacks. The balance of this chapter is devoted to a discussion of such attributes.

Reversionary Interests

Probably one of the first thoughts which occurs to a taxpayer considering a trust and leaseback involves the permanency of the arrangement. Since the taxpayer is making the transfer primarily for tax reasons, he obviously doesn't want to give up any more of the property than he has to, particularly where it might appreciate in value. One way around the problem is to retain a reversionary interest, i.e., to provide in the trust instrument that the property will revert to the transferor after a certain number of years.

> *Example:* Taxpayer transfers the building in which he conducts his medical practice to a trust and then leases the property back. The terms of the trust provide that the income is to be paid yearly to taxpayer's two minor children and at the end of 15 years the trust is to terminate and the building is to be returned to the taxpayer.

Unfortunately, the retention by the taxpayer of a reversionary interest may result in a loss of the rental deduction. The problem is caused by Section 162(a)(3) of the Internal Revenue Code which provides that there can be no rental deduction for property in which the taxpayer has an equity interest. Although there is no legislative history as to what constitutes an equity interest, some courts have construed a reversion to be an equity interest. For example, in the *Alden B. Oakes* case, the Tax Court defined a person having an equity in property as including one who ". . . has a right of redemption, a *reversionary interest,* a right to specific performance or, in general, any right respecting property which traditionally would have been enforceable by means of an equitable remedy" (emphasis added).[12] Similarly, the *Hall* case[13] found an equity interest where a doctor and his wife placed a jointly-owned building in trust for their two children pursuant to a trust and leaseback arrangement, but provided that the trust was to terminate on the death of either child or either of the grantors, in which case the property was to revert to the surviving grantor or his estate.

To be contrasted with the *Hall* case is *Duffy v. U.S.,*[14] a 1972 district court case. In the *Duffy* case, a doctor and his wife set up a trust and transferred a building to it. The doctor then leased the building for use in his practice. The trust was irrevocable for a period of ten years

---

[12] 44 T.C. 524 at 531 (1965).
[13] *Hall v. U. S.,* 208 F. Supp. 584 (D.C. N.Y., 1962).
[14] 343 F. Supp. 4 (D.C. Ohio, 1972); *rev'd on other grounds,* 32 A.F.T.R.2d 72-6164 (6th Cir., 1973).

and 30 days and was amendable by joint action of the grantors upon the expiration of this period.

The Treasury attacked the rental deduction on several grounds, one of which was that the rent was not deductible because the taxpayer had an equity interest in the property since the trust agreement was amendable after ten years and 30 days. The district court, however, conceding that there was "equity" in the legal sense, took the position that, since the trust fell within the ten-year exception of Section 676, it would frustrate the purpose of Sections 671 and 677 to disallow the rental deduction. The court, therefore, allowed the deduction despite the taxpayer's equity interest in the property.

It is interesting to note that the Tax Court in a 1968 case, *Sidney W. Penn,*[15] reached a different conclusion, taking the position that Sections 671–677 of the Code are not applicable to trusts and leasebacks.

Notwithstanding its opinion in the *Penn* case, the Tax Court has recently reached the same result as the *Duffy* case, but on different theory. Repudiating its statement in the *Oakes* case that a reversionary interest constitutes an equity in property, the Tax Court, in the *Mathews*[16] case, held that a reversionary interest was not an equity interest within the meaning of Section 162(a)(3).

Whether the concept of equity interest can go beyond that of a reversionary interest is difficult to say. A recent case, the *Chace* case,[17] seems to hold that a right in the grantor to renew a three-year lease for three additional periods of three years each at the same rental also constitutes an equity in the property. While the *Chace* case, which also involved a reversionary interest, probably goes too far in construing what is meant by the term, "equity," it should be taken into consideration in drafting any leaseback.

Interestingly enough, even prior to the *Mathews* case, the Tax Court held that the fact that the property will pass to the transferor's wife on termination of the trust is not the retention of an equity interest by the transferor within the meaning of Section 162(a)(3).[18] This is so even though a joint return is filed. Thus, even though a transferor cannot retain a reversionary interest in himself he can provide that on termination of the trust the property will pass to his wife.

Independence of Trustee

Obviously, since the transferor is going to have to deal with the trustee of the property, he would like the trustee to be a friendly party, preferably himself.

Until a few years ago, it was more or less taken for granted that the transferor should not be the trustee if he was to get the benefit of the rental deduction. Recently, the Ninth Circuit cast doubt on this assumption with its decision in the *Brooke*[19] case.

---

[15] 51 T.C. 144 (1968); See also, *Jack Wiles,* P-H T.C. ¶59.29 (1972).

[16] *James Mathews,* 61 T.C. (No. 3), P-H T.C.R. 61.3.

[17] *Chace v. U. S.,* 422 F.2d 292 (5th Cir., 1970), *affirming* 303 F. Supp. 513 (D. C. Fla.).

[18] *Alden B. Oakes,* 44 T.C. 524 (1965), but see *White v. Fitzpatrick,* 193 F.2d 398 (2nd Cir., 1952), *cert. denied,* 343 U.S. 928.

[19] *Brooke v. U. S.,* 30 A.F.T.R.2d 72-5284 (9th Cir., 1972).

In the *Brooke* case, the taxpayer was a Montana physician earning from $26,000 to $30,000 a year with six children ranging in age from 6 to 14. In order, according to the testimony of the taxpayer, to provide for the health and education of the children and insulate some of his assets from the threat of malpractice suits, he gave to his children a piece of real estate which contained a rental apartment, a pharmacy, and the offices used for his medical practice. Following the conveyance, the Montana State Probate Court appointed the taxpayer as guardian of the children.

In his capacity as guardian for the children, the taxpayer collected the rents from the apartment and the pharmacy and without a written lease paid to himself as guardian for the children the reasonable rental value of the medical offices he occupied. The amounts so collected were used to pay insurance premiums for the children, to provide private school tuition, musical instruments, music, swimming and public speaking lessons, to purchase an automobile for the oldest child when he became old enough to drive, and to pay travel expenses to New Mexico for an asthmatic child. The Internal Revenue Service challenged the taxpayer's rental deductions on a number of grounds, one of which was that, since the taxpayer was the trustee, the trust did not have an independent trustee.

In sustaining the rental deduction, the Ninth Circuit adhered to the rule that the trustee must be independent in order for there to be an effective trust and leaseback, but held that the necessary independence of the trustee was achieved by the guardianship. The court pointed out that the Montana Probate Court administers guardianships with the same requisite independence as any court-administered trust, that the court would see that the rental obligations were met and accountings rendered, and that there should be no lack of confidence in the supervision by the courts. In short, the court held that "A court appointed trustee—even though the taxpayer—offers sufficient independence."[20] The court suggested that should the taxpayer at some future date breach the fiduciary obligation to his children, the Internal Revenue Service might renew its challenge to the validity of the gift.

Despite the decision by the Ninth Circuit in the *Brooke* case, it would still be best to avoid having the taxpayer act as trustee. In the first place, unless the Treasury concedes that *Brooke* is correct it will probably continue to contest the matter in other circuits. Thus, a taxpayer who names himself as trustee in a trust-leaseback situation may be insuring a lawsuit. Second, even if the Treasury concedes that *Brooke* is correct, it will probably try to limit its application by focusing on the fact that the guardianship was court-administered.[21] Finally, although selecting an independent trustee does not guarantee success, it can play a very important role in convincing a court that a trust-leaseback has economic reality.[22]

Assuming that the taxpayer should not be the trustee, who should be chosen as trustee?

The next most logical choice would seem to be a member of the taxpayer's family. Unfortunately, if one concludes that it is unwise to name the taxpayer as trustee, it is probably also unwise to name another member of the family as trustee. Theoretically, of course, there would seem to be no reason why a member of the transferor's family could not be a trustee, as

---

[20] *Supra* fn. 19 at 72-5285.
[21] See *Jack Wiles*, P-H T.C. ¶59.29 at 59-204.
[22] *Alden B. Oakes, supra* fn. 18.

the *Potter*[23] case, which upheld the validity of an arrangement where the transferor's wife and father were trustees, illustrates. Practically speaking, there is considerable question as to whether such a person would act independently and thus the situation is ripe for attack by the Internal Revenue Service.

As a general rule then, the trustee should be completely independent of the transferor. This does not necessarily mean that an institutional trustee, such as a bank, must be appointed. A noninstitutional trustee will suffice provided the person appointed functions as an independent trustee. This is not always the case. Business associates of the transferor who are appointed as trustee may take their duties and obligations as trustee lightly, in effect relinquishing their independence. For instance, in the *Audano*[24] case, the transferor named his attorney and C.P.A. as trustees. Unfortunately, the attorney and C.P.A. failed to take any real interest in the trust and certainly did not act as trustees would normally be expected to act. For example, among other things, they failed to determine that the rentals were fair, failed to determine whether higher rentals could have been obtained elsewhere, and neglected to obtain written leases. The result was that the taxpayer lost the rental deduction. The important thing to remember is that if a noninstitutional trustee is to be appointed, he must be independent and act truly so. If it is not possible to find such a party, then the transferor should appoint an institutional trustee.

Even the appointment of an institutional trustee may not eliminate attacks by the Internal Revenue Service where the transferor attempts to maintain control over the trustee. The retention of a power to change the trustee could raise a question as to its independence, and one court[25] has taken the position that an institutional trustee cannot be independent where the transferor has the right to settle the account of the trustee. Although this latter position might be somewhat extreme,[26] the case does illustrate the importance of the transferor not reserving any powers which might bring the trustee's independence into question.

Prearrangements As to Leaseback

Obviously, no one is going to be interested in transferring property that he has been using to a trust unless he is reasonably sure that he can lease it back. There can be problems, however, where the leaseback is required as a condition of the transfer.

> *Example:* A doctor transfers the building in which he maintains his offices to a trust for the benefit of his son. Because he wants to make sure that he can continue to use the building for his practice, he insists that the terms of the trust require the trustee to lease the building back to him.

A number of cases have attached great significance to such a condition in denying the transferor a rental deduction,[27] and it would be far better if the transfer were made first and the

---

[23] *John T. Potter,* 27 T.C. 200 (1956), *acq.* 1957-2 C.B. 6.
[24] *Audano v. U. S.,* 428 F.2d 251 (5th Cir., 1970).
[25] *Supra* fn. 13.
[26] The Tax Court reached the opposite conclusion in *Alden B. Oakes, supra* fn. 18.
[27] E.g., *Van Zandt v. Comm.,* 341 F.2d 440 (5th Cir., 1965).

leaseback then negotiated independently of the transfer. Moreover, as a practical matter, so long as the transferor is willing to pay fair rental value there is little reason to believe that the trustee would not be willing to lease the property back to him, particularly where leasing the property to others might involve additional costs such as painting and remodeling. Thus, the reservation of a specific right to lease the property is not only dangerous, but is probably unnecessary.

Rent

Obviously, the transferor has an incentive to have the rent as high as possible since that will enable him to shift more income to the lower bracket taxpayer. The rent, however, must be reasonable and must be justifiable in comparison with other rental property of a similar nature.

Frequently, rents are set at obviously inflated levels. An example would be the *Audano*[28] case, mentioned previously, where the rent over a five-year period averaged $11,700 a year for equipment with an original cost of $15,000, and the taxpayer offered no expert testimony regarding the reasonableness of such rent. The transferor must remember that the burden of proving that the rent is reasonable rests on him and he must be prepared to back it up with independent appraisals and the like.

Formalities

Since the trust-and-leaseback area is so fraught with the possibility of attack by the Internal Revenue Service, it seems almost unnecessary to emphasize that the normal formalities should be strictly followed, i.e., the lease between the transferor and trustees should be written and should be appropriate to the property and area, rental payments should be made promptly, and the terms of the lease strictly complied with. In short, the formalities should be as complete as possible.

Business Purpose

The concept of "business purpose" is an illusive one which has crept into the trust-leaseback area. Basically, it means that there must be a business reason for the transaction. If the test were applied literally to the trust-leaseback, it could not be met since there is usually no business purpose for an essential element in the transaction, i.e., the transfer in trust. The better approach is to apply the test only to the leaseback aspect of the transaction as the Tax Court did in the *Oakes* case[29] where it expressly rejected the idea that there must be a business reason for the transfer to the trust. Unfortunately, not all the courts have done this and there is language in some of the cases which suggests that the test must be applied to the transfer in trust as well as the leaseback.[30]

---

[28] *Supra* fn. 24.
[29] *Supra* fn. 18.
[30] E.g., *Van Zandt, supra* fn. 27.

The cases which have taken this view, however, all involved situations that called for disallowance of the rental deduction on other grounds such as lack of independence of trustee or the retention of a reversionary interest by the transferor. Since the business-purpose test seems to be called into play only when these other factors are present, there is serious question as to whether it has independent significance even in those courts which advocate the stricter view.

This does not mean that the Internal Revenue Service will not continue to raise the issue as the *Brooke* case,[31] which was discussed previously, indicates. In addition to arguing the independent trustee issue, the Service also relied heavily on a lack of business purpose for the transfer in trust as a ground for disallowing the rental deduction.

The Ninth Circuit responded to this argument by finding that there was a business purpose for the transfer, namely, the taxpayer made the transfer to avoid friction with his partners, protect his assets from malpractice judgments, and (for ethical considerations) to divorce himself from technical legal ownership of the pharmacy. The difficulty with the court's response, as the dissenting opinion points out, is that the trial court had found as a fact that the transfer served no substantial business purpose. Thus, in the view of the dissenting judge, the majority decided the case in the taxpayer's favor not because there was a valid business purpose but because it did not want to apply the business-purpose doctrine to the transfer in trust.

If the dissent is correct in this respect, it is unfortunate that the Ninth Circuit did not meet the issue of business purpose head-on rather than evade it. An outright rejection of the business-purpose test would have been helpful in dispelling the notion that there must be a business purpose for both the gift and the leaseback rather than for just the leaseback.

Using Trust Income to Satisfy Legal Obligations of the Transferor

Since the purpose of the trust-leaseback arrangement is to shift income from the high-bracket transferor to the lower-bracket beneficiary, it is important that the income of the trust be handled in such a manner as not to jeopardize this purpose.

Section 677(b) of the Internal Revenue Code provides that when distributions from a trust are used for the support and maintenance of a beneficiary whom the transferor is legally obligated to support, then such distributions are taxable to the transferor. Thus, it is important where the income from the trust is to be distributed to, or used for, the benefit of minor children of the transferor, that it not be used to provide items which the transferor is legally obligated to provide.

> *Example:* Taxpayer transfers some equipment which he has been using in his business to a trust for the benefit of his minor children and then leases it back at a rental of $5,000 a year. The trustee, the transferor's brother, uses $1,000 of the trust income to buy the children

---

[31] *Supra* fn. 19.

clothing and other items which the transferor would normally provide pursuant to his legal obligation to support the children. The transferor will be taxed on the $1,000 expended for such purposes.

Income used for purposes other than the maintenance and support of dependents is not taxable to the transferor. For instance, in the *Brooke* case, distributions of trust income were used to provide private schooling, music, swimming, and public speaking lessons for the transferor's children. Despite this, the income used to pay for these items was not taxable to their father, a physician earning between $26,000 and $30,000 a year, because they were not considered part of the father's support obligation under Montana law.

It should be recognized that the scope of what is support is determined under local law, and local law has been expanding this concept so that items which were formerly not considered support may very well be considered support in the future. For example, whereas years ago a college education would not have been considered part of a parent's support obligation, it probably would be today for a father who makes enough money to take advantage of a trust-leaseback arrangement.

Mortgaged Property

Frequently, the property to be transferred in trust is subject to a mortgage on which the transferor may or may not be personally liable and the amount of which may or may not exceed the tax basis of the property. Where the transferor is personally liable on the mortgage and continues to be personally liable after the transfer (i.e., the trustee does not assume the mortgage but merely takes subject to it), then payments on the mortgage by the trustee may constitute income to the transferor under the discharge of an obligation theory mentioned above, i.e., trust income used to discharge a legal obligation of the transferor is taxable to him. The *Jenn* case[32] illustrates the problem.

In the *Jenn* case, a taxpayer transferred real estate to trusts for the benefit of his minor children while retaining a reversionary interest. The real estate was subject to two mortgages but the taxpayer remained personally liable on them since there was no written provision for the trustee to assume the mortgages. Since the real estate was taken subject to the mortgages, the trustee continued the payments on them. The Internal Revenue Service took the position, and the court agreed, that the trust income used to make payments on the mortgages was taxable to the taxpayer.

Unfortunately, the language of the *Jenn* case is somewhat confusing. The court initially seemed to base its holding on the fact that the income was used to discharge a legal obligation of the transferor. It then went on, however, to hold that the release by the transferor of his reversionary right as to one-third of the corpus at the end of 1962 meant that he was liable for tax on only two-thirds of the trusts' 1963 income. Thus, despite the language of the opinion, the decision was apparently based on the retention of the reversionary interest rather than the use of the income to satisfy the transferor's legal obligation.

---

[32] *Jenn v. Commissioner*, 25 A.F.T.R.2d 70-756 (D.C. Ind., 1970).

It should be noted that although the *Jenn* Court seems to have based its decision on the fact that the taxpayer retained the reversion, the retention of the reversionary interest is, under the regulations, actually irrelevant. The regulations take the position that a taxpayer is subject to tax under Section 677 on income used to satisfy his legal obligation whether he has a reversionary interest or not.[33]

Obviously, having the transferor taxed on the trust income used to make mortgage payments thwarts the basic purpose of the arrangement. In order to avoid this possibility, the transferor should, if possible, prior to making the transfer to the trust, secure a release of personal responsibility so that at the time the mortgage payments are made by the trustee there is no satisfaction of an indebtedness of the transferor through such payments. The Service has conceded in Revenue Ruling 54–516[34] that where mortgaged property is transferred in trust, the trust income used to satisfy the mortgage will not be taxed to the grantor where the grantor is not liable on the underlying mortgage obligation.[35]

If the holder of the mortgage is not willing to release the transferor from personal liability unless the trustee assumes liability on the mortgage, then the taxpayer should consider having the trustee assume, rather than merely take subject to, the mortgage. This can cause difficulties, however, if the tax basis of the property is less than the amount of the mortgage. Where a taxpayer sells property which is subject to a mortgage, the amount of the mortgage is considered to be part of the proceeds of the sale whether the buyer assumes the mortgage or merely takes subject to it.[36] Although, generally speaking, most people do not feel that a gift, as opposed to a sale, of mortgaged property results in income to the donor, even where the amount of the mortgage is in excess of the tax basis of the property, the situation is somewhat different where the donee actually assumes the obligation as opposed to merely taking subject to it. Thus, if a trustee in a trust leaseback arrangement assumes a mortgage obligation rather than simply taking the property subject to it, the transfer of the mortgaged property to the trust will probably be treated as a sale resulting in income to the transferor to the extent the indebtedness exceeds the tax basis of the property. This conclusion is confirmed by the *Malone* case.[37]

In the *Malone* case, the taxpayer established an irrevocable trust for the benefit of his minor grandchildren. He then conveyed 546 acres of farm land to the trust. The taxpayer had an adjusted basis in the land of $13,350 and at the time of the transfer the property was subject to a mortgage in the amount of $32,000 on which the taxpayer was personally liable. Although the trustee did not expressly assume liability for the mortgage, the trust instrument did direct the trustee to "deduct" the annual payments on the mortgage from the trust income.

The Internal Revenue Service took the position that under the trust agreement the trustee had actually assumed the mortgage debt, thereby relieving the taxpayer of the primary liability

---

[33] Reg. 1.677(a)–1(d). See also, Rev. Rul. 54–516, 1954-2 C.B. 54.

[34] *Supra* fn. 33.

[35] Should, however, the taxpayer retain a reversionary interest in the property then he may still be subject to tax notwithstanding his release from personal liability. See, Price, *Eat, Drink and Be Merry at the Expense of the Federal FISC*, TAXES—THE TAX MAGAZINE, March, 1971, p. 175 at 183.

[36] *Crane v. Comm.*, 331 U.S. 1 (1947).

[37] *Malone v. U. S.*, 326 F. Supp. 106 (D.C. Miss., 1971); *affirmed per curiam*, 455 F.2d 502 (5th Cir., 1972).

thereon. As a result, the Service argued, the transfer in trust was really part gift and part sale and the taxpayer had realized a long-term capital gain of $18,650, i.e., the difference between the $32,000 debt and the taxpayer's basis for the property of $13,350.

Unfortunately for the taxpayer, the district court agreed with the Service pointing out that under Mississippi law an express assumption is not necessary, and it is sufficient that the language of the instrument in question show a clear intent on the part of the grantee to assume the liability for paying the mortgage debt. The court held such intent was shown by the language of the trust instrument directing the trustees to deduct the payments on the mortgage from trust income since such language necessarily implied a direction to pay the deducted amount to the mortgagee. The agreement of the trustees to accept such an obligation amounted to an assumption of the debt.

The case is important not only because it supports the conclusion that the assumption by the trustee of a mortgage on property transferred to a trust will result in income to the transferor where the amount of the mortgage exceeds the basis of the property and the transferor is personally liable on the mortgage, but also because it shows that assumption need not be express but may be implied.

Chapter 8

Purchasing—the Critical Tax Aspects
of Financing the Purchase

Assuming a business decides to purchase rather than lease, it must make a second decision and that is how to finance the purchase.

It is important to realize that all purchases are financed, even where the buyer uses its own cash. It may not appear, at first, that a company that uses its own cash is financing but it should be recognized that cash which is used to purchase equipment or business property is not available for other revenue-producing purposes such as sales promotion. Thus, the cost of paying cash for equipment or property (internal financing) is the loss of the earnings which the cash would otherwise have generated. Where these earnings would exceed the cost of borrowing from someone else (external or outside financing), it is customary to borrow.

The decision whether to finance internally or externally is a fairly easy one for most buyers. Although there are situations where buyers chose to finance internally, for the majority of purchasers the question is not whether to use outside financing, but rather the type of outside financing to use.

There are, of course, a number of options open to the average purchaser. The first is an installment or conditional sales contract with the seller. Alternatively, the purchaser may borrow the necessary funds from a bank or other lender, with the purchased asset or assets securing the loan. Where the property to be purchased is subject to an existing mortgage, the buyer may simply take over the mortgage. Finally, where the amount involved is sufficiently large, the buyer may borrow the necessary funds from the public by issuing bonds or debentures.[1]

COSTS OF BORROWING (OTHER THAN INTEREST EXPENSE)

Most financing arrangements involve certain costs other than the basic interest charge. In many cases these costs are nominal, but there are situations where they can be substantial. For

---

[1] A corporation also has the option of securing funds by issuing additional stock.

example, the cost to a businessman of entering into a typical conditional sales agreement may involve no more than the expense of having his lawyer examine the agreement; whereas the buyer who finances his purchases through the issuance of bonds or debentures can expect to incur substantial legal, accounting, and other fees.

The general rule regarding costs of borrowing (other than interest) is that they are not deductible immediately but must be amortized over the life of the loan. Thus, if a borrower pays a commission or other fee to secure a loan, the cost is not currently deductible, but must be amortized.[2]

> *Example:* X corporation wishes to borrow $3,000,000 to purchase a new plant. Unable to secure the necessary financing on its own, it engages a broker to arrange a mortgage. The broker arranges a 20-year loan and charges a commission of $30,000. X may not deduct the commission as a current expense but must amortize it over the term of the loan, i.e., 20 years.

The same is true of those costs involved in the issuance of bonds or debentures such as the costs of printing and listing and the related legal and accounting expenses involved in the issuance of such securities.[3]

> *Example:* Y corporation wants to buy new equipment which will cost in the neighborhood of $10,000,000. Rather than purchase the equipment under conditional sales agreements, Y decides to issue $10,000,000 of 15-year debentures, the proceeds of which will be used to purchase the equipment. Because the issuance of the debentures will be a "public offering," Y is forced to incur substantial legal and accounting expenses amounting to $50,000. Printing costs and the cost of listing the debentures run another $50,000. The $100,000 cost of issuing the debentures may not be deducted currently but must be amortized over the 15-year term of the debentures.

It should be noted that amortization is required even where the taxpayer is on the cash method of accounting.[4] Should the loan be paid off prematurely, as would normally be the case where the property is sold, the remaining balance of the costs may, of course, be written off.[5]

> *Example:* A corporation borrows $400,000 on a ten-year note to purchase equipment. The commission for arranging the loan is $4,000. In the fourth year of the loan, A decides to pay it off and does so. The unamortized portion of the commission ($2,800) should be written off in the fourth year.

This would be true even where, as in the case of some mortgages, the loan is paid off by means of a subsequent purchaser assuming the mortgage as part of the purchase price.[6]

---

[2] Rev. Rul. 70–360, 1970-2 C.B. 103.
[3] *Denver & Rio Grande Western Railroad Co.*, 32 T.C. 43, (1959) *aff'd on another issue* 279 F.2d 368.
[4] *Lovejoy*, 18 B.T.A. 1179 (1930).
[5] *S & L Building Corp.*, 19 B.T.A. 788 (1930), acq. X-1 C.B. 60, *aff'd on another point*, 288 U.S. 406 (1933).
[6] *Metropolitan Properties Corp.*, 24 B.T.A. 220 (1931), acq. XI-1 C.B. 5.

It is important to realize that the costs of acquiring a loan are not treated as part of the cost of acquiring the property which is purchased with the proceeds of the loan. Thus, where the property is sold, and the loan paid off, the borrower is entitled to claim an ordinary deduction for the unamortized costs of borrowing even though the sale results in a capital gain.[7]

> *Example:* X corporation borrows $500,000 to purchase a tract of land for investment. The costs of securing the loan, which is for 20 years, are $20,000. After ten years, the land is sold for $800,000. The gain on the sale is $300,000 ($800,000 − $500,000) and it is taxed at capital gains rates. The unamortized costs of securing the loan ($10,000) do not reduce the amount of the capital gain but may be taken as an ordinary deduction.

INTEREST EXPENSE

Although the cost of borrowing can, as discussed, include costs other than interest, by far the greatest cost of borrowing is the interest charge levied by the lender.

Interest charges are deductible as current expenses under Section 163(a) of the Internal Revenue Code and normally their deductibility will not be contested by the Internal Revenue Service. Like most rules, however, there are exceptions.

Interest Cost Assumed As Part of the Purchase Price

One exception involves the buyer who purchases property by assuming a mortgage on which there is delinquent interest. In such cases, the buyer is not entitled to an interest deduction when he pays the interest because the payment is really a part of the purchase price, not a charge for the use of money. Instead of deducting the payment, the buyer must capitalize it and treat it as part of the basis of the property.[8]

Prepaid Interest

Prepaid interest is not a problem where accrual basis taxpayers are involved since an accrual basis taxpayer deducts interest for the year in which the liability to pay accrues regardless of when payment is actually made.

> *Example:* A, an accrual basis taxpayer, borrows $100,000 to be repaid at the end of ten years, interest to be paid annually at the rate of 8 percent. On these facts, A will be entitled to deduct $8,000 in the first and each succeeding year. An immediate prepayment of $40,000 in interest will not increase the amount of A's deduction since the time when payment is made is irrelevant where the taxpayer is on the accrual basis.

The situation is somewhat different where the taxpayer is on the cash basis. Here, the time of payment is critical and a prepayment would normally accelerate the year in which an

---

[7] *Supra* fn. 5.
[8] *Rodney, Inc. v. Comm.*, 145 F.2d 692 (2d Cir., 1944).

item can be deducted. For example, in the *Fackler* case,[9] the Tax Court allowed a taxpayer to take a current deduction for a payment that represented the prepayment of several years interest, and the *Konigsberg* case,[10] a Tax Court memorandum decision, allowed a current deduction for the payment in advance of five-years interest.

Unfortunately, the Internal Revenue Service, refuses to follow these cases. The Service's position is that the deduction of prepaid interest by a cash-basis taxpayer may not clearly reflect income for the taxable year of payment and therefore should be allowed only under certain circumstances. The rules the Service will follow in determining whether or not to contest a deduction for prepaid interest are set forth in Revenue Ruling 68–643,[11] as modified by Revenue Ruling 69–582,[12] and are as follows:

1. If interest on an indebtedness is prepaid for a period not in excess of 12 months of the taxable year immediately following the taxable year in which the prepayment is made, a deduction will be considered on a case-by-case basis to determine whether a material distortion of income has resulted.

2. If interest is prepaid for a period extending more than 12 months beyond the taxable year of payment, the deduction will automatically be considered as distorting income and, if the distortion is material, the taxpayer will be required to change its method of accounting for the interest and allocate it over the taxable years involved.

3. The above rules do not apply to interest prepayments for periods not in excess of five years made before November 25, 1968, or to an interest prepayment for a period not in excess of five years made on or after November 26, 1968, pursuant to a legal obligation incurred before such date to make the prepayment.

Prepayment Penalties

A prepayment penalty is an additional amount that a borrower must pay under the terms of a loan when he chooses to pay off the loan over a shorter period than originally anticipated. It is intended to compensate the lender for the shortening of the loan period and it is really additional interest rather than a penalty.

Example: X corporation wants to borrow $200,000 repayable over ten years. Because the money market is tight, X has to agree to a 10 percent interest rate and a prepayment penalty of 5 percent of the unpaid balance should he pay off the loan earlier than agreed. Some time later, after money has become more available, X decides to refinance the note, which now has a balance due of $150,000. It does so with money it has borrowed from another lender at

---

[9] *J. D. Fackler*, 39 B.T.A. 395, *acq.* C.B. 1939-1 (Part 1) 11, *acq. withdrawn* Rev. Rul. 68–643, 1968-2 C.B. 76, *aff'd* 132 F.2d 509.

[10] *Joseph H. Konigsberg*, 1946 P-H T.C. Memo ¶74,258.

[11] 1968-2 C.B. 76.

[12] 1969-2 C.B. 29.

a substantially reduced interest rate. Pursuant to the prepayment penalty provisions of the old note, X must pay a $7,500 penalty for prematurely paying off the old loan.

Although the Commissioner originally took the position that prepayment penalties were not deductible as interest,[13] he subsequently reversed his position and now agrees that an interest deduction is proper.[14] He has, however, tried to disallow an immediate deduction where the purpose of the prepayment is to enable the borrower to refinance through another lender. In such cases, he takes the position that the penalty is really a cost of obtaining the new financing and should be amortized over the period of the new loan.

Despite the seeming logic of the Commissioner's position, the Tax Court in the *12701 Shaker Boulevard* case[15] allowed an immediate writeoff in a situation involving refinancing. The court focused on the fact that the old and new mortgagees were different and unrelated parties and therefore treated the repayment of the old debt and the new borrowing as separate transactions.

Excessive or Usurious Interest

Although it would seem that there might be some limit on the rate of interest for which the taxpayer can claim a deduction, this is generally not true. As one court expressed it, there is nothing in the Internal Revenue Code to limit the interest deduction to what is ordinary and necessary or reasonable.[16] Even where the interest paid is clearly usurious, a deduction has been allowed. For example, in *Cuba Railroad Co. v. U.S.*,[17] a company which agreed to pay 3 percent interest on bonds was allowed a deduction for such interest even though local (Cuban) law limited the interest rate on such obligations to 1 percent. Similarly, the Tax Court allowed a Maine Corporation doing business in Cuba, and paying interest on its bonds at a rate in excess of the 1 percent limit authorized by Cuban law, to deduct such excess interest notwithstanding the statutory limitation.[18]

As a matter of fact, an interest deduction may be allowed even where interest payments are described as something else in order to avoid a usury statute. This was the situation in *A.R. Jones Syndicate*,[19] a Seventh Circuit case, where because of an Illinois usury statute it was agreed that a loan at the rate of 14 percent was to be evidenced by preferred stock, redeemable at par and bearing a dividend of 14 percent per annum regardless of earnings, rather than a note. Despite the formal designation of the payments as dividends, the taxpayer was allowed to deduct them as interest.

Although interest payments to related parties will be carefully scrutinized to insure that

---

[13] See Rev. Rul. 168, 1953-2 C.B. 19, and Rev. Rul. 55–12, 1955-1 C.B. 259, which, although denying an interest deduction for prepayment penalties, concede their deductibility as business expenses where the loan was a business as opposed to a personal loan.

[14] Rev. Rul. 57–198, 1957–1 C.B. 94.

[15] The *12701 Shaker Blvd. Co.*, 36 T.C. 255 (1961), *aff'd without opinion* 312 F.2d 747 (6th Cir., 1963).

[16] *Dorzback v. Collison*, 195 F.2d 69 (3rd Cir., 1952).

[17] 254 F.2d 280 (2nd Cir., 1958).

[18] *Guantanamo & Western Railroad Co.*, 31 T.C. 842 (1959).

[19] 23 F.2d 833 (7th Cir., 1927).

the payments are really interest, once it is decided that they are true interest a deduction will be allowed, notwithstanding the apparent excessiveness of such payments. This is perhaps best illustrated by *Dorzback v. Collison*[20] in which a taxpayer agreed to pay his wife 25 percent of the net profits of his clothing store business "in lieu of interest," the wife having been substituted as creditor for a bank. Despite the fact that during two of the years in question 25 percent of the net profits equalled the amount of the loan, and in the third year actually exceeded it, the Tenth Circuit allowed an interest deduction for the payments.

One situation in which an interest deduction will not be allowed is where the interest payment is made gratuitously. For instance, in *Bakhaus and Burke, Inc.*,[21] where the taxpayer paid 5 percent interest when the loan agreement specified 4 percent, the Tax Court denied a deduction for the excess 1 percent on the ground that it was gratuitous. When there is an adequate reason for the excess payment, however, a deduction will be allowed. This was the case in *Hypotheek Land Co. v. Commissioner*,[22] where a deduction was allowed for a retroactive increase from 3 percent to 5 percent in the interest due under a contract because the other party to the agreement could have repudiated the contract in view of the low interest rate.

Allocation of Payments between Principal and Interest

Rather than have separate payments of principal and interest, many financing arrangements call for periodic payments that cover both principal and interest.

> *Example:* A borrows $10,000 for use in his hardware business. His monthly payment on the loan is $300 which covers both interest and amortization of principal.

Since each payment is in part principal and in part interest, it must be divided into its principal and interest elements in order to determine the borrower's interest deduction. Usually, this is done in accordance with the financing agreement which either sets forth a schedule showing the principal and interest portions of each payment or gives a formula for determining them.

Where the financing agreement allocates or provides a method for allocating payments between principal and interest, this is normally determinative for tax purposes unless the agreement conflicts with the imputed interest rules of Section 483 or involves related parties. Even where the financing agreement does not allocate periodic payments between principal and interest, an agreement at the time of payment as to the interest portion will normally control for tax purposes. The same is true even where the agreement is made after the payment so long as it is made in the same taxable year as the payment.[23]

> *Example:* X borrows $10,000 from Y at 8 percent interest. The agreement provides for monthly payments of $200 but does not apportion the payments between principal and interest. At the time of the first payment, X and Y agree that $50 of each payment will be

---

[20] 195 F.2d 69 (3rd Cir., 1952).
[21] 1955 P-H T.C. Memo ¶55,227.
[22] 200 F.2d 390 (9th Cir., 1952).
[23] *Huntington-Redondo Co.*, 36 B.T.A. 116 (1937), *acq.* 1937-2 C.B. 14.

principal and the balance interest. Such agreement will control for purposes of determining the amount of interest which can be deducted by X and must be reported as income by Y.

If the parties fail to agree as to the proper allocation, and the governing local statutes either allocate the payment or give one of the parties the right to make the allocation, and he does, then that allocation will control for tax purposes.[24]

> *Example:* A borrows $35,000 from B at 9 percent interest. The agreement provides for repayment at the rate of $500 a month and makes no allocation of the payments as to principal or interest. A and B are unable to come to any agreement as to the proper allocation. The governing statute provides that in such cases the borrower shall have the right to make the allocation. A notifies B that he will apply all payments first to interest and then to principal. Such allocation is controlling for tax purposes.

In the absence of any allocation by the parties, the Commissioner's allocation will prevail provided it is not patently unreasonable.

Related Parties

One circumstance, which can have a definite effect on an interest deduction, is the fact that the debtor and creditor are related. Although there is no reason why a creditor cannot lend to a related party, the existence of the relationship can raise a question as to whether the debt is "true debt." For instance, there have been numerous cases[25] where interest deductions on loans to corporations by their shareholders were denied because the loans were not considered to be true debt, i.e., the court concluded they were in reality disguised capital contributions.[26]

A similar problem can arise where a parent corporation borrows money from a subsidiary and makes no attempt at repayment. Here the Commissioner may argue that the "loan" was a disguised dividend.

> *Example:* A corporation, habitually in need of funds, borrows $5,000,000 from a subsidiary at 7 percent interest. No schedule is set for repayment of the loan and five years pass without any repayment of principal. Under these circumstances, the Service may take the position that the original loan was really a dividend and therefore there can be no deduction for the "interest" payments to the subsidiary.

Even where the debt is conceded to be *bona fide,* this does not necessarily mean that all of the interest paid is deductible. The Internal Revenue Service may still contend that, although the debt is true debt, the interest rate is excessive and attempt to deny a deduction for the "excessive" portion as in the *Dorzback* case[27] discussed previously.

---

[24] *Estate of Paul M. Bowen,* 2 T.C. 1 (1943), *acq.* 1943 C.B. 3; *Millar Brainard,* 7 T.C. 1180 (1946).

[25] E.g., *Gooding Amusement Co. v. Comm.,* 236 F.2d 159 (6th Cir., 1956), *aff'g.* 23 T.C. 408 (1954).

[26] Sec. 385, added to the Code by the 1969 Revenue Act, gives the Commissioner authority to issue regulatory guidelines for determining whether a corporate obligation constitutes stock or indebtedness.

[27] *Supra* fn. 16.

Finally, even though the debt is conceded to be *bona fide*, and the interest rate not excessive, an interest deduction may still be disallowed because of failure to make timely payment within the meaning of Section 267 of the Code. What Section 267 provides is that a deduction by an accrual-basis taxpayer for accrued interest due a related lender[28] who is on the cash method of accounting will be lost if not paid to the lender within the borrower's taxable year or two and a half months thereafter.

> *Example:* A corporation, an accrual-basis taxpayer, borrows $50,000 from B, a 60-percent cash-basis shareholder. Both A and B are on a calendar year. The interest on the loan for 1972 is $4,000. A accrues the $4,000 as an expense but does not actually pay the interest until June of 1974. On these facts, A will lose the deduction for the interest payment.

It should be noted that the Service takes the position that the deduction is permanently lost since Reg. 1.267(a)–1(b)(2) provides that ". . . , if the accrued expenses or interest are paid after the deduction has become disallowed under Section 267(a)(2), no deduction would be allowable for the taxable year in which payment is made, since an accrual item is deductible only in the taxable year in which it is properly accruable."

Section 267 is, of course, no problem where the creditor is on the accrual basis. It is also possible to avoid Section 267 without actually paying the interest due in cash, even where the creditor is on the cash basis, by distributing to the creditor a note having a face value equal to the accrued interest. Revenue Ruling 55–608[29] specifically provides that a deduction will be allowed where a note is issued by an accrual-basis taxpayer to a cash-basis, related taxpayer provided:

1. the taxpayer is solvent;

2. the note is issued within the taxpayer's taxable year or within 2½ months thereafter;

3. the note has a fair market value, when issued, equal to its face value.

---

[28] The related taxpayers referred to in Section 267 are as follows:
1. Members of a family, as defined in Section 267(c)(4);
2. An individual and a corporation, more than 50 percent in value of the outstanding stock of which is owned, directly or indirectly, by or for such individual;
3. Two corporations, more than 50 percent in value of the outstanding stock of each of which is owned, directly or indirectly, by or for the same individual, if either one of such corporations, with respect to the taxable year of the corporation preceding the date of the sale or exchange was, under the law applicable to such taxable year, a personal holding company or a foreign personal holding company;
4. A grantor and a fiduciary of any trust;
5. A fiduciary of a trust and a fiduciary of another trust, if the same person is a grantor of both trusts;
6. A fiduciary of a trust and a beneficiary of such trust;
7. A fiduciary of a trust and a beneficiary of another trust, if the same person is a grantor of both trusts.
8. A fiduciary of a trust and a corporation, more than 50 percent in value of the outstanding stock of which is owned, directly or indirectly, by or for the trust or by or for a person who is a grantor of the trust; or
9. A person and an organization to which Section 501 (relating to certain educational and charitable organizations which are exempt from tax) applies and which is controlled directly or indirectly by such person or (if such person is an individual) by members of the family of such individual.

[29] 1955-2 C.B. 546.

Finally, even where a note is not issued, Section 267 may be avoided through application of the constructive receipt doctrine.[30]

Imputed Interest

Up to this point, we have assumed that there is an interest charge which the borrower is trying to deduct. This has not always been the case. In the past, sellers would sometimes negotiate sales calling for a higher sales price in lieu of interest in an attempt to convert ordinary income into capital gain.

> *Example:* A, an individual in the 70-percent bracket, agrees to sell a tract of land to B for $100,000 on an installment note. The interest on such a note would normally amount to $30,000. Because A would have to pay a tax of 70 percent on such interest, he insists that the note be non-interest bearing and that instead the purchase price of the land be set at $130,000 so that the $30,000 will be taxed at capital gain rather than ordinary income rates.

Congress responded to such arrangements by adding Section 483 to the Internal Revenue Code. Section 483 imputes interest in contracts which fail to provide for a reasonable rate of interest. The Commissioner is allowed to determine what a reasonable rate of interest is, and at the present time he has set the rate at 4 percent per annum simple interest. Thus, a contract which calls for interest of at least 4 percent will not be attacked by the Internal Revenue Service.[31] Failure to provide a rate of at least 4 percent simple will result in the imputing of interest at 5 percent.[32] This rule applies to sales for a price in excess of $3,000 where payment is deferred for more than one year.[33] The rule does not apply to a seller, however, where the sale would give rise to ordinary income in any event.[34]

It should be noted that Section 483 applies to buyers as well as sellers and to the extent that the seller is required to report interest income by virtue of Section 483, the buyer is entitled to an interest deduction.[35]

> *Example:* Assume the same facts as in the prior example except that the sale falls within the coverage of Section 483. Under the regulations, an interest rate of 5 percent will be imputed and a portion of each payment will be considered interest and taxed at ordinary income rates. The buyer will be entitled to a corresponding deduction for interest expense.

Election to Capitalize Interest Payments

Although most taxpayers deduct interest payments currently, Section 266 of the Internal Revenue Code permits a taxpayer, under certain circumstances, to capitalize interest charges by adding them to the basis of the property with respect to which they were incurred.

---

[30] See Reg. 1.267(a)–1(b)(1)(iii); *McKee v. Comm.*, 18 T.C. 512 (1952); *W. C. Leonard & Co.*, 324 F. Supp., 422 (D.C. Miss., 1971).

[31] Reg. 1.483–1(d)(2).

[32] Reg. 1.483–1(c)(2).

[33] Sec. 483(f)(1); Sec. 483(c)(1)(A).

[34] Sec. 483(f)(3). It would still apply to the buyer. (Reg. 1.483–2(b)(3)(ii)).

[35] Reg. 1.483–2(a)(1).

The election is available for mortgage interest and carrying charges on real property that is unimproved and unproductive[36] and for carrying charges on real property in the process of development but only during the period of such development.[37] It is also available for personal property but only until the later of the date the property is installed or is first put into use by the taxpayer.[38]

> *Example 1:* A company buys a tract of land to be used eventually for a factory, borrowing the necessary funds. The tract lies unused for three years, during which time the carrying charges on it amount to $15,000. At the end of the third year, A starts to erect the factory, a process which takes an additional two years, during which time carrying charges amount to another $30,000. A may, if it wishes, capitalize the carrying charges incurred while the land was vacant ($15,000) and during the period of construction ($30,000) rather than deduct them currently.

> *Example 2:* X buys a machine to be used to manufacture a new product. Unfortunately, because of certain problems involved in the development of the product, the machine cannot be used for six months. During this six month period, the carrying charges on the machine amount to $1,000. X may elect to capitalize the $1,000 in carrying charges.

An election to capitalize interest expense is made by filing with the original tax return for the year for which the election is made a statement indicating the item or items with respect to which the election is made.[39] If the election is made as to unimproved and unproductive real estate, it may be made each year and the taxpayer is not bound to a similar election in the following year. An election as to property in the process of development, however, is binding for the duration of the project and the same is true for an election covering machinery, i.e., the election is binding until the machinery is installed or put into use, whichever is later.[40]

An election to capitalize interest payments would normally be made only by a business which is not able to use an immediate deduction.[41] To the extent that the election is made with respect to interest charges incurred in the process of construction or with respect to machinery, the capitalized interest expense may be recovered, at least in part, through an increased allowance for depreciation. If the property involved is unimproved, or if it is improved, but is sold before the deferred charge is recovered by way of depreciation, then the only benefit of the deferral has been an increase in basis. This increase in basis could turn out to be as valuable as an ordinary deduction if the property should subsequently be sold at a loss since such property would normally be Section 1231 property. If the property is sold at a gain, then the increase in basis will be less valuable in that it will probably only reduce what would normally be a capital gain.

------

[36] Reg. 1.266–1(b)(i).

[37] Reg. 1.266–1(b)(ii).

[38] Reg. 1.266–1(b)(iii).

[39] Reg. 1.266–1(c)(3).

[40] Reg. 1.266–1(c)(2).

[41] The net operating loss carryback and carryforward provisions should not be overlooked in determining whether or not the deduction can be used.

DISPOSING OF FINANCED PROPERTY

A discussion of the tax aspects of financing purchases of business property and equipment would be less than complete if it did not give some consideration to the problems involved in disposing of such financed property.

We might start by pointing out that the disposition of financed property is governed by the same rule which governs the disposition of property which has not been financed, i.e., gain or loss is determined by the extent to which the basis of the property is greater or lesser than its sale price.

Debt in Excess of Basis

It is important to realize, however, that where property which has been financed is sold, the sales price includes, in addition to the cash or other property received, any debt on the property which the buyer assumes or takes subject to.[42] What this means is that the seller may realize gain in excess of the cash or other property received. To illustrate how this works, let us assume that X purchases a building for $100,000 by paying $10,000 cash and giving a mortgage for $90,000. Let us further assume that when X sells the building for $30,000 cash, subject to the mortgage, he has paid $10,000 off on the mortgage and has taken depreciation amounting to $25,000. X's gain on the sale is computed as follows:

Cash received	$30,000
Mortgage	80,000
Total consideration received by seller	$110,000
Basis of property ($100,000 − $25,000)	− 75,000
Gain to Seller	$ 35,000

Application of the above rule should cause no difficulty where the seller is personally liable on the debt since the buyer's agreement to pay it is obviously a benefit to the seller. It does cause difficulty where the seller is not personally liable on the debt since the buyer's agreement to pay it produces no direct benefit to the seller. Nevertheless, even in this case it is clear that the debt must be taken into account in computing the seller's gain.[43]

It is important to realize that the rule that the price which the seller receives includes the debt which is assumed or taken subject to by the buyer is not limited to situations where the property is actually sold. It also applies to situations where the property in question is exchanged for other property and even where it is surrendered for the debt obligation itself.[44]

---

[42] *Crane v. Comm.*, 331 U.S. 1 (1947).

[43] Actually the seller received the benefit when it took the depreciation deductions which resulted in the lower basis.

[44] *Parker v. Delaney*, 186 F.2d 455 (1st Cir., 1950), *cert. denied*, 341 U.S. 926.

Example 1: A owns land which cost $15,000 and is subject to a mortgage of $10,000. He exchanges it with B for machinery worth $20,000. Since the exchange does not come within the "like kind" provisions of Section 1031, it results in the recognition of gain the same as an outright sale. The price realized on the sale includes the mortgage to which the property is subject. A's gain is $15,000 computed as follows:

Fair market value of machinery received	$20,000
Mortgage	10,000
Total consideration received by A	$30,000
Basis of property	−15,000
Gain to A	$15,000

Example 2: X owns machinery with an undepreciated cost of $10,000 on which he still owes the seller $12,000. The seller agrees to accept the machinery in full payment of X's note. X realizes a gain of $2,000 (the excess of the face value of the note over the undepreciated cost of the machinery) on the transaction.

Even where the transfer is otherwise nontaxable under the "like kind exchange" rule of Section 1031, gain will be recognized where the transferee assumes or takes the property subject to indebtedness. The rule here is that the amount of the debt assumed or taken subject to is treated as "boot,"[45] and gain is recognized, even in like kind exchanges, to the extent of the boot received.[46]

Example: A owns a building with an undepreciated cost of $20,000 which is subject to a mortgage of $10,000. During the year, he exchanges this building, subject to the mortgage, for a building owned by B which is unencumbered and which is worth $40,000. The exchange qualifies as a "like kind" exchange under Section 1031. Despite the applicability of Section 1031, A will realize $10,000 of gain in that year since the $10,000 mortgage to which A's property was subject is treated as boot and therefore $10,000 of A's $30,000 gain ($40,000 + $10,000 − $20,000) is realized immediately.

The one exception to this rule involves the situation where the property received in the exchange is also encumbered. In such cases, the indebtedness on the property transferred is treated as boot only to the extent it exceeds the indebtedness on the property received.[47]

Example: X owns land which cost $20,000 and which is subject to a mortgage of $15,000. He exchanges it in a transaction qualifying under Section 1031 for land worth $40,000 which is subject to a mortgage of $12,000. Of X's $23,000 gain on the transaction ($40,000 − $12,000 − $20,000 + $15,000) $3,000 (the excess of the mortgage on the property he gave up over the mortgage on property he received) is realized immediately.

---

[45] Sec. 1031(d).
[46] Sec. 1031(b).
[47] Reg. 1.1031(d)–2.

Although the rule requiring the seller to include in the purchase price any debt assumed or taken subject to by the buyer applies whether the property is sold or exchanged, and even where the exchange would otherwise be tax free, there is one situation where it may not apply, and that is where the property is abandoned. An owner would, of course, normally not abandon property if his equity in it had value, i.e., if the value of the property exceeded the amount of the liability to which the property was subject. Where, however, the value of the property is less than the amount of the liability, and the owner is not personally liable on the debt, there is no reason why he should not abandon the property. The difficulty this causes the Internal Revenue Service is that, unlike the transactions discussed previously, there is no taxable sale or exchange to trigger the recognition of gain to the extent the liability exceeds basis.

Despite this lack of a triggering event, there is language in *Parker v. Delaney,*[48] a 1950 First Circuit case, which indicates that were the court to be faced with the problem, it would find that a taxpayer does realize income on the abandonment of property to the extent that the amount of non-recourse obligations exceeds the basis of such property. Notwithstanding the language of *Parker v. Delaney,* neither the First Circuit nor any other court has as yet specifically dealt with the problem of abandonment and until some court does deal directly with the problem, the answer to the question of whether abandonment triggers gain to the extent non-recourse liabilities exceed basis must remain unanswered.

Foreclosures

The preceding discussion dealt only with voluntary dispositions of financed property. Not all dispositions are voluntary, of course, and the tax problems created by foreclosure should also be considered.

Generally speaking, the tax consequences of foreclosure, insofar as the debtor is concerned, are much the same as the tax consequences of a regular sale, i.e., his gain or loss is computed as though he had voluntarily sold the property.[49] This means, of course, that the net proceeds considered to be realized by the debtor include the entire amount of the debt outstanding at the time of the foreclosure.[50]

> *Example:* A purchases a tract of land, subject to a mortgage of $30,000, for $5,000. After paying off $5,000 of the mortgage, he defaults and the property is sold at a foreclosure sale for $20,000. Since the proceeds of the sale include the entire debt outstanding at the time of the foreclosure, A's loss on the foreclosure is computed as follows:

Basis for property	$35,000
Amount of mortgage at time of foreclosure sale	−25,000
Loss on foreclosure sale	$10,000

---

[48] *Supra* fn. 44.
[49] *Helvering v. Hammel,* 311 U.S. 504 (1941); *Electro-Chemical Engraving Co. v. Comm.,* 311 U.S. 513 (1941).
[50] *Supra* fn. 42.

The only time when this might not be true is where the debt was not related to the acquisition or improvement of the encumbered property. In such a case, the debt would not have been considered in determining the basis of the property, and therefore, should not be considered in determining the gain or loss on the sale of the property.[51]

> *Example:* A bought a tract of land for $40,000. Subsequently, he pledged the land as collateral for a loan of $30,000 to be used for working capital. The loan was defaulted on and the land sold at a foreclosure sale for $20,000. A's loss on the foreclosure sale is computed as follows:

Basis for land	$40,000
Amount realized on fore-closure sale	−20,000
Loss on foreclosure sale	$20,000

Deficiencies

The foreclosure process involves a sale of the secured property in satisfaction of the debt owed on it. To the extent the sales price is sufficient to pay off the note, the creditor is satisfied and the debtor is freed of any further obligation with respect to the indebtedness. But assume that the sales price is not sufficient to pay off the debt, what then?

Where the obligation is nonrecourse, i.e., the debtor is not personally liable on the note, the fact that there is a deficiency is irrelevant to the debtor since he is under no obligation to make it good. Where the obligation is a recourse obligation, however, the debtor remains personally liable and to the extent the sales proceeds are not sufficient to pay off the debt he is obligated to satisfy the deficiency. Where he does satisfy this deficiency, the amount of it is usually added to his basis for the property in order to determine his loss on the transaction.[52]

> *Example:* A company borrows $100,000 to buy a building, giving a mortgage to secure the loan. A defaults on the loan shortly thereafter and the property is sold at a foreclosure sale for $90,000. Since A is personally liable on the mortgage, it pays the mortgagee the deficiency of $10,000. A's loss on the transaction is as follows:

Original basis for building	$100,000
Payment of deficiency	+ 10,000
Adjusted basis	$110,000
Amount of mortgage at time of foreclosure	−100,000
Loss on foreclosure	$ 10,000

Suppose the debt in question was not incurred to acquire or improve the property in question but was incurred for some other purpose, e.g., to finance the purchase of inventory.

---

[51] Anderson, *Tax Factors in Real Estate, Third Edition* p. 230. Prentice-Hall, Inc.
[52] *Harry H. Diamond,* 43 B.T.A. 809 (1941).

Anderson[53] takes the position, and properly so, that the payment of the deficiency should not affect the basis of the foreclosed property any more than the original loan did, and therefore, the loss suffered by the debtor on the foreclosure sale is not affected by the payment of the deficiency.

> *Example:* B borrows $100,000 from C on a recourse note, pledging a building with a basis of $90,000 as collateral. B defaults on the note shortly thereafter and the property is sold for $80,000 at a foreclosure sale. B's loss on the foreclosure is $10,000 ($90,000 basis of building less $80,000 proceeds of sale) and it is not affected by B's subsequent payment of the $20,000 deficiency ($100,000 mortgage − $80,000 proceeds of sale).

Time for Deducting Losses on Foreclosure

Normally, a seller recognizes gain or loss in the year the property is actually sold. Foreclosure sales are unlike most sales, however, because the seller in a foreclosure sale generally has a right of redemption for a certain time after foreclosure. Thus, the time for deducting losses on foreclosure sales, where there is such a right of redemption, is not the year of the sale but the year in which the redemption right expires.[54]

> *Example:* X owns land which he paid $100,000 for and on which $50,000 is still owed. He is unable to make additional payments on the mortgage and in June of a given year the property is sold at a foreclosure sale for $50,000. Under the applicable state law, X has one year within which to redeem the property from the purchaser. Because X has a right of redemption, the sale of the property is not final until X's right of redemption lapses and thus X's loss on the foreclosure sale of $50,000 cannot be claimed prior to June of the following year.

Where a debtor who has a right of redemption wants to accelerate the recognition of a loss, he can do so either by abandoning his right of redemption[55] or by delivering a quitclaim deed to the mortgagee.[56] Since it may be difficult to prove abandonment, other than through the giving of a quitclaim deed, a debtor who wishes to abandon his right of redemption would be well advised to give a quitclaim deed.

A debtor who exercises his right of redemption realizes no loss on the sale. At the same time, it does not necessarily follow that a debtor has exercised his right of redemption where he reacquires the property. For instance, in *Tompkins v. Commissioner*,[57] although one of the mortgagors purchased the property at the foreclosure sale, the purchase was not, under the circumstances involved, treated as a redemption and the mortgagors were allowed to claim the

---

[53] *Supra* fn. 51.

[54] *Derby Realty Corp.*, 35 B.T.A. 335 (1937), *acq.* 1938-1 C.B. 9; *J. C. Hawkins*, 34 B.T.A. 918 (1936), *acq.* 1937-2 C.B. 13, *aff'd* 91 F.2d 354 (5th Cir., 1937).

[55] *Jacob Abelson*, 44 B.T.A. 98, *non-acq.* 1941-2 C.B. 14.

[56] *Sherwin A. Hill*, 40 B.T.A. 376, *non-acq.* 1939-2 C.B. 53, *reversed on another ground*, 119 F.2d 421 (6th Cir., 1941).

[57] 97 F.2d 396 (4th Cir., 1938).

loss on foreclosure. Similarly, in *McCarthy v. Cripe*,[58] a loss was allowed on foreclosure even though the property was purchased by an agent for a corporation, more than 50 percent of whose stock was owned by the mortgagor.

Gain on Foreclosure

Although foreclosure will frequently result in a loss to the debtor, this is not an inevitable result and there can be cases where it results in the realization of taxable gain. This would certainly be true where the foreclosed property is sold for more than its original cost. It would also be true where the debtor had taken depreciation in excess of the payments made with respect to the property and was either not personally liable on the obligation or was released from liability as a result of the sale.[59]

> *Example 1:* X owns land subject to a mortgage of $30,000 with a basis of $30,000. X defaults on the mortgage and the property is sold for $40,000. X has a $10,000 gain from the foreclosure sale ($40,000 realized on sale less $30,000 basis).

> *Example 2:* Y purchased a building for $5,000 subject to a $50,000 mortgage on which Y is not personally liable. Y subsequently defaults on the mortgage, at which time, the basis of the property has been reduced by depreciation to $20,000 and the mortgage has been reduced to $30,000. The property is sold at a foreclosure sale for $30,000. Y has a gain on the sale, even though he receives none of the sales proceeds, computed as follows:

Amount realized on foreclosure sale	$30,000
Basis of building	−20,000
Gain to Y	$10,000

Since a foreclosure is treated as a sale by the debtor even in those cases where the property is not actually sold but is merely surrendered to the creditor in exchange for cancellation of the indebtedness,[60] the nature of the gain is determined under those rules which normally govern the disposition of assets in the case of business property and equipment, i.e., Sections 1231, 1245, and 1250.

---

[58] 201 F.2d 679 (7th Cir., 1953).
[59] *Parker v. Delaney*, 186 F.2d 455 (1st Cir., 1950); *R. O'Dell & Sons Co.*, 169 F.2d 247 (3rd Cir., 1948).
[60] *Ibid.*

Chapter 9

Techniques for Reducing the Tax Bite
Through Depreciation, Repairs,
and Improvements on Property

A taxpayer who purchases business property and equipment is usually entitled to depreciate its cost. The first part of this chapter will discuss the circumstances in which depreciation may be claimed and the alternative methods of depreciation.

THE PURPOSE OF DEPRECIATION

The purpose of depreciation, both from an accounting and a tax viewpoint, is to allow the owner of an asset with a limited useful life to recover its cost over such useful life. It is important to realize that depreciation is not a valuation process and that the depreciation allowance for a particular year does not necessarily represent the decline in value of the asset during the year. As a matter of fact, in some cases, particularly where buildings are involved, there may have been no decrease in value during the year. The conceptual problem of depreciating property which has not actually decreased in value has been taken care of to some extent with the introduction into the Internal Revenue Code of depreciation recapture.[1]

WHAT IS DEPRECIABLE PROPERTY?

Not all property is depreciable, unimproved land[2] being the prime example of nondepreciable property. Inventory, stock in trade, and other items sold in the normal course of the taxpayer's business[3] are also nondepreciable assets.

---

[1] Sections 1245 and 1250.
[2] Reg. 1.167(a)–2.
[3] *Ibid.*

Intangibles such as patents, copyrights, and franchises have a limited useful life and their cost may be amortized over such life.[4] The cost of intangibles not having a limited useful life cannot be amortized. An example of the latter would be goodwill which is considered to have an indefinite useful life. Although natural resources such as oil, gas, and coal are subject to exhaustion, the Internal Revenue Code provides for such exhaustion by means of a depletion as opposed to a depreciation allowance.

Tangible property (e.g., machines, trucks, etc.) and buildings are depreciable since such assets have a limited useful life. Even these items are not always depreciable, however, since in order to depreciate an asset the taxpayer must have the economic interest in the property. Thus, a lessee may not depreciate a building which he leases since he does not own the building.[5] As a matter of fact, even ownership of property does not always entitle one to depreciate such property. An example would be the lessor who has leased property under a lease which requires the lessee not only to keep the property in as good a condition as it was at the beginning of the lease, but also to restore the value of the property at the expiration of the term.[6] Since the restoration clause protects the lessor against economic loss, he is not entitled to depreciate the property.

The fact that buildings are depreciable, but the land on which they are located is not, can cause problems where a taxpayer purchases land and buildings as a unit. In such cases, the purchase price must be allocated between the land and buildings in order to determine the depreciable (buildings) and nondepreciable (land) portion. The regulations[7] indicate that the allocation of purchase price to the buildings should be made on the basis of the fair market value of the buildings at the time of purchase as compared with the fair market value of the entire property at the time of purchase.

> *Example:* A purchases land with a building on it for $20,000. The fair market value of the building is $15,000 and the fair market value of the entire tract is the same as the price paid for it, i.e., $20,000. The purchase price is allocated by assigning $15,000 to the building and $5,000 to the land.
>
> If the value of the tract had been $25,000 (even though the purchaser paid only $20,000—a bargain purchase), only $15/25$ths of the purchase price of $20,000 or $12,000 would be allocated to the building and the remaining $8,000 would be allocated to the land.

Notwithstanding the regulations, the Internal Revenue Service has in one case,[8] involving a somewhat unusual situation, allowed the price paid for property to be allocated first to improvements to the extent of their fair market value and only the remainder to land.

---

[4] Reg. 1.167(a)–3. Amortization involves the same basic concept as depreciation, the difference being that the cost of an asset subject to amortization must be written off in equal annual installments over its useful life, while the cost of an asset subject to depreciation can frequently, through use of the accelerated methods of depreciation, be written off in uneven installments.

[5] A lessee would, however, be entitled to depreciate a building which he himself had constructed on leased property.

[6] *Terre Haute Electric Company, Inc. v. Comm.*, 96 F.2d 383 (1938); See also, Rev. Rul. 62–8, 1962–1 C.B. 31, which distinguishes between obligations to restore value and obligations to restore only to the condition at the beginning of the lease, and which allows the lessor to claim some allowance for depreciation in the latter case.

[7] Reg. 1.167(a)–5.

[8] Rev. Rul. 68–362, 1968–2 C.B. 334.

The ruling in question involved the situation where a taxpayer leased land that it owned to a developer who, under the terms of the lease, was obligated to construct a shopping center on the land. The developer borrowed the construction funds, executing a mortgage on the shopping center improvements to secure the loan. In addition, the taxpayer as part of the transaction subordinated its fee interest in the land to the mortgage. Eventually, the developer defaulted on the loan and the lender advised the taxpayer that it intended to foreclose unless the mortgage was paid off. At the time, the combined value of the land and improvements was in excess of the unpaid balance on the mortgage although the balance of the mortgage exceeded the fair market value of the improvements. In order to protect its interest, the taxpayer assumed the mortgage and acquired legal title to the improvements.

On these facts, the Service held that the assumption of the mortgage was in effect a purchase which resulted in the taxpayer not only acquiring legal title to the improvements, but also protected its title to the land. The Service then allowed the taxpayer to allocate the cost of the assumption of the mortgage by apportioning to the improvements an amount equal to their fair market value. Only the excess of the mortgage assumed over the fair market value of the improvements was required to be added to the basis of the land.

METHODS OF DEPRECIATION

The Internal Revenue Code offers a number of different methods of computing depreciation. In general, these methods allow the taxpayer to claim the same depreciation allowance for each year of useful life, to allocate more depreciation to the early years than to the later years, or to allocate less depreciation to the early years and more to the later years. In addition, provision is made for computing depreciation in terms of output where that is more appropriate than computing it in terms of years.

Straight Line

The simplest method of computing depreciation is the straight line method. It produces the same depreciation allowance each year and is easy to work with. Under the straight line method, the annual depreciation allowance for an asset is normally determined by reducing the cost or other basis of the asset by its estimated salvage value and dividing the result by the number of years of its estimated useful life.[9]

> *Example:* A company buys a building with an expected useful life of 40 years for $40,000. Salvage value at the end of the building's useful life is estimated to be $4,000. A's annual depreciation allowance under the straight line method will be $900. ($40,000 − $4,000 = $36,000 ÷ 40 = $900.)

Although in the above example the full amount of the salvage value was deducted in arriving at the annual depreciation allowance, this is not always required. Where the property

---

[9] Reg. 1.167(b)–1(a).

involved is depreciable personal property (acquired after October 16, 1962) with a useful life of three years or more, the taxpayer is required to take salvage value into account only to the extent it exceeds 10 percent of the basis of the property.[10]

> *Example:* X Company buys a machine with a useful life of ten years for $5,000. Salvage value is estimated to be $800. Assuming X chooses to take advantage of the above rule, its annual depreciation allowance for the machine will be $470, not $420, since only salvage value in excess of 10 percent of cost will be taken into account.

It is important to realize that in any case where the taxpayer does not elect another acceptable method of depreciation he will be considered to be on the straight line method.[11] Application of this rule can present difficulties where the taxpayer has elected another method of depreciation and it is subsequently discovered that the asset in question did not qualify for such method. A typical example would be the case where a taxpayer elects 200 percent declining balance depreciation with respect to used equipment. Since, as will be discussed later, the maximum percentage of declining balance depreciation that can be claimed with respect to used personal property is 150 percent it is clear that the election to use 200 percent is invalid. The question is whether, since the taxpayer obviously intended to claim accelerated depreciation, he will be allowed to use 150 percent declining balance depreciation or is limited to straight line.

The Internal Revenue Service originally took the position that in the situation outlined above the taxpayer was limited to straight line depreciation notwithstanding his obvious intent to be on an accelerated method.[12] The Tax Court took a more liberal approach and in two cases[13] involving an erroneous election of 200 percent declining balance depreciation allowed the taxpayer to adopt the 150 percent declining balance method. Subsequently, the Service reversed its position and in Revenue Ruling 72–491[14] conceded that a taxpayer who had erroneously selected an unallowable depreciation method could adopt any permissible method, not just straight line, on discovery of the error.

Declining Balance

Although straight line depreciation is easy to compute and produces uniform depreciation deductions, it has been overshadowed to some extent with the advent of accelerated, principally declining balance, depreciation. Under the declining balance method of depreciation, the depreciation allowances in the earlier years tend to be considerably higher than under the straight line method. This enables a business to reduce its taxes in such years and can be an important factor in terms of cash flow.

---

[10] Section 167(f).
[11] Reg. 1.167(a)–10(a).
[12] Rev. Rul. 67–338, 1967–2 C.B. 102.
[13] *Silver Queen Motel,* 55 T.C. 1101 (1971); *Robert M. Foley,* 56 T.C. 765 (1971) *acq.* 1972 P-H ¶55,441.
[14] 1972 P-H ¶55,444.

Depreciation is computed under the declining balance method by applying a uniform rate of depreciation, expressed in terms of a percentage, to a steadily decreasing base which is the unrecovered cost of the asset.[15] In the first year, unrecovered cost is the original cost. In subsequent years, unrecovered cost is original cost less the depreciation taken in prior years.

> *Example:* Assume a taxpayer buys a new machine with a useful life of ten years for $10,000 and elects double declining balance depreciation. The depreciation rate will be 20 percent (double means double the straight line rate) and the first-year's depreciation will be $2,000. The second-year's depreciation will be $1,600 which is computed by applying the depreciation rate of 20 percent to the unrecovered cost of $8,000 (original cost of $10,000 less prior depreciation of $2,000).

In addition to illustrating how declining balance depreciation is computed, the above example also illustrates the more rapid writeoff inherent in the use of the declining balance method. The table below shows the depreciation deductions for the first three years under the double declining balance as opposed to the straight line method.

Year	Double Declining Balance	Straight[16] Line
1	$2,000	$1,000
2	1,600	1,000
3	1,280	1,000
	$4,880	$3,000

As the table indicates, the depreciation deductions for the first three years under the double declining balance method are substantially in excess of those under the straight line method. At the same time, it should be noted that as the years pass the annual depreciation allowance under the double declining balance method is dropping, so that by the third year it is approaching in amount the straight line allowance, and by the fifth year it will be less than the corresponding straight line allowance. At this point, depreciation of the remaining cost on a straight line basis will produce a faster writeoff over the remaining useful life of the property and it is customary to switch to the straight line method. This can be done without obtaining the permission of the Internal Revenue Service.[17]

Although the preceding discussion involved the use of the double declining (200 percent of the straight line rate) method not all property qualifies for the double declining or even the declining balance method. Insofar as tangible personal property is concerned, only new property with a useful life of three years or more qualifies for double declining balance depreciation.[18] Depreciation on used tangible personal property is limited to 150 percent of the

---

[15] Reg. 1.167(b)–2(a).
[16] The salvage value is assumed to be less than 10 percent and is therefore ignored in the computations.
[17] Sec. 167(e).
[18] Sec. 167(c).

straight line rate.[19] The regulations permitting the 150 percent method with respect to used tangible property do not limit it to property having a useful life of three years or more, but the Internal Revenue Service has taken the position in Revenue Ruling 67–248[20] that the 150 percent declining balance method may not be applied to used property with a useful life of less than three years except in very unusual circumstances. Revenue Ruling 67–248 was preceded by a Tax Court decision[21] holding that the 150 percent declining balance method may not be used for property having a useful life of less than three years and thus is not without judicial support.

The situation with respect to real estate (essentially buildings) is somewhat different. Until the 1969 Tax Reform Act, new real estate generally qualified for 200 percent declining balance depreciation and used real estate for 150 percent declining balance.

The Tax Reform Act changed this and now only new residential housing qualifies for 200 percent declining balance depreciation,[22] the maximum available on all other new real estate being limited to 150 percent of the straight line rate.[23] Accelerated depreciation is not permitted at all with respect to used realty[24] except that 125 percent declining balance depreciation is permitted for used residential rental property with a remaining useful life of 20 years or more.[25]

Sum of the Years-Digits

Although the declining balance method applies a fixed rate to a decreasing base, the sum of the years-digits method applies a steadily decreasing rate to a constant base.[26] The base is the original cost (or original cost less salvage value) of the property. The rate is a fraction, the numerator of which is the number of years of useful life remaining and the denominator the sum of all the years' digits in the useful life of the property.

> *Example:* An asset which cost $1,000 has no salvage value and a useful life of four years. The yearly depreciation allowance under the sum of the years-digits method is determined first by adding the sum of all the years' digits in the useful life $(4 + 3 + 2 + 1 = 10)$. This gives the denominator of the fraction with the numerator being the remaining useful life. The computations are as follows:

First Year	$4/10 \times \$1,000 =$	$400
Second Year	$3/10 \times \$1,000 =$	300
Third Year	$2/10 \times \$1,000 =$	200
Fourth Year	$1/10 \times \$1,000 =$	100
		$1,000

---

[19] Rev. Rul. 57–352, 1957–2 C.B. 150.
[20] 1967–2 C.B. 98.
[21] *Holder-Driv-Ur-Self, Inc.*, 43 T.C. 202 (1964), *nonacq.* 1965–2 C.B. 7.
[22] Sec. 167(j)(2).
[23] Sec. 167(j)(1).
[24] Sec. 167(j)(4).
[25] Sec. 167(j)(5).
[26] Reg. 1.167(b)–3(a).

The use of the sum of the years-digits method is restricted to new property with a useful life of three years or more.[27] Like 200 percent declining balance depreciation it was available for all new buildings prior to the 1969 Tax Reform Act, but when the Tax Reform Act limited the use of the double declining balance method to new residential housing it also limited the use of sum of the years-digits depreciation to new residential housing.[28] Thus today, the sum of the years-digits method is available only as to new tangible personal property with a useful life of three years or more, or new residential housing.

It should be noted that, unlike the declining balance method, in computing depreciation under the sum of the years-digits method, salvage value must be taken into account,[29] although in the case of certain tangible property it need be taken into account only to the extent it exceeds 10 percent of the basis of the property.[30]

Methods Which Produce More Depreciation in Later Years

Since very few taxpayers are interested in depreciation methods which produce less depreciation in the early years and more in later years, the discussion of such methods will be limited. There are such methods, however, and two which have been used to some extent are the retirement and replacement methods.

Under the retirement method, the entire cost of an asset is deducted in the year the asset is retired. Under the replacement method, the cost of an item which is retired, but not replaced, is handled in the same way as under the retirement method, i.e., it is written off in the year of retirement. It is the cost of the item which is retired and replaced that is handled differently. Rather than write off the cost of the item which is replaced, the cost of the replacement item is written off.

Although the retirement and replacement methods make no sense at all in terms of depreciating individual assets, they can be very useful to industries using large quantities of identical items which must be periodically replaced. Thus, such methods are still used by railroads for such assets as rails and ties.

Computing Depreciation in Terms of Output

There are times when it is more helpful to measure the useful life of an asset in terms of output rather than in terms of years. The Internal Revenue Service has recognized this, and accordingly will, in appropriate circumstances, allow depreciation based on the unit of production method[31] and the income forecast method.[32]

The unit of production method is particularly appropriate where the extraction of natural resources is involved, although it can be useful in other situations as well. Under the unit of

---

[27] Sec. 167(c).
[28] Sec. 167(j)(1) and (2).
[29] Reg. 1.167(b)–3(a)(1).
[30] Sec. 167(f).
[31] Reg. 1.167(b)–0(b).
[32] Rev. Rul. 60–358, 1960–2 C.B. 68.

production method, an estimate is first made of the total number of units to be produced by or in connection with the asset in question. The cost of the asset to be depreciated, less salvage value, is then allocated among the units to be produced with each unit bearing an equal share of the depreciation. Thus, the depreciation for a particular year will vary with the number of units produced during the year.

> *Example:* It is estimated that a particular machine, costing $40,000, will produce 20,000 units before it wears out. If we assume the machine has no salvage value, then the depreciation per unit of production will be $2 and the depreciation allowance for a year when 8,000 units are produced will be $16,000.

Notwithstanding the usefulness of the unit of production method, there are times when useful life can be more meaningfully measured in terms of hours or days of use rather than units of production. In these cases, it is permissible to estimate the useful life of assets in such terms.[33]

> *Example:* A machine which cost $15,000 is estimated to have a useful life of 30,000 hours. Assuming the machine has no salvage value, the depreciation per hour of use will be $.50. If the machine is used 10,000 hours in a year, the depreciation for the year will be $5,000.

Since the unit of production method assumes that physical wear and tear will be the principal factor in determining an asset's useful life, the method should not be used where obsolescence has an important effect on useful life.

The "income forecast" method is a variation of the unit of production method which measures production in terms of anticipated revenues rather than actual units of production. The Internal Revenue Service has approved its use in computing depreciation on television films and taped shows leased to others for exhibition[34] and has also extended its use to motion picture films.[35] The income forecast method is particularly appropriate to such assets since the useful life of a film or show cannot be measured in terms of physical wear or tear but must be measured in terms of anticipated viewer interest. The only meaningful measure of such interest is estimated revenues.

Under the income forecast method, depreciation is allocated equally to each dollar of anticipated revenue and the depreciation allowance for a particular year is determined by reference to revenue for the year.

> *Example:* A television film which cost $100,000 to make is expected to produce revenues of $500,000. The depreciation per dollar of revenue will be $.20 and depreciation in a year in which revenues are $200,000 will be $40,000.

---

[33] Rev. Rul. 56–652, 1956–2 C.B. 125.
[34] Rev. Rul. 60–358, 1960–2 C.B. 68.
[35] Rev. Rul. 64–273, 1964–2 C.B. 62.

Although the Internal Revenue Service has so far accepted the use of the income forecast method only for movie and television films and tapes,[36] there would seem to be no reason why the method should not apply to any asset where anticipated revenue, rather than wear and tear, is the more meaningful measure of useful life.

Electing a Method of Depreciation—Change of Method

The initial selection of a method of depreciation is a fairly simple matter. There is no formal election, the election of a particular method being made by claiming depreciation under that method on the first tax return on which the taxpayer is entitled to claim depreciation for the item in question.[37] Should a taxpayer fail to elect a method, Regulation 1.167(b)–1(a) provides that the straight line method shall be used. The election applies only to the item with respect to which it is made, and does not preclude a different election for another asset even where the asset is of the same kind.

Once made the election is binding[38] and the taxpayer can switch to another method only with the consent of the Commissioner. The one exception to this rule is that a taxpayer may change from the double declining balance method to the straight line method at any time.[39] The problem of erroneous elections, i.e., mistakenly selecting a method one is not entitled to, was discussed earlier in this chapter.[40]

As mentioned, in order to effect a change of method (other than from double declining balance to straight line) the taxpayer must secure the consent of the Commissioner. This is done by submitting an application on Form 3115. If the change of method is one covered by Revenue Procedure 67–40[41] and the taxpayer meets the conditions of the Revenue Procedure, consent to the requested change will be automatic. For changes not covered by Revenue Procedure 67–40 the Commissioner must affirmatively grant permission.

Additional First Year Depreciation

In addition to the normal depreciation allowance for tangible personal property, any taxpayer, except a trust, may elect to write off 20 percent of the cost of such property, with a useful life of six years or more, in the year in which the property is first depreciable.[42] The amount of tangible personal property that can qualify for this extra depreciation is limited to $10,000 a year. Thus, the total additional first-year depreciation in any one year is limited to $2,000. In computing the additional depreciation, salvage value is ignored,[43] but the additional depreciation reduces basis in computing normal depreciation.[44]

---

[36] See *KIRO, Inc. v. Comm.*, 51 T.C. 155 for the use of a sliding scale variation of the income forecast method.
[37] Reg. 1.167(c)–1(c).
[38] Reg. 1.167(e)–1(a).
[39] Sec. 167(e)(1).
[40] See the discussion under the heading, "Straight Line Method."
[41] 1967–2 C.B. 674.
[42] Sec. 179.
[43] Reg. 1.179–1(d).
[44] Sec. 179(d)(8).

Example: Taxpayer purchases a new machine with a useful life of ten years, and no salvage value, for $10,000 and elects to claim the additional first-year depreciation. The additional first-year depreciation will be $2,000 and normal depreciation, assuming the straight line method is chosen, $800 ($10,000 − $2,000 = $8,000 ÷ 10).

A separate election must be made each time the allowance for additional first-year depreciation is claimed. The election is made by showing in the appropriate place in the taxpayer's return for the year in question the amount of additional first-year depreciation claimed.[45] The election may cover one item or several items or portions of the cost of several items so long as the $10,000 limit is not exceeded.[46]

SALVAGE VALUE

As pointed out in the discussion of the straight line method, salvage value must be taken into account in computing depreciation with two exceptions. First, salvage value is not taken into account in computing the annual depreciation allowances under the declining balance method of depreciation provided, of course, that an asset may not be depreciated below its salvage value.[47] Second, salvage value need be taken into account in depreciating personal property having a useful life of three years or more only to the extent that it exceeds 10 percent of the cost of the property,[48] with again the proviso that a property may not be depreciated below its salvage value.[49]

Since salvage value represents the amount which a taxpayer can reasonably expect·to realize when he disposes of an asset, an asset's salvage value will vary with the practices of the taxpayer involved. For example, for a taxpayer who normally uses machines until they are worn out, salvage value will be the scrap value of the machines, usually a fairly low figure. The situation is different for taxpayers who seldom keep an asset for its full useful life. A business which trades in its automobiles every two years will have a fairly substantial salvage value for the automobiles since a two-year-old car usually has a fairly significant resale value.

In computing the salvage value to be taken into account in determining the depreciation allowance for a particular asset, the Regulations allow a taxpayer to compute it on either a gross or a net basis. If the taxpayer computes salvage on a gross basis, he does not take the costs of removal into account until disposal, at which time he deducts them in full. If he computes salvage value on a net basis, he takes the costs of removal into account initially in determining salvage value and deducts them at the time of salvage only to the extent they exceed the original estimate. Whichever method is chosen must be consistently followed.[50]

Once the salvage value of an asset has been set, it normally is not changed unless the

---

[45] Reg. 1.179–4(a).
[46] Reg. 1.179–1(c).
[47] Reg. 1.167(b)–2(a).
[48] Sec. 167(f). This provision is limited to property acquired after October 16, 1962.
[49] Reg. 1.167(f)–1.
[50] Reg. 1.167(a)–1(c)(1).

useful life of the asset is changed, in which case the salvage value can also be redetermined.[51] In no event, of course, may an asset be depreciated below salvage value; however, the mere fact that an asset is sold at a gain does not allow the Commissioner to redetermine salvage value for the purpose of disallowing depreciation in the year of sale as the *Fribourg*[52] case illustrates.

In the *Fribourg* case, the taxpayer, a shipping company, purchased a ship in December of 1955 to use in its business. The taxpayer determined the useful life of the ship to be three years and depreciated the ship on that basis, using a salvage value suggested by the Internal Revenue Service. Because of the Suez crisis in 1956 and 1957, the value of ships rose sharply and in June of 1957 the taxpayer agreed to sell the ship for an amount substantially in excess of its remaining cost. The sale actually took place in December of 1957.

Since the ship had been sold at a gain, the Commissioner argued that the taxpayer was not allowed to claim any depreciation in the year of sale. This was consistent with his position in Revenue Ruling 62–92[53] that depreciation for the year of sale is limited to the amount, if any, by which the adjusted basis of the property at the beginning of the year exceeds the amount realized from the sale. Both the Tax Court and the Second Circuit upheld the Commissioner, the Second Circuit pointing out that to allow a depreciation deduction in the year in which an asset is sold for more than its adjusted basis contravenes the basic purpose of the depreciation deduction.

The Supreme Court, however, reversed the Tax Court and the Second Circuit and held that the position of the Commissioner as expressed in Revenue Ruling 62–92 was erroneous, thus rejecting the proposition that the sale of a depreciable asset for an amount in excess of its adjusted basis *automatically* bars a deduction for depreciation for the year of sale.

Subsequently, the Service issued Revenue Ruling 67–272[54] which modified Revenue Ruling 62–92 so as to bring it into accord with the no-automatic-disallowance rule of *Fribourg* but reserved the right to challenge depreciation in the year of sale in any case in which the original estimate of useful life or salvage value was unreasonable. As a practical matter, the incentive of the Commissioner to attack depreciation in the year of sale has been sharply reduced with the advent of depreciation recapture.

USEFUL LIFE

Obviously, an estimate of useful life is essential in computing depreciation for an asset. Unfortunately, the useful life of an asset can depend on a number of variables and taxpayers will frequently find themselves engaged in a battle with the Internal Revenue Service over the correctness of the useful life claimed for a particular asset or assets. Since the burden of proof is on the taxpayer, he will usually try to justify the useful life used by reference to his own or

---

[51] *Ibid.*
[52] *Fribourg Navigation Co.*, 383 U.S. 272 (1966).
[53] 1962–1 C.B. 29.
[54] 1967–2 C.B. 99.

other's experience with similar assets. The Service may, in turn, challenge the appropriateness of the comparison, or may rely on its own engineers in contending for a longer life.

Because of the difficulties involved in determining useful lives, and in order to bring some certainty into the area, the Internal Revenue Service has a number of times published lists of useful lives acceptable to the Service.

Bulletin F

The first of these lists was Bulletin F, issued in 1942, which set forth useful lives for various assets on an item-by-item basis. Although the lives listed were intended to serve as guidelines rather than absolutes, it was inevitable that Revenue Agents would begin to consider them authoritative and Bulletin F was for many years a formidable barrier to those claiming lives shorter than those listed.

Eventually, the Internal Revenue adopted a broader approach to useful lives with the introduction in 1962 of the "guideline lives."[55]

Guideline Lives

The guideline lives were intended to supersede Bulletin F and, although their use was not mandatory, a taxpayer who chose not to use the guidelines, at least in theory, could not rely on Bulletin F.

One of the purposes of the guideline lives was to eliminate the need to choose a specific useful life for each asset. Thus, assets were grouped into various classes with each class having a useful life determined by reference to the average lives of the assets contained therein. Despite the seeming simplicity of this approach, its usefulness was complicated by the Reserve Ratio Test. This was a complicated test designed to insure that taxpayers' replacement policies were consistent with the assumptions on which the guideline lives were based. Fortunately, it passed into history with the advent of the ADR regulations.

ADR Regulations

The ADR regulations were introduced by the Treasury in an attempt to further liberalize depreciation by giving taxpayers a choice, within limits, as to the useful life of an asset. The regulations applied to property placed in service after 1970 and, among other things, allowed a taxpayer to use a life 20 percent shorter or longer than the guideline life. Since the ADR regulations were elective, taxpayers were allowed to continue to use the old guideline life or lives based on "facts and circumstances."

The introduction of the new ADR regulations created quite a furor, with some people taking the position that the Treasury had no authority to allow a taxpayer to write off assets over periods that were less than their useful lives. The dispute was resolved by the Revenue Act of 1971 which in effect adopted, with certain modifications, the ADR regulations.

---

[55] Rev. Proc. 62–21, 1962–2 C.B. 418.

STATUTORY ADR RULES

The statutory ADR rules introduce a "class life" system. Under this system, a taxpayer can elect to use a class life for eligible property placed in service during the taxable year for which the Treasury has prescribed a class life. The class lives set by the Treasury are to reflect reasonably the anticipated useful lives of the assets in question but the Treasury may allow a variance of not more than 20 percent from such lives, the same as under the ADR regulations.[56]

> *Example:* The class life for automobiles is three years but a taxpayer may use a life as short as two and one-half years or as long as three and one-half years.

The property eligible for the class life system is tangible property which is subject to the allowance for depreciation provided by Section 167(a) but only if:

1. An asset guideline class and asset guideline period are in effect for such property for the taxable year of election.

2. The property is first placed in service after December 31, 1970.

3. The property is either—
   a. Section 1245 property as defined in Section 1245(a)(3), or
   b. Section 1250 property as defined in Section 1250(c).[57]

The Election

If the class life system is elected with respect to a particular taxable year, it covers, with certain exceptions, all assets qualifying for the class life system that are placed in service during that year.[58] Thus, a taxpayer may not elect to use the system with respect to one class of additions for a particular year but not another.

> *Example:* A taxpayer has both machinery and office furniture additions during the year. He may not elect the class system as to the machinery additions but not the office furniture additions. He must elect the system as to both or neither.

A taxpayer may, however, elect to use the system for one year's additions but not another's since the election is an annual one.[59]

Since the election of the class life system for a particular year covers all assets placed in

---

[56] Sec. 167(m).
[57] Reg. 1.167(a)–11(b)(2).
[58] Reg. 1.167(a)–11(b)(5)(ii).
[59] Reg. 1.167(a)–11(a)(1).

service during the year, a taxpayer who wants to elect the system for new assets placed in service during the year must also use it for used assets placed in service during such year [60] even though the lives of such used assets might actually be shorter than the guideline lives. There is an exception to this rule where the unadjusted basis of used Section 1245 property placed in service during the year in question exceeds 10 percent of the unadjusted basis of all Section 1245 property placed in service during the year. In such a case, the taxpayer may elect to apply the class life system only to the new property.[61] This is an all or nothing election and if the taxpayer chooses to exclude any used Section 1245 property for a particular year, he must exclude all used Section 1245 property for that year. The "unadjusted basis" means the cost or other basis of an asset without regard to adjustments for depreciation or amortization (other than depreciation under Section 179) but with the other adjustments required under Section 1016 or other applicable provisions.[62] A similar election is available for Section 1250 property.[63]

> *Example 1:* The cost of a taxpayer's Section 1245 additions during the year was $11,000. Of this, $1,000 represents used additions and the balance new. Since the cost of the used additions is less than 10 percent of the total cost of additions during the year, an election to use the class life system covers both the used and new additions. If the cost of the used additions had been $2,500, then the cost of the used assets would have exceeded 10 percent of the total cost of additions for the year and the taxpayer could have elected the system as to new additions only.

> *Example 2:* The cost of a taxpayer's Section 1245 additions during the year is $10,000 of which $1,000 represents the cost of used additions. Since the cost of the used additions does not exceed 10 percent of the adjusted basis of the total additions, an election to use the class life system will cover used as well as new additions. If, however, the taxpayer elects to claim the 20 percent additional first-year depreciation as to certain of its new additions, then it may exclude the used additions from the class life election since the 20 percent additional first-year depreciation will reduce the unadjusted basis of the new additions and bring the unadjusted basis of the used to over 10 percent of the total.

It is important to realize that an election to use the class life rules covers more than useful lives. The class life rules encompass a complete system of depreciating assets, and an election to use them requires following the system not only as to useful life, but also as to methods of depreciation, computation of depreciation, treatment of retirements, first-year conventions, etc.[64] Thus, in determining whether or not to make the election, it is important to at least be aware of the other aspects of the system.

---

[60] Reg. 1.167(a)–11(b)(5)(ii).
[61] Reg. 1.167(a)–11(b)(5)(iii)(a).
[62] Reg. 1.167(a)–11(c)(1)(v)(a).
[63] Reg. 1.167(a)–11(b)(5)(iii)(b).
[64] Reg. 1.167(a)–11(a)(1).

Asset Grouping

We might start out by looking at the asset grouping rules.

Under the class life system, all eligible property must be carried in what are known as "vintage accounts" and separate vintage accounts must be set up for each guideline class represented in a year's acquisitions. An account may not include assets from more than one guideline class or from more than one year.[65]

> *Example:* A taxpayer's additions for last year include $8,000 of office equipment and $6,000 of automobiles. This year's additions include another $4,000 of office equipment. If the taxpayer elects the class life system for both years, then he must set up three vintage accounts; one for last year's office equipment, one for last year's automobiles, and one for this year's office equipment. Last year's office equipment and automobiles may not be placed in the same vintage account since they fall into different guideline classes. In addition, even though last year's and this year's office equipment additions fall into the same guideline class, separate vintage accounts must be set up since different years are involved.

The fact that there must be a separate vintage account for each guideline class represented in the year's acquisitions does not mean that all assets of a class must be carried in the same account, and more than one account may be established for different assets of the same guideline class.[66]

> *Example:* A manufacturer acquires various items of factory equipment in the same year, including lathes and drill presses. Although both of these items are in the same guideline class, the taxpayer may establish a separate vintage account for each of them.

Moreover, certain assets may not be included in the same account even though they are in the same guideline class. For instance, new and used assets must be kept in separate accounts as must assets for which additional first-year depreciation has been elected.[67]

In addition to classifying additions into vintage accounts, the taxpayer must maintain a depreciation reserve for each vintage account and the amount of the reserve for each account must be stated in each income tax return on which depreciation under the system is claimed.[68]

Useful Life

Having set up vintage accounts, the taxpayer must then specify the useful life he wishes to apply to each account. Different lives may be assigned to different vintage accounts, even

---

[65] Reg. 1.167(a)–11(b)(3)(i).
[66] *Ibid.*
[67] Reg. 1.167(a)–11(b)(3)(ii).
[68] Reg. 1.167(a)–11(c)(1)(ii).

though such accounts are in the same guideline class, so long as all the lives assigned are within the asset depreciation range established for the class.[69]

> *Example:* A acquires two different types of machines, both of which are covered by the same guideline class with a guideline life of five years. If A chooses, he may put each machine in a different vintage account and claim a useful life of four years (the lower limit of the guideline life) for one, and six years (the upper limit of the guideline life) for the other.

The asset depreciation ranges for the class life system are set forth in Rev. Proc. 72–10.[70] Rev. Proc. 72–10 provides the asset guideline period for each guideline class, the asset guideline periods being for the most part identical with the guideline lives established under Rev. Proc. 62–21. The asset depreciation range for each class can then vary from 80 percent of the asset guideline period to 120 percent of the guideline period, provided that any fractional part of a year must be rounded to the nearest whole year or the nearest half year.

Salvage Value

Salvage value must be determined as to each vintage account based on the facts and circumstances existing at the end of the year in which the account is established.[71] It is important to realize, however, that under the class life system, salvage value serves only as a limit on total depreciation. Thus, in computing annual depreciation allowances, salvage is ignored until the final years of an asset's useful life. In the final years, salvage value must be considered since an asset may not be depreciated below its salvage value.[72]

The salvage value of a vintage account is its gross salvage value without reduction for the costs of removal, dismantling, demolition, or similar operations.[73] These costs may not be taken into consideration in computing salvage value but must be deducted as current expenses in the year paid or incurred.[74] This is in sharp contrast with the normal depreciation rules which allow the use of net salvage value, i.e., gross salvage value less related costs such as removal. As is true under the normal depreciation rules, the salvage value of new or used personal property with a life of three years or more may be reduced by an amount up to 10 percent of the unadjusted basis of the account.[75] This, of course, does not mean the salvage value can be reduced below zero.

In order to avoid minimal adjustments, a taxpayer's estimated salvage value will ordinarily not be changed unless the correct salvage value for a vintage account is higher than the taxpayer's estimated salvage value by more than 10 percent of the unadjusted basis of the account at the close of the taxable year in which the account is established.[76] For example, if

---

[69] Reg. 1.167(a)–11(b)(4)(i).
[70] 1972 P-H ¶15,466.10.
[71] Reg. 1.167(a)–11(d)(1)(iii).
[72] Reg. 1.167(a)–11(c)(1)(i).
[73] Reg. 1.167(a)–11(d)(1)(i) and (ii).
[74] Reg. 1.167(a)–11(d)(3)(x).
[75] Reg. 1.167(a)–11(d)(1)(ii).
[76] Reg. 1.167(a)–11(d)(1)(v).

the unadjusted basis of an asset in a vintage account at the end of its first year is $30,000, and the taxpayer has estimated a salvage value of $5,000, the Service will not change the taxpayer's estimate of salvage value unless it feels that the correct salvage value is more than $8,000 (i.e., taxpayer's estimate of salvage value ($5,000) plus 10 percent of the $30,000 unadjusted basis of the asset at the end of the first year ($3,000)).

This 10 percent leeway does not, of course, mean that a taxpayer can regularly underestimate salvage in order to take advantage of the 10 percent rule. If the Service finds that the taxpayer is consistently doing this, the leeway will not be allowed.[77]

Methods of Depreciation

A taxpayer who elects to use the class life system must, subject to a limited exception, use the straight line, declining balance or the sum of the years-digits methods of depreciation. Assets which are depreciated under other methods, such as the unit of production method, may not be included in the election.[78] With one difference, the class life rules allow the use of accelerated methods under the same conditions established by Section 167(c) and (j). That is to say, insofar as tangible personal property is concerned, the double declining balance and sum of the years-digits method may be used only for new property in a vintage account with a class life of three years or more. The straight line method may be used for any property, and the 150 percent declining balance method may be used for new or used property provided the vintage account in question has a class life of three years or more. The only difference between the use of the accelerated methods under Section 167(c) and the use of the accelerated methods under the class life system is that under the class life system, in determining whether an asset has a useful life of three years or more, it is the depreciation period which was selected for the account in which the asset is placed, rather than the actual estimated useful life of the asset, that is critical.[79] The extent to which accelerated depreciation can be used with respect to real estate is, of course, governed by Section 167(j).

Two types of changes in depreciation method are allowed under the class life system. At any time, the taxpayer can change to the straight line method from the declining balance or sum of the years-digits method. Also, at any time, a change may be made from the declining balance to the sum of the years-digits method.[80]

The class life system assumes, as did the depreciation guideline lives in Rev. Proc. 62–21, that the asset depreciation period chosen already reflects the salvage value. As a result, the straight line and sum of the years-digits computations do not take salvage value into account. Again it must be emphasized, however, that no account may ever be depreciated below estimated salvage value.[81]

---

[77] *Ibid.*
[78] Reg. 1.167(a)–11(b)(5)(v)(a).
[79] Reg. 1.167(a)–11(c)(1)(iv)(b).
[80] Reg. 1.167(a)–11(c)(1)(iii)(a).
[81] Reg. 1.167(a)–11(c)(1)(i).

Retirements

The class life system distinguishes between ordinary and extraordinary retirements. The term, "ordinary retirement," is defined as including any retirement of Section 1245 property from a vintage account which is not treated as an "extraordinary retirement." The retirement of an asset from a vintage account is an "extraordinary retirement" if:[82]

A. The asset is Section 1250 property;

B. The asset is Section 1245 property which is retired as the direct result of fire, storm, shipwreck, or other casualty and the taxpayer, at his option consistently applied (taking into account type, frequency and the size of such casualties) treats such retirements as extraordinary; or

C. (1) The asset is Section 1245 property which is retired (other than by transfer to supplies or scrap) in a taxable year as the direct result of a cessation, termination, curtailment, or disposition of a business, manufacturing, or other income-producing process, operation, facility, or unit, and

    (2) The unadjusted basis (determined without regard to subdivision (vi) of Reg. 1.167(a)–11(d)(3)) of all such assets so retired in such taxable year from such account as a direct result of the event described in (C)(1) of this subdivision exceeds 20 percent of the unadjusted basis of such account immediately prior to such event.

For the purposes of (C), all accounts (other than a special basis vintage account containing Section 1245 property of the same vintage in the same asset guideline class, and from which a retirement as a direct result of such event occurs within the taxable year) are treated as a single vintage account.

Generally speaking, gain is not recognized upon a normal retirement from a multiple-asset account. Instead, the proceeds of the retirement are added to the depreciation reserve of the vintage account from which the asset is retired,[83] and gain is recognized only to the extent the reserve at the end of the taxable year exceeds the unadjusted basis of the account.[84] Since the proceeds are added to the depreciation reserve rather than used to reduce the cost of the assets in the account, the annual depreciation allowance under the straight line or sum of the years-digits methods will not be affected until such time as the balance of the reserve equals the original cost or other basis of the assets in the account. The same is not true of the declining balance method, and here the annual depreciation allowance will be immediately affected since declining balance depreciation is computed by applying a fixed percentage to the original

---

[82] Reg. 1.167(a)–11(d)(3)(ii).
[83] Reg. 1.167(a)–11(d)(3)(iii).
[84] Reg. 1.167(a)–11(d)(3)(ix).

cost or other basis of the assets in the account as reduced by the depreciation reserve for the account.[85]

The rule as to extraordinary retirements is different. Extraordinary retirements ordinarily result in the recognition of gain or loss unless one of the nonrecognition provisions of the Code is involved.[86] In addition, the annual depreciation allowance is affected since the cost or other basis of the asset is removed from the vintage account, and the portion of the reserve for depreciation attributable to the asset is removed from the reserve.[87]

First-Year Convention

Under the class life system, a taxpayer has a choice as to first-year conventions.

He may use the half-year convention and treat all additions as placed in service on the first day of the second half of the taxable year and treat all extraordinary retirements as occurring on the first day of the second half of the taxable year.[88] Alternatively, he may use a modified half-year convention in which he treats additions and extraordinary retirements during the first half of a taxable year as occurring on the first day of such taxable year; and additions and extraordinary retirements during the second half of the taxable year as occurring on the first day of the succeeding taxable year.[89]

Whichever convention is adopted for a particular year must be adopted for all vintage accounts of such taxable year, but the same convention need not be adopted for the vintage accounts of another taxable year.[90]

Formal Election of the Class Life System

An election to use the class life system is made in the income tax return filed for the taxable year in which the property is first placed in service.[91] The election must specify:

1. That the taxpayer makes the election and consents to, and agrees to apply all the provisions of Reg. 1.167(a)–11;

2. The asset guideline class for each vintage account of the taxable year;

3. The asset depreciation period selected for each vintage account;

4. The first-year convention adopted for the taxable year of election and (if the taxpayer applies the modified half-year convention) the total cost or other basis of all eligible property first placed in service in the first half of the taxable year and the total cost or other basis of all eligible property first placed in service in the last half of the taxable year;

---

[85] Reg. 1.167(a)–11(c)(1)(i)(d).
[86] Reg. 1.167(a)–11(d)(3)(iv).
[87] *Ibid.*
[88] Reg. 1.167(a)–11(c)(2)(iii).
[89] Reg. 1.167(a)–11(c)(2)(ii).
[90] Reg. 1.167(a)–11(c)(2)(i).
[91] Reg. 1.167(a)–11(f)(2).

5. The unadjusted basis and salvage value for each vintage account, and the amount, if any, by which gross salvage value was decreased under Section 167(f);

6. Whether the 10 percent used property rule described in Reg. 1.167(a)–11(b)(5)(iii) has been applied to exclude used property from the election;

7. Each asset guideline class for which the taxpayer elects to apply the asset guideline class repair allowance, the amount of property improvement for each such class as determined under paragraph (d)(2)(VII)(a) of Reg. 1.167(a)–11, and whether or not the taxpayer elects for the taxable year to allocate the unadjusted basis of a special basis account for the taxable year in accordance with paragraph (d)(3)(VI) of Reg. 1.167(a)–11;

8. Whether any eligible property for which the taxpayer was not required or permitted to make an election was excluded because of the special rules of paragraph (b)(5)(V), (VI) or (VII), or (6), or (e)(3)(1);

9. Whether any "Section 38 property" was excluded from the election;

10. Such other information as may reasonably be required.[92]

In addition, a taxpayer must also file the following information with respect to each asset guideline class for the taxable year of election:

a. The total unadjusted basis of all assets retired during the taxable year from each asset guideline class, and the proceeds realized during the taxable year from such retirements;

b. The vintage (that is, the taxable year in which established) of the assets retired during the year;

c. Such reasonable information with respect to expenditures for the repair, maintenance, rehabilitation, or improvement of assets as shall be prescribed by the Commissioner, and;

d. Such other information as may be prescribed by the Commissioner.

REPAIRS, MAINTENANCE, AND IMPROVEMENTS

In addition to claiming depreciation on business property and equipment, a taxpayer is also entitled to deduct the cost of maintaining and repairing such items.[93] A taxpayer may not, however, expense improvements. The cost of improvements must be capitalized and recov-

---

[92] Reg. 1.167(a)–11(f)(4)(ii).
[93] Sec. 162(a).

ered through the allowance for depreciation. Unfortunately, it is not always clear whether certain items constitute maintenance, repairs, or improvements, and a taxpayer will on occasion find the Internal Revenue Service disputing the expensing of a particular item.

There are, of course, certain costs that everyone concedes are deductible and should be written off currently. These include items such as janitorial and caretaker services. Such expenses are recurring costs and obviously do nothing more than preserve the value of the asset.

Even where the item in question seems to add to the value of an asset, it will still be treated as deductible if the addition of value is temporary and the expenditure must be repeated at frequent intervals. A typical example is the cost of repainting a building. Most people would agree that repainting adds some value to a building and normally the increase in value will last more than one year. Despite this, repainting has been generally held to be an item of maintenance, the cost of which can be expensed currently.[94] This expensing can be justified on the theory that repainting merely preserves the building, and therefore does not represent a true increase in value; or, on the theory that the increase in value is so temporary and so insubstantial that capitalization is not practical. In either case, the result is the same.

This is not to say that painting can never be a capital item. Just like many other items of maintenance or repair, even painting may, under certain circumstances, constitute a capital item. For example, where painting is done as part of, or in connection with, a general reconditioning project, its cost must be capitalized even though it would be a proper expense item were it not part of the reconditioning cost.[95]

In addition to painting, there are a number of other costs that would normally be considered maintenance or repairs. These would include items such as the cost of mending leaks in a roof,[96] pointing and cleaning the walls of a building,[97] repairing sidewalk lights,[98] the cost of rebuilding one wall of a building,[99] and the cost of realigning roof supports.[100]

Where an item is improved, as opposed to merely repaired, the cost must be capitalized and cannot be expressed currently. For example, the cost of replacing a wall,[101] the cost of resurfacing an entire roof,[102] and the cost of constructing a concrete wall around a warehouse building to replace a worn-out wooden one,[103] have all been held to be improvements—the cost of which must be capitalized.

It should be noted that even where the cost of a replacement must be capitalized because it

---

[94] *Rose v. Haverty Furniture Co.*, 15 F.2d 345 (5th Cir., 1926); *Max Kurtz*, 8 B.T.A. 679 (1927) *acq.* VII-1 C.B. 18; *Kirkland v. U.S.*, 267 F. Supp. 259 (D.C. Neb.).

[95] *J. M. Jones*, 242 F.2d 616 (5th Cir., 1957); *Bank of Houston*, 1960 P-H T.C. Memo ¶60,110 (1960).

[96] *Pierce Estates, Inc.*, 16 T.C. 1020 *acq.* 1951–2 C.B. 3. *Reversed and remanded on another issue*—195 F.2d 475, (3rd Cir., 1952).

[97] *City National Bank*, 1952 P-H T.C.M. ¶52,112.

[98] *Crocker Co., Inc.*, 15 B.T.A. 175 (1929) *acq.* VIII–2 C.B. 12.

[99] *O. L. Thomas*, 1962 P-H T.C.M. ¶62,134.

[100] *Gopcevic*, 1944 P-H T.C.M. ¶44,373.

[101] *Stewart Supply Co., Inc.*, 324 F.2d 233, (2nd Cir., 1963).

[102] *Southwest Ornamental Iron Co.*, 1953 P-H T.C.M. ¶53,171.

[103] *Alexander Sprunt & Son, Inc.* 24 B.T.A. 599 (1931).

constitutes an improvement, the taxpayer is entitled to write off the remaining cost of the item being replaced if it is abandoned.

> *Example:* A owns a building surrounded by a wooden fence with a remaining undepreciated cost of $5,000. For security reasons, A decides to tear down the old fence and replace it with a new steel fence. The cost of the new fence is $15,000. The cost of tearing down the old fence is $2,000. Although A must capitalize the cost of the new fence, the remaining undepreciated cost of the old fence ($5,000), less any salvage value, and the cost of tearing it down ($2,000) may be written off in the year of replacement.

REPAIRS UNDER THE CLASS LIFE SYSTEM

A taxpayer who elects the class life system may also elect to use the "repair allowance" rule. Under this election, a taxpayer may deduct, without challenge by the Internal Revenue Service, expenditures for the repair, maintenance, or improvement of a class of property up to a certain amount (the repair allowance) even though the expenditures clearly prolong the life of an asset or assets. Only the excess over the amount of the repair allowance must be capitalized.[104]

The repair allowance for a class is determined by multiplying the percentage prescribed for the class by the average of the beginning and end-of-the-year asset basis of the repair allowance property.[105]

> *Example:* The annual asset guideline repair allowance percentage for office furniture and fixtures is 7.5 percent. If the average of the beginning and end-of-the-year asset basis of a vintage account for office furniture and fixtures is $10,000, then the repair allowance for the class for the year is $750.

Obviously, making the repair allowance election can be helpful to a taxpayer since it allows him to deduct expenditures currently, even though they prolong the life of an asset, so long as the total deduction does not exceed the repair allowance. At the same time, the election does not solve all problems since certain expenditures do not qualify for the election. The expenditures not qualifying for the election (excluded additions) are:

A. An expenditure which substantially increases the productivity of an existing identifiable unit of property over its productivity when first acquired by the taxpayer;

B. An expenditure which substantially increases the capacity of an existing identifiable unit of property over its capacity when first acquired by the taxpayer;

---

[104] Reg. 1.167(a)–11(d)(2)(iv)(a).
[105] Reg. 1.167(a)–11(d)(2)(iii).

C. An expenditure which modifies an existing identifiable unit of property for a substantially different use;

D. An expenditure for an identifiable unit of property if (1) such expenditure is for an additional identifiable unit of property or (2) such expenditure (other than an expenditure described in (E)) is for replacement of an identifiable unit of property which was retired;

E. An expenditure for replacement of a part in, or a component or portion of, an existing identifiable unit of property (whether or not such part, component or portion is also an identifiable unit of property) if such part, component or portion is for replacement of a part, component or portion which was retired in a retirement upon which gain or loss is recognized (or would be recognized but for a special nonrecognition provision of the Code or §1.1502-13).

F. In the case of a building or other structure (in addition to (B), (C), (D), and (E) which also apply to such property), an expenditure for additional cubic or linear space; and

G. In the case of those units of property of pipelines, electric utilities, telephone companies, and telegraph companies consisting of lines, cables, and poles (in addition to (A) through (E) which also apply to such property), an expenditure for replacement of a material portion of the unit of property.

Notwithstanding the above, the term "excluded addition" does not include any expenditure in connection with the repair, maintenance, rehabilitation, or improvement of an identifiable unit of property which does not exceed $100. In addition, for purposes of (A), (B) and (F) an increase in productivity or capacity is substantial only if the increase is more than 25 percent.[106]

If a taxpayer repairs, rehabilitates, or improves property for sale or resale to customers, the repair allowance rule does not apply to expenditures for the repair, maintenance, rehabilitation, or improvement of such property. Where a taxpayer follows a practice of acquiring property for his own use and the property needs repair, rehabilitation, or improvement to be suitable for such use, then any expenditures made for such repair, rehabilitation, or improvement do not qualify under the repair allowance rule.[107]

---

[106] Reg. 1.167(a)–11(d)(2)(vi).
[107] Reg. 1.167(a)–11(d)(2)(v)(c).

Chapter 10

Making Tax-Wise Decisions in the Disposition of Purchased Property

Just as the purchase of property has tax consequences, so does disposing of property have tax implications.

There are a number of ways of disposing of property. The most obvious is by sale. Exchanges in full or partial payment for other property have also become fairly common, particularly where they afford a tax advantage. Occasionally, property can neither be sold nor exchanged and must be abandoned. Finally, property may be destroyed by fire or other disaster or taken through condemnation.

TAX CONSEQUENCES OF SELLING BUSINESS PROPERTY AND EQUIPMENT

Unlike exchanges, which can offer an opportunity for tax deferral, the tax consequences of a sale of business property or equipment are generally immediate in the sense that the gain or loss from the sale is recognized currently rather than deferred to some future period. This may or may not be beneficial depending on whether the sale results in gain or loss and the nature of such gain or loss.

Determining whether the sale of property will result in gain or loss is usually not difficult and generally involves nothing more than a comparison of the undepreciated cost or other basis of the property with the sales price. Determining the nature of the gain or loss is somewhat more involved, particularly where depreciation recapture comes into play.

If the property has been held six months or less, there is no problem since any gain or loss will be treated as ordinary. Where the property has been held for more than six months, reference must be made to Section 1231 of the code to determine whether the gain or loss will be capital or ordinary.

Section 1231

Section 1231 provides that where real or depreciable property used in the taxpayer's trade or business and held for over six months is sold, the classification of the gain or loss as ordinary or capital will depend on whether the net result of all sales of Section 1231 assets for the year is a gain or a loss. If the net result is a gain, then all the gains and losses on the sale of Section 1231 assets are treated as capital gains and losses. If the net result is a loss, then all the gains and losses are treated as ordinary gains and losses.[1]

Although Section 1231 is obviously favorable to businessmen, its emphasis on the net result of Section 1231 sales for the year allows astute planners to gain even greater benefits through careful timing of sales.

> *Example:* Y corporation plans to sell two Section 1231 assets. One of the assets will be sold at a $20,000 loss; the other at an $18,000 gain. If Y sells both in the same year, the net result will be a $2,000 ordinary loss resulting in a tax saving of approximately $1,000. If, on the other hand, Y plans the sales so that one falls in one year and the other in a second year, and there are no other Section 1231 sales in either year, then the net result will be an $18,000 capital gain, taxable at the rate of 30 percent, and an ordinary loss of $20,000, deductible at the rate of 48 percent, resulting in a net tax saving of $4,200.

Depreciation Recapture

The rather generous provisions of Section 1231 were, unfortunately, somewhat restricted with the advent of depreciation recapture. Depreciation recapture was introduced into the Internal Revenue Code in 1962 through the addition of Section 1245. Under Section 1245, gain on the sale of depreciable personal property is taxed as ordinary income to the extent of post-1961 depreciation. Since Section 1245 overrides Section 1231,[2] a gain that would normally be capital under Section 1231 because there was a net Section 1231 gain for the year becomes ordinary to the extent of the post-1961 depreciation.

The same concept was introduced with respect to depreciable realty in 1964 when Section 1250 was added to the Code. Section 1250, unlike Section 1245, provided for only partial recapture of depreciation in most situations and even this could be eliminated if the property was held long enough. The rule was that where property was held less than 21 months, all post-1963 depreciation was subject to recapture. Once the property had been held at least 20 months, only the excess of accelerated over straight line depreciation was recapturable and the percentage recaptured declined by 1 percent for each month the property was held in excess of 20 months so that there was no recapture after the property had been held for ten years (120 months).

> *Example:* X sold a factory on June 30, 1969, which it had owned for five years. The excess of accelerated depreciation over straight line depreciation for the five-year period was

---

[1] Sec. 1231(a).
[2] Sec. 1245(d).

$10,000. The factory was sold at a gain of $40,000 and there were no other sales of Section 1231 assets during the year in question. Since the property had been held for a total of 60 months, the percent of excess depreciation recapturable is reduced by 40 percent (one percent for each month the property is held in excess of 20 months) and only 60 percent or $6,000 of the gain attributable to the excess depreciation of $10,000 must be treated as ordinary income.

Section 1250 was, unfortunately, modified in 1969 to provide for full recapture of excess depreciation taken after 1969, regardless of how long the property is held except where the property in question is residential rental property (e.g., apartment buildings).[3] Thus, if in the prior example the building were purchased in 1970 and sold in 1975, all, not merely 60 percent of the excess depreciation would be recapturable.

The old rule continues to apply, however, to depreciation taken prior to 1970, and thus, where property acquired prior to 1970 is sold, the recapture applicable to pre-1970 depreciation is determined under the old rules and the recapture applicable to post-1969 depreciation under the new.[4]

> *Example:* X sold an office building on December 31, 1973, at a gain of $20,000 having held it six years. Pre-1970, excess depreciation was $10,000, and post-1969 excess depreciation $5,000. Under Section 1250 only 48 percent or $4,800 of the pre-1970 excess depreciation will be recapturable; whereas, 100 percent of the post-1969 excess depreciation is recapturable.

Investment Credit Recapture

In addition to the problems caused by depreciation recapture, a business considering the sale of property must also take into account the investment credit implications of disposing of property.

Starting in 1962, businesses were allowed a tax credit of 7 percent of the cost of *new* depreciable property with a useful life of at least eight years. If property had a useful life of six years or more but less than eight years, two-thirds of its cost qualified for the credit. If the useful life was four years or more but less than six, then only one-third of the cost of the property qualified for the credit. No credit was allowed where the property had a useful life of less than four years.[5] The credit, referred to as "the investment credit" was, with some exceptions suspended between October 10, 1966, and March 9, 1967,[6] and repealed generally

---

[3] Where the property is residential rental property, the percentage of excess depreciation recapturable is reduced by one percentage point for each month in excess of 100 during which the property is held by the seller (Sec. 1250(a)(1)(C)(iii)). The recapture provisions are even more favorable where the mortgage is insured under Sections 221(d)(3) or 236 of the National Housing Act (or comparable provisions of local law) and certain other conditions are met (Sec. 1250(a)(1)(C)(ii)).

[4] Sec. 1250(a)(2).

[5] The credit was also allowed for up to $50,000 of the cost of used depreciable personal property (Sec. 48(c)). Later, the brackets were shortened so that now property with a three-to-five-year useful life qualifies for the credit to the extent of one-third of its cost, property with a useful life of five to seven years qualifies for the credit to the extent of two-thirds of its cost and property with a useful life of seven years or more qualifies for the full amount of the credit (Sec. 46(c)(2)).

[6] Sec. 48(h).

effective April 18, 1969.[7] It was reintroduced in the Revenue Act of 1971 to apply to property acquired after August 15, 1971.[8]

Since a taxpayer claims the investment credit at the time of purchase of the asset, and not after he has held the asset for the requisite period, the Internal Revenue Code provides for the recapture of investment credit where the property is disposed of prematurely. The amount of recapture is determined, and recapture effected, by increasing the taxpayer's tax for the year of disposal by the difference between the investment credit originally claimed and the amount which would have been claimed had the period the taxpayer actually held the property been used.[9]

Because investment credit recapture can be quite substantial in particular cases, it is important for a taxpayer who is considering the sale of property to take it into consideration.

Installment Sales

Although most sales result in the immediate recognition of gain or loss, a seller may under certain circumstances elect to defer recognition of gain on a sale by making an installment sale election. Under an installment sale election, a taxpayer reports as gross profit from the sale only that proportion of the payments received during the year which the gross profit realized, or to be realized when payment is completed, bears to the total contract price.

The installment sale election is available for casual sales of personal property, other than inventory, for a price exceeding $1,000 and for any sales of real property.[10] In both cases, the sale must contemplate payments in two or more taxable years[11] and the payments in the year of sale may not exceed 30 percent of the selling price.[12] Payments received in the year of sale include payments in cash or property but do not include evidences of indebtedness of the buyer[13] unless such evidences of indebtedness are readily tradable in an established securities market or are payable on demand.[14] It should be noted that the installment sale election does not apply to losses and thus it is not possible to defer losses to future periods by means of such an election.

Although the installment sale election provides obvious advantages to a seller who receives 30 percent or less of the sales price in the year of sale, there are a number of technical points which should not be overlooked. The first is that where the contract of sale provides for no interest or an unreasonably low rate of interest on the deferred payments, then a portion of the deferred payments will under Section 483 be treated as interest rather than as part of the sales price.[15] This will reduce the sales price for purposes of the 30 percent test and could result in payments in the year of sale in excess of 30 percent.

---

[7] Sec. 49(a).

[8] Sec. 50.

[9] Sec. 47.

[10] Sec. 453(b)(1).

[11] Rev. Rul. 69–462, 1969–2 C.B. 107, amplified Rev. Rul. 71–595, 1972–1 C.B. 223.

[12] Sec. 453(b)(2)(A)(ii).

[13] *Ibid.*

[14] Sec. 453(b)(3).

[15] Sec. 483. The imputed interest rules apply only to payments due more than six months after sale under a contract

> *Example:* X sells a piece of real estate for $100,000 with $30,000 payable in the year of sale and the balance over five years. The contract provides for no interest on the deferred payments. Under Section 483, a portion of the $100,000 sales price will be treated as interest with the result that payments in the year of sale will exceed 30 percent of the adjusted sales price, making the sale ineligible for the installment sale election.

The second point to be noted is that gain deferred through an installment sale election will be recognized if the installment sale obligations are sold or disposed of.[16]

> *Example:* A sells a tract of land in 1973 for $80,000, payable $20,000 at closing and the balance in equal payments over the next three years at 5 percent interest. Since A's basis for the land is only $20,000, he makes an installment sale election and reports in 1973 a gain of only $15,000. Assuming A does not dispose of the installment sales obligations received in the sale, he will report an additional $15,000 of gain in each of the next three years. Should A sell the purchaser's note a year after making the election, then he will have to recognize the remaining $45,000 of gain in that year.

EXCHANGES AS ALTERNATIVES TO SALES

As the preceding discussion indicates, sales of property, except to the extent the installment sale provisions apply, result in the immediate recognition of gain. The same is not true of exchanges. Exchanges can, in certain situations, offer considerable opportunity for tax deferral.

Section 1031

The key to tax deferral where exchanges are involved is Section 1031 of the Internal Revenue Code. This section provides that no gain or loss shall be recognized where property held for productive use in a trade or business or for investment is exchanged solely for property of a "like kind" also to be held either for productive use in a trade or business or for investment. Certain types of assets are specifically excluded from the coverage of Section 1031, however, and these include stock in trade or other property held primarily for sale, stocks, bonds, notes, securities, and other evidences of indebtedness.[17]

Despite its exclusions, Section 1031 can be extremely helpful to a businessman since it covers all business property and equipment except what is held primarily for sale. Thus, Section 1031 can apply to anything from a machine tool to a jet airplane.

---

providing for one or more payments due more than one year from the date of sale. The contract must provide for a selling price of more than $3,000 and there is no imputed interest where the contract provides for interest at the rate of at least 4 percent annum simple (Reg. 1.483–1 and 2).

[16] Sec. 453(d).

[17] Sec. 1031(a).

The "Like-Kind" Requirement of Section 1031

Although Section 1031 can apply to a broad variety of exchanges, the requirement that the property received in the exchange be of "like kind" imposes a rather basic restriction, although it is not usually a problem in most exchanges involving business property or equipment. For example, the most common exchange involving business property or equipment is the trade-in, i.e., a business buys a new piece of equipment, say a truck, by trading in an older truck and making a cash payment in addition. Such a transaction clearly satisfies the "like-kind" requirement of Section 1031.[18]

It should be noted that the definition of "like kind" is fairly broad and the term is not restricted to those situations where the asset exchanged is exactly the same type or quality as the asset received. Rather "like kind" refers to the general nature or character of the property.[19] For example, it is clear where exchanges of real estate are involved that the fact that one piece is improved and the other unimproved does not prevent the application of Section 1031.[20] Even the exchange of land for a leasehold interest will qualify provided the leasehold is for a sufficiently long term to be considered the equivalent of the fee. For example, the exchange of a factory for the right to lease it for 99 years would certainly qualify as a Section 1031 transaction and the Internal Revenue Service takes the position that the exchange of a fee interest for a lease with 30 years or more to run is a like-kind exchange.[21]

Although the concept of "like kind" is rather broad, this does not mean that any exchange will qualify for Section 1031 treatment. Thus, an exchange of real for personal property clearly does not fall under Section 1031. Nor, as implied above, is an exchange of a fee interest for a leasehold of less than 30 years a like-kind exchange.

Inability to Claim Losses in Section 1031 Transactions

It is important to realize that Section 1031 is not elective and that it applies to losses as well as to gains. Thus, taxpayers who want to recognize a loss on the disposition of business property should be careful not to dispose of the property in a Section 1031 transaction. This can be a particularly troublesome problem where the property involved would normally be used as a trade-in. In such cases, an attempt to sell the loss property and purchase a replacement in separate transactions with the same person may prove unsuccessful under a constructive trade-in theory, and the taxpayer would be well advised to sell the loss item to a third party, if possible.[22]

---

[18] Reg. 1.1031(a)–1(c)(1).
[19] Reg. 1.1031(a)–1(b).
[20] Reg. 1.1031(a)–1(c)(2).
[21] *Ibid.*
[22] Am Jur 2d, Vol. 34 para. 4188.

Section 1031 Transactions Involving the
Receipt of Cash or Other Property

In many Section 1031 transactions, the asset exchanged or traded in is less valuable than the asset received and the taxpayer must make a payment in addition to the trade-in. There are cases, however, particularly when the subject of the exchange is real estate, where the asset exchanged is more valuable than that received. In such cases, the taxpayer will receive cash or other property in addition to the like-kind property.[23]

The fact that money or other property is received in an exchange of like-kind property does not make Section 1031 inapplicable to the transaction. Rather, the transaction will still be governed by Section 1031 but gain will be recognized to the extent of the money and fair market value of the other property received.[24]

> *Example:* A taxpayer exchanges unimproved land with a basis of $100,000 for unimproved land worth $150,000 and cash of $50,000. Although the taxpayer's gain on the exchange is $100,000, the gain will be recognized only to the extent of the cash received, i.e., $50,000.

Where the property involved in the exchange is real estate, it is necessary to take mortgages into consideration in determining whether the taxpayer has received other property, necessitating the recognition of gain. The rule here is that where a taxpayer exchanges property subject to a mortgage for property not subject to a mortgage, the amount of the mortgage on the property given up is treated as the receipt of other property and gain is recognized to the extent of the mortgage liability.[25]

> *Example:* A exchanges real estate with a tax basis of $100,000, and subject to a $50,000 mortgage, for unencumbered real estate worth $200,000. A's gain of $150,000 is recognized to the extent of the mortgage of $50,000.

If both the property exchanged and the property received are subject to mortgages, the mortgages are netted and the taxpayer will be considered to have received other property only to the extent there is a net reduction in indebtedness in his favor as a result of the exchange.[26]

> *Example:* A exchanges a property subject to a mortgage of $10,000 for property subject to a mortgage of $15,000. A is not considered to have received other property as a result of the exchange since the mortgage on the property received exceeds the mortgage on the property surrendered. Had the mortgage on the new property been only $5,000, A would have received other property of $5,000.

---

[23] Such money and property is frequently referred to as "boot."
[24] Sec. 1031(b).
[25] Sec. 1031(d).
[26] Reg. 1.1031(d)–2, Example (2).

Up to this point, it has been assumed that the fair market value of the property surrendered exceeded, or was at least equal to, the amount of the mortgage to which the property was subject. Suppose the fair market value of the property is less than the amount of the mortgage to which the property is subject—does this affect the result? One writer has suggested that it does and has concluded that where the taxpayer is not personally liable on the mortgage, the amount of the mortgage should not be construed as other property to the extent that it exceeds the fair market value of the property surrendered.[27]

Finally, it is important to realize that although the receipt of money or other property can result in the recognition of gain to the extent of such money or property, the same is not true where a loss is involved. The receipt of money or other property does not change the basic rule that loss is not recognized in a Section 1031 exchange.[28]

Three-Party Transactions

Generally, exchanges under Section 1031 involve only two parties. There have, however, been a number of cases involving three parties which have been held to qualify as tax-free under Section 1031. Such cases can arise under a variety of circumstances. One of the more common is where a buyer wishes to purchase a tract of land from the owner, but the owner is reluctant to pay the tax which would result from a sale, although he would be willing to exchange the land tax-free for similar land. In such circumstances, the buyer will commonly try to work out a three-way exchange with a third party who owns land which would be acceptable to the owner of the first tract. The arrangement would be for the buyer to buy the second tract for cash and then exchange it for the first tract, intending to qualify the exchange under Section 1031 so that the owner of the first tract does not realize any gain as a result of the transaction.

Three-party exchanges are not limited to the above circumstances and sometimes the situation is reversed so that the initiative to bring a third party into the picture comes from the owner of land who wants to exchange his land for another tract of land. Where the owner of the second tract is unwilling to exchange his tract but demands cash for it, the owner of the first tract has no alternative but to try to arrange with some third party, who is interested in the first tract, to buy the second tract for cash and then exchange it for the first tract.

Although there may be some question as to whether specific three-party exchanges are covered by Section 1031, the Internal Revenue Service has conceded, at least in principle, that three-party exchanges can qualify under Section 1031. The Service's admission is contained in Revenue Ruling 57–244[29] which involved the situation where A, B, and C each owned a tract of land. A wanted to acquire the tract owned by C. C in turn was interested in B's tract and B wanted to acquire A's tract. The parties handled the problem by having A convey his lot to B, B then conveyed his tract to C and C conveyed his tract to A. The Service held that the

---

[27] Tax Management Portfolio #61–2nd, page A-21, citing *Crane v. Comm.*, 331 U.S. 1 (1947), but acknowledging the existence of *Mendham Corporation*, 9 T.C. 320 (1947).

[28] Sec. 1031(c).

[29] 1957–1 C.B. 247.

exchanges qualified under Section 1031, notwithstanding the fact that three rather than two parties were involved. Despite its admission that Section 1031 can apply to three-party exchanges, the Service has vigorously contested its application in situations other than that described in Revenue Ruling 57–244.

The typical situation involving three-party exchanges today is the one mentioned previously where a purchaser wants to buy land but the owner refuses to sell, although he would be willing to exchange the property tax-free for other land.

> *Example:* A owns a tract of land that B would like to buy for cash. A is not interested in selling the land for cash because of the tax involved, but is willing to exchange it for a similar tract owned by C.

In such cases the purchaser (B) will buy property satisfactory to the owner (A) of the land the purchaser is interested in, and then effect an exchange. In some cases, the party insisting on the exchange will personally select, and even negotiate for, the property to be exchanged.

The Service's attacks on such transactions can generally be expected to be based on the theory that the purchaser (B) was acting as an agent for A when he purchased the property to be exchanged. Thus, it will be argued that A really sold his property for cash and then reinvested the proceeds. This argument can be particularly appealing where A was involved in the selection of, and negotiations for, the property which he subsequently accepted in exchange for his property.

Despite the Service's attacks, it seems reasonably clear that a taxpayer can successfully effect a three-party Section 1031 exchange, provided the transaction is set up properly. For example, consider the situation mentioned where A owns a tract of land which B wants to acquire for cash, but A is interested only in a tax-free exchange. In such a case, the proper way to set up the transaction is for A and B to enter into an agreement for A to exchange his land for suitable land to be acquired by B. B should then go out and acquire land suitable to A and exchange it for A's land. Under these facts, the exchange by A will clearly qualify for Section 1031 treatment notwithstanding the fact that B acquired the property turned over to A solely for the purpose of exchanging it for A's property.

Does it make any difference if B has the new property deeded directly to A, rather than to B and then to A? Apparently not, so long as A never had a right to, nor obtained control of, the funds used to purchase the new property since the net effect to A is still an exchange of property for property.[30] Nor does it matter that, pursuant to the exchange agreement between A and B, B deposits the funds to be used for the purchase of the new property in escrow, provided A has no right to, or control over, such funds.[31]

The importance of not allowing A, the party seeking the benefit of Section 1031, any

---

[30] *Three-party Exchanges; How to Assure Tax Benefits by Careful Planning,* Paul E. Anderson, 34 Journal of Taxation, January, 1971, pp. 58–59; *Leslie Q. Coupe,* 52 T.C. 394 (1969), *acq.* 1970–1 C.B. XV; *Haden v. Comm.,* 165 F.2d 588 (5th Cir., 1948).

[31] *Alderson v. Comm.,* 317 F.2d 790 (9th Cir., 1963).

control over the funds to be used for the purchase of the property he is to receive in the exchange cannot be overemphasized, as the *Carlton* case[32] illustrates.

In the *Carlton* case, the taxpayers owned a ranch that a corporation agreed to acquire under a contract which provided that the taxpayers could require the corporation to acquire other land, designated by the taxpayers, to be exchanged for the taxpayer's land in fulfillment of the contract. The taxpayers found suitable land and the corporation entered into agreements to purchase it. Unfortunately, in order to avoid having title to the new property pass through the corporation, the corporation assigned its rights and obligations under the purchase agreements to the taxpayers and paid them the amount required to be paid under such contracts. The taxpayers then fulfilled the purchase agreements by paying the money over to the sellers. Although it was quite clear that the taxpayers had intended a tax-free Section 1031 exchange, the Fifth Circuit found against them and held the transaction to be a taxable sale, rather than a tax-free exchange, because they had received cash, rather than like-kind property for their property.

In the preceding discussion, we assumed that we were dealing with an owner of property who was not interested in selling his property but would consider only a tax-free exchange. There are cases, however, where an owner of property would like to exchange it for other property tax-free, but would be willing to sell it for cash if property suitable to him cannot be located within a reasonable time. Does the taxpayer's willingness to take cash if suitable property can't be found affect his right to claim Section 1031 treatment if suitable property is found?

It would appear fairly clear that it does not, as the *Alderson* case[33] illustrates. In that case, the taxpayers entered into an agreement to sell certain property for cash. Subsequently, they discovered property similar to their own and executed an amendment to the contract so as to provide that in lieu of paying cash, the buyer would acquire and convey to taxpayers the like-kind property which the taxpayers had discovered. This was done and the taxpayers claimed Section 1031 treatment. Although the Tax Court ruled against the taxpayers, the Ninth Circuit reversed the Tax Court and held that the exchange qualified under Section 1031.

As a result of the *Alderson* case, it is now possible for a taxpayer who wants to dispose of certain property, but would like a tax-free exchange if possible, to provide in the agreement for a like-kind exchange if suitable property can be located, and, if not, for a cash purchase.

CONDEMNATION AND INVOLUNTARY CONVERSION

Sometimes property is disposed of involuntarily. This would be the case where it is condemned, or stolen, or destroyed by fire or other casualty. Despite the involuntariness of such dispositions, a taxpayer will normally realize gain or loss, just the same as he would on voluntary dispositions. Section 1033, fortunately, provides an exception to this general rule,

---

[32] *Carlton v. U.S.*, 385 F.2d 238 (5th Cir., 1967).
[33] *Supra* note 31.

insofar as gain is concerned, where the proceeds[34] of the disposition are converted into property similar or related in service or use to the property so converted.

It should be emphasized that Section 1033 applies only to gains; it does not affect the recognition of losses. It should also be emphasized that the concept of "similar in use" is a much more restrictive concept than that of "like kind" and that property can be "like kind" without being "similar in use."

Basically, what Section 1033 provides is that where property has been involuntarily converted, and the owner of the property reinvests the proceeds of such conversion in "property similar or related in service or use to the property so converted" within two years after the close of the first taxable year in which any part of the gain on the conversion is realized, then gain will be recognized only to the extent that the cash proceeds of the conversion exceed the purchase price of the replacement property.

As mentioned, the concept of "similar or related in service or use" is somewhat restrictive, and there has been considerable litigation over its meaning. Anderson[35] points out that some courts have adopted a "functional use" test while others have chosen the "same general class" test. Under the functional use test, which has been adopted by the Third[36] and Ninth[37] circuits, the replacement property must serve the same function as the converted property in order to qualify as "similar in use." Thus, the conversion of a rental parking lot into a rental warehouse would not qualify for Section 1033 treatment[38] nor would the conversion of a rental farm and drive-in theatre into a rental office building.[39]

Other courts have been more liberal and adopted the "same general class" test which focuses on the purpose for which the taxpayer held the property. Thus in *Liant Record, Inc. v. Commissioner*[40] a rental office building was held to be similar to a rental apartment building; and in *Pohn v. Commissioner*,[41] a rental service station was held to be similar to land leased for the construction of apartments. The Internal Revenue Service's position is set forth in Revenue Ruling 64–237[42] in which the Service adopts, with certain restrictions, the "same general class" test for property which is held for rental or investment purposes and the functional use test for property which the owner himself is using.

It is important to note that Section 1033 provides for an exception to the similar use test where real property held for productive use in a trade or business or for investment is taken or sold under the threat of condemnation. In such cases, the like-kind test of Section 1031 is substituted for the similar use test.[43] Section 1033 also allows a taxpayer to satisfy the similar

---

[34] This would be the condemnation award in the case of a condemnation and the insurance proceeds or other recovery where theft or destruction is involved.

[35] Anderson, *Tax Planning of Real Estate*, ALI-ABA Practice Handbook (1970) pp. 141–143.

[36] *McCaffrey v. Comm.*, 275 F.2d 27 (3rd Cir., 1960), *cert. denied*, 363 U.S. 828 (1960).

[37] *Filippini v. U.S.*, 318 F.2d 841 (9th Cir., 1963), *cert. denied*, 375 U.S. 922 (1963).

[38] *Supra* note 36.

[39] *Supra* note 37.

[40] 303 F.2d 326 (2nd Cir., 1962).

[41] 309 F.2d 427 (7th Cir., 1962).

[42] 1964–2 C.B. 319.

[43] Sec. 1033(g). The exception does not cover stock in trade or other property held primarily for sale.

use test by using the proceeds of the condemnation or other involuntary conversion to acquire control of a corporation owning similar property.[44]

Severance Damages and Special Assessments

In condemnation cases, a taxpayer will occasionally find that only a portion of his property has been taken. In such cases, the taxpayer may receive an award not only for the property taken (condemnation award), but also for damage to the remaining property (severance damages).

Where the severance damages are set apart in a separate award, the award, to the extent it is not expended in making improvements (such as fences) required by the severance, is applied in reduction of the basis of the remaining property and to the extent it exceeds such basis it constitutes taxable income.[45] Where the severance damages are not separately set forth or separately designated, then they may not be offset against the basis of the remaining property but must be treated as part of the condemnation award.[46] This can be a significant disadvantage where the condemnation award is not going to be reinvested pursuant to Section 1033, and the basis of the property taken is such that taxable gain will be realized. In such a case, the inability to apply the severance damages against the basis of the remaining property will increase the gain, and corresponding tax, on the property surrendered to the condemning authorities.

As a practical matter, it may be very difficult to separate severance damages from the basic condemnation award since many condemning authorities give only lump sum awards. The Internal Revenue Service has held, however, that even where the award is a lump sum award, severance damages will be considered to be established where the taxpayer receives at the time of settlement from the condemning authority an itemized statement indicating the specific amount of the total award which is for severance damages.[47]

Sometimes the condemnation of particular portions of the taxpayer's property may actually benefit, rather than damage, the remaining portion. In such cases, the condemning authority may make a special assessment against the remaining property. Where this is done, the assessment is offset against the condemnation award for the property taken. Any excess of the assessment over the condemnation award is added to the basis of the retained property.[48]

TAX CONSEQUENCES OF ABANDONMENT

There are times when an owner of property no longer has any use for it but finds himself unable to sell or exchange it. In such cases, he may simply choose to abandon the property.

---

[44] Control is defined to mean ownership of stock possessing at least 80 percent of the total combined voting power of all classes of voting stock and at least 80 percent of the total number of shares of all other classes of stock of the corporation. Sec. 1033(a)(2).

[45] If the damage is to only a portion of the remaining property, then the award can be applied only in reduction of the basis of the damaged portion and the excess constitutes taxable gain. Rev. Rul. 68–37, 1968–1 C.B. 359. See Rev. Rul. 54–575, 1954–2 C.B. 145, which points out the conditions under which such income would be capital gain.

[46] *Marshall C. Allaben*, 35 B.T.A. 327 (1937).

[47] Rev. Rul. 64–183, 1964–1 C.B. 297.

[48] Reg. 1.1033(a)–2(c)(10).

The abandonment of property is not treated as a sale or exchange. Rather, the tax consequences of abandonment are determined by Section 165(a) which allows the owner of the property to claim an ordinary loss to the extent the adjusted basis of the property exceeds the salvage received. In order to claim such a loss, however, there must be some act of abandonment. The execution of a quitclaim deed[49] where real estate is involved would clearly meet this requirement but lesser acts may also suffice. For instance, in *Denman v. Brumbak*[50] the Sixth Circuit allowed an abandonment loss where the evidence of abandonment was the writeoff of the property on the owner's books. Similarly, in *Intercounty Operating Co.*,[51] failure to pay real estate taxes was sufficient under the circumstances to prove abandonment.

---

[49] *William H. Jamison,* 8 T.C. 173 (1947), *acq.* 1947–1 C.B. 2.
[50] 58 F.2d 128 (6th Cir., 1932).
[51] 4 T.C. 55 (1944), *acq.* 1944 C.B. 15.

Chapter 11

The Use of Industrial Development
Bonds in Purchasing or Leasing
Business Property and Equipment

Industrial development bonds have been used extensively by states and their political subdivisions as a means of attracting industry. Since such bonds can be used to finance both leases and purchases of business property and equipment, a discussion of the rules governing their use follows.

BACKGROUND

If we were to take a brief look at the history of industrial development bonds, we would find that they have generally been used to bring companies into an area by offering them the opportunity to rent plants and equipment at a lower than normal rental.

> *Example:* X county wants to attract manufacturing to its area in order to provide more jobs for its inhabitants. It therefore issues $5,000,000 in 4 percent 20-year bonds and then offers to build and rent to Y, a manufacturer seeking a new plant location, a new plant at a rental equal to the amount necessary to pay the principal and interest on the bonds. Since the rental under such an arrangement is usually substantially less than the rental Y would otherwise pay, Y will, assuming other factors are equal, usually accept X's offer and locate the new plant in X county.

Where a company preferred to own rather than lease, this could also be arranged. In such cases, the municipality would acquire the plant or equipment and then sell it to the company on a deferred payment sale with the interest rate on the deferred payments corresponding to the interest rate the municipality was paying on the bonds used to acquire the plant or equipment.

Example: City A would like to have X build its new manufacturing facility in A. In order to induce X to do so, A offers to issue $5,000,000 of 4¼ percent 25-year bonds and use the proceeds to construct a plant for X. Upon completion of the plant, A will sell it to X, at cost, on a deferred payment arrangement, with the deferred payments bearing interest at the rate of 4¼ percent. X accepts A's offer since the interest cost on the deferred payments is substantially less than X would otherwise pay.

The difficulty with such industrial development bonds was that they were in a sense not really municipal obligations. Although the bonds were issued in the name of the municipality or other political subdivision, they were generally either revenue bonds payable only out of the rent which secured them or, in the case where the plant was actually sold, payable only out of the proceeds of the sale and secured only by a mortgage on the plant. Thus, frequently the municipality had no real liability, either direct or indirect, with respect to the obligations. Actually, the real debtor was the company which leased or bought the plant or equipment and the municipality was merely placing its name on the bonds to enable the true borrower to get the lower interest rate normally associated with tax-free bonds.

As time went on, the problem became more acute. Whereas initially both the amount of the individual issues and the total amount of issues were relatively small, as additional communities became aware of the advantages offered by industrial development bonds their popularity increased and more and more communities turned to them as a means of encouraging economic development. This created a number of problems. First, the increased number of industrial development bonds started to put pressure on the interest rates carried by regular municipal bonds and forced municipalities to increase the interest rates on such bonds. Second, the usefulness of industrial development bonds, i.e., as a means of attracting industry to a particular area, was reduced as more and more communities began to offer them. Finally, the federal government began to develop increasing concern over the amount of federal revenue that was being lost through the use of such bonds.

REVERSAL OF TREASURY'S POSITION

The Treasury's concern over the growing use of industrial development bonds ultimately resulted in a reversal of its former position[1] that such bonds qualified as tax exempt under Section 103 of the Internal Revenue Code.

The first indication of the Treasury's change in position came in TIR 972 which was released on March 6, 1968, and announced that the Treasury was re-examining its position that industrial development bonds would be considered "obligations" within the meaning of Section 103, and stated that the Treasury would shortly publish proposed regulations dealing with such bonds. Proposed regulations were issued on March 23, 1968, but these were subsequently withdrawn and new proposed regulations issued in their place. These new

---

[1] See, Revenue Ruling 54–106, 1954–1 C.B. 28; 57–187, 1957–1 C.B. 65; and 63–20, 1963–1 C.B. 24.

proposed regulations, which were to be applicable to industrial development bonds initially sold after March 15, 1968, provided that interest on industrial development bonds would no longer be exempt under Section 103. The theory of the proposed regulations was that such bonds were not obligations of a state or political subdivision within the meaning of Section 103 since the primary obligor was not a state or political subdivision.

THE REVENUE ACT OF 1968

The clamor that greeted the issuance of the Treasury's proposed regulations led Congress to conclude that the problem of industrial development bonds should be handled legislatively rather than administratively, and accordingly the Revenue Act of 1968 incorporated provisions designed to end the "abuses" of industrial development bonds. This was done by providing[2] that, in general, interest on industrial development bonds issued after a certain date would no longer be tax-exempt. It was felt, however, that a complete bar on such bonds would be unwise and therefore exceptions were provided. These exceptions relate to bonds used to provide certain types of facilities and certain small issues.

INDUSTRIAL DEVELOPMENT BONDS: QUALIFICATIONS AND USAGE

The new legislation added section 103(c) to the Internal Revenue Code. Section 103(c) provides that, subject to certain exceptions, the interest on industrial development bonds issued after December 31, 1968, no longer qualifies as tax exempt. Section 103(c)(2) defines industrial development bonds to include any obligation—

A. Which is issued as part of an issue, all or a major portion of the proceeds of which, are to be used directly or indirectly in any trade or business carried on by any person who is not an exempt person (within the meaning of Section 103(c)(3)), and

B. The payment of the principal or interest on which (under the terms of such obligation or any underlying arrangement) is, in whole or in major part—

    (i) Secured by any interest in property used or to be used in a trade or business or in payments in respect of such property, or

    (ii) To be derived from payments in respect of property, or borrowed money, used or to be used in a trade or business.

The term "exempt person" is then defined in Section 103(c)(3) to mean a governmental unit or an organization described in Section 501(c)(3) and exempt from tax under Section 501(a)

---

[2] Sec. 103(c).

(but only with respect to a trade or business carried on by such organization which is not an unrelated trade or business, determined by applying Section 513(a) to such organization).

In reading the definition of industrial development bonds, it is important to note that by defining the term "industrial development bond" to mean any obligation which is issued as part of an issue *where all or a major portion* of the proceeds are to be used directly or indirectly in a trade or business carried on by a person who is not an exempt person, Congress indicated that it is permissible for a portion of the proceeds to be used in the trade or business of a nonexempt person so long as the portion in question does not represent a major portion of the proceeds of the issue.[3]

Unfortunately, both the Statute and the Committee reports fail to define what is meant by a "major portion of the proceeds" and thus the usefulness of this exception is limited to some extent by uncertainty as to its broadness. The regulations remove some of the uncertainty by specifically defining the term "major portion" as the direct or indirect use of more than 25 percent of the proceeds of an issue by nonexempt persons in their trades or businesses.[4] In determining whether the test is satisfied, use by all nonexempt persons must be aggregated. The regulations further provide that where nonexempt persons use a major portion of the output of facilities such as electrical energy, gas or water facilities constructed, reconstructed, or acquired with the proceeds of an issue, the issue will be an industrial development issue if such use has the effect of transferring to the nonexempt persons the benefits of ownership and the burden of paying the debt service on the obligations used directly or indirectly to finance such facilities.[5]

It is also important to note that the fact that a state or local government has pledged its full faith and credit with respect to a particular obligation will not prevent the obligation from being an industrial development bond if the issue is also secured by an interest in property used in a trade or business carried on by any private business user of proceeds of the issue.[6]

The regulations give a number of examples designed to illustrate their application to various situations. Two of the more pertinent examples are set forth below:

> *Example 1:*[7] J, a political subdivision of a state, will issue several series of bonds from time to time and will use the proceeds to rehabilitate urban areas. More than 25 percent of the proceeds of each issue will be used for the rehabilitation and construction of buildings which will be leased or sold to nonexempt persons for use in their trades or businesses. There is no limitation either on the number of issues or the aggregate amount of bonds which may be outstanding. No group of bondholders has any legal claim prior to any other bondholders or creditors with respect to specific revenues of J, and there is no arrangement whereby revenues from a particular project are paid into a trust or constructive trust, or sinking funds, or are otherwise segregated or restricted for the benefit of any group of bondholders. There

---

[3] Reg. 1.103–7(b)(3)(i).
[4] Reg. 1.103–7(b)(3)(iii).
[5] Reg. 1.103–7(b)(5).
[6] Reg. 1.103–7(b)(4).
[7] Reg. 1.103–7(c), Example (14).

is, however, an unconditional obligation by J to pay the principal and interest on each issue of bonds. Further, it is apparent that J requires the revenues from the lease or sale of buildings to nonexempt persons in order to pay in full the principal and interest on the bonds in question. The bonds are industrial development bonds because a major portion of the proceeds will be used in the trades or businesses of nonexempt persons and, pursuant to an underlying arrangement, payment of the principal and interest is, in major part, to be derived from payments in respect of property or borrowed money used in the trades or businesses of nonexempt persons.

Example 2:[8] A. State D and corporation Y enter into an agreement under which Y will lease for 20 years three floors of a 12-story office building to be constructed by D on land which it will acquire. D will occupy the grade floor and the remaining eight floors of the building. The portion of the costs of acquiring the land and constructing the building which are allocated to the space to be leased by Y is not in excess of 25 percent of the total costs of acquiring the land and constructing the building. Such costs, whether attributable to the acquisition of land or the acquisition, construction, reconstruction, or improvement of the building, were allocated to leased space in the same proportion that the reasonable rental value of such leased space bears to the reasonable rental value of the entire building. From the facts and circumstances presented, it is determined that such allocation was reasonable. The agreement between D and Y provides that D will issue $10 million of bonds, that the proceeds of the bond issue will be used to purchase land and construct an office building, that Y will lease the designated floor space for 20 years at its reasonable rental value, and that such rental payments and the building itself shall be security for the bonds. The bonds are not industrial development bonds since a major portion of the proceeds is not to be used, directly or indirectly, in the trade or business of a nonexempt person.

B. The facts are the same as in paragraph A of this example except that corporation Y will lease four floors, and the costs allocated to these floors are in excess of 25 percent of D's investment in the land and building. The bonds are industrial development bonds because (1) a major portion of the building is to be used in the trade or business of a nonexempt person, and (2) a major portion of the principal and interest on such issue is secured by the rental payments on the building.

EXEMPTIONS

In addition to allowing a portion (no more than 25 percent according to the regulations) of the proceeds of state or local bond issues to be used for industrial development purposes, Congress also decided that there were certain cases where the use of the entire proceeds of an issue for industrial development purposes should be permitted notwithstanding the general prohibition against industrial development bonds. These cases can be divided into two categories, i.e., exemptions for specific types of facilities ("exempt activities") and exemptions for "small issues."

---

[8] Reg. 1.103–7(c), Example (7).

Exempt Facilities

The exemption for specific facilities[9] covers any obligation which is issued as part of an issue substantially all the proceeds of which are to be used to provide—

    A. Residential real property for family units,

    B. Sports facilities,

    C. Convention or trade show facilities,

    D. Airports, docks, wharves, mass commuting facilities, parking facilities, or storage or training facilities directly related to any of the foregoing,

    E. Sewage or solid waste disposal facilities or facilities for the local funishing of electric energy or gas,

    F. Air or water pollution control facilities, or

    G. Facilities for the furnishing of water, if available on reasonable demand to members of the general public.

Although the statute itself says nothing about public use, the regulations impose the additional requirement that to qualify under Section 103(c)(4) as an exempt facility, the facility must serve or be available on a regular basis for general public use, or be a part of facilities so used.[10] Thus facilities which are constructed for the use of a limited number of nonexempt persons in their trades or businesses would not qualify even though they are the type facility listed in Section 103(c)(4). Also the Section 103(c)(4) exemption does not apply with respect to an obligation for any period during which it is held by a person who is a substantial user of the facilities or a related person.[11]

> *Example 1:*[12] City D issues $100 million of its bonds and uses the proceeds to finance construction of an airport for the use of the general public. D will own and operate the airport. A major portion of the rentable space in the terminal building is leased on a long-term basis to common carrier and nonscheduled airlines none of which will own any of the bonds in question. The bonds will be secured by the airport landing and runway charges and by payments with respect to such long-term leases from such commercial airlines. Such commercial airline payments are expected to constitute more than 50 percent of the total revenues from the airport. The bonds are industrial development bonds, but since the proceeds are to be used for an airport for use by the general public and by carriers serving the general public, it is an exempt facility under Section 103(c)(4)(D). The result would be the same if D hired an airport management firm to operate the airport.

---

[9] Sec. 103(c)(4).
[10] Reg. 1.103–8(a)(2).
[11] Sec. 103(c)(7).
[12] Reg. 1.103–8(h), Example (5).

Example 2:[13] City E issues $6 million of its bonds and uses the proceeds to finance construction of a landing strip for airplanes to be located adjacent to the factories of corporations Y and Z. The landing strip will be used in the trades or businesses of Y and Z and by any member of the general public wishing to use it. However, due to its location, general public use will be negligible. The lease payments by Y and Z for the use of the facility are the security for the bonds. The bonds are industrial development bonds and the facility is not an exempt facility under Section 103(c)(4)(D) because it is not a facility constructed for general public use.

In addition to the Section 103(c)(4) exemption for specific types of facilities, Section 103(c)(5) provides an exemption for any obligation issued as part of an issue substantially all the proceeds of which are to be used for the acquisition or development of land as the site for an industrial park.

The term "development of land" is defined to include the providing of "water, sewage, drainage or similar facilities, or transportation, power, or communication facilities, which are incidental to the use of the site as an industrial park, but, except with respect to such facilities, does not include the provision of structures or buildings."

Example 1:[14] City A and corporations X, Y, and Z (unrelated companies) enter into an arrangement under which A is to acquire a tract of land suitable for use as an industrial park. The arrangement provides that: (1) A will issue $10 million of bonds to be used for the acquisition and development of a suitable tract of land; (2) the tract will be controlled and administered by A, pursuant to a comprehensive zoning plan, for the use of a group of enterprises; (3) A will install necessary water, sewer, and drainage facilities on the tract; (4) A will sell substantial portions of the developed tract to X for use as a factory site and to Y for use as a warehouse site; (5) A will lease a sizable portion of the tract to Z for 20 years as a distribution center site; and (6) the developed tract and the proceeds from the sale or lease or parts of the tract will be the security for the bonds. The bonds are industrial development bonds. Since, however, the proceeds of the issue are to be used for the acquisition and development of a tract of land as the site for an industrial park, the issue is exempt under Section 103(c)(5) unless the provisions of Section 103(c)(7) apply. (Section 103(c)(7) provides that the exceptions allowed by paragraphs 4, 5 and 6 of 103(c) shall not apply with respect to an obligation for any period during which it is held by a person who is a substantial user of the facilities or a related person.)

Example 2:[15] The facts are the same as in example (1) except that $1 million of the proceeds of the $10 million issue are to be used for the construction of a factory by corporation W or X. The bonds are industrial development bonds. Under these circumstances, substantially all of the proceeds are treated as used or to be used for the acquisition and development of a tract of land as the site for an industrial park described in Section 103(c)(5), and the issue will still be exempt unless the provisions of Section 103(c)(7) apply.

---

[13] Reg. 1.103–8(h), Example (6).
[14] Reg. 1.103–9(d), Example (1).
[15] Reg. 1.103–9(d), Example (2).

Small Issues—the $1,000,000 Exemption

Although the specific exemptions mentioned above will be of help to some businesses, the important exemption from the viewpoint of most businessmen is the exemption for small issues.

The exemption for small issues is set forth in Section 103(c)(6), which defines a small issue as an issue:

> . . . the aggregate authorized face amount of which is $1,000,000 or less and substantially all the proceeds of which are to be used (i) for the acquisition, construction, reconstruction, or improvement of land or property of a character subject to the allowance for depreciation, or (ii) to redeem part or all of a prior issue which was issued for purposes described in clause (i) or this clause.[16]

The regulations then go on to give the following examples of issues qualifying for the exemption.

> *Example 1:*[17] County A and corporation X enter into an arrangement under which the county will provide a factory which X will lease for 25 years. The arrangement provides (1) that A will issue $1 million of bonds on March 1, 1970, (2) that the proceeds of the bond issue will be used to acquire land in County A (but not in an incorporated municipality) and to construct and equip a factory on such land in accordance with X's specifications, (3) that X will rent the facility for 25 years at an annual rental equal to the amount necessary to amortize the principal and pay the interest on the outstanding bonds and (4) that such payments by X and the facility itself shall be the security for the bonds. Although the bonds issued are industrial development bonds, the bonds are an exempt small issue under Section 103(c)(6)(A) and this section [of the regulations] since the aggregate authorized face amount of the bond issue is $1 million or less and all of the proceeds of the bond issue are to be used to acquire and improve land and acquire and construct depreciable property. The result would be the same if the arrangement provided that X would purchase the facility from A.

> *Example 2:*[18] The facts are the same as in example (1) except that, instead of acquiring land and constructing a new factory, the arrangement provides that A will acquire a vacant existing factory building and rebuild and equip the building in accordance with X's specifications. The bonds are an exempt small issue for the same reasons as in example (1).

As the definition of "small issue" indicates, the exemption also covers an issue of $1,000,000 or less, the proceeds of which are to be used to redeem all or part of a prior exempt small issue or prior refunding issue. The exemption does not apply, however, where the proceeds are

---

[16] Sec. 103(c)(6)(A).
[17] Reg. 1.103–10(f), Example (1).
[18] Reg. 1.103–10(f), Example (2).

loaned to a borrower for use as working capital or to finance the purchase of inventory unless the amount used for such purposes is an insubstantial part of such proceeds.[19]

In applying the $1,000,000 limitation to a particular new issue, the face amount of prior outstanding small issues, to the extent they are not to be redeemed from the current issue, must be aggregated with the face amount of the new issue. The aggregation is made, however, only to the extent that the proceeds of the new issue are to be used primarily with respect to facilities located in the same incorporated municipality or located in the same county (but not in any incorporated municipality) as the facilities for which the prior issue was used, and then only if the principal user of the facilities is the same or a related person.[20] What this means is that a municipality can issue as many bonds not exceeding $1,000,000 per issue as it cares to, provided the person for whom the facilities are to be constructed or acquired does not have other facilities constructed with the proceeds of prior exempt small issues, whether issued by the same issuer or not, in the same incorporated municipality or located in the same county (but not in any incorporated municipality). If the prior issue was issued before the effective date of the statute (May 1, 1968), the prior facilities are ignored.[21]

> *Example 1:* City X agrees to issue $1,000,000 in bonds and lend the proceeds to company A for use in acquiring a new plant in city X. X also agrees to issue another $1,000,000 in bonds, the proceeds of which will be used by company B in building a new factory in city X. A and B are not related to each other and neither has any other facilities in city X. Both issues will qualify for the small issue exemption since aggregation would be required only if A and B were related or they had other facilities in City X which were acquired with the proceeds of a prior exempt small issue.

> *Example 2:* City Y, an incorporated municipality, agrees to issue $500,000 of bonds the proceeds of which are to be loaned to company A for use in constructing a plant in city Y. A has another plant in city Y which was constructed with the proceeds of a $1,000,000 bond issue by the state in which city Y is located. $500,000 of face value of these bonds is still outstanding. Since the aggregate of the new issue ($500,000) plus the face amount of the outstanding bonds used to construct the older plant ($500,000) does not exceed $1,000,000 the new issue will qualify as tax exempt under the small issue exemption. If $600,000 of the prior issue were still outstanding, then the new issue would not qualify for the small issue exemption since the aggregate of the outstanding portion of the old issue and the new issue would be in excess of $1,000,000. The only exception would be where the prior issue was issued before May 1, 1968. Bonds issued before May 1, 1968, (the effective date of the changes affecting industrial development bonds) do not count against the $1,000,000 limit.

As pointed out, the exemption for small issues does not apply if more than an insubstantial amount of the proceeds of an issue is loaned to a borrower for use as working capital or to

---

[19] Reg. 1.103–10(b)(ii).

[20] Sec. 103(c)(6)(B). The term "related person" is defined in Sec. 103(c)(6)(C) to include persons related within the meaning of Sections 267 or 707(b) or members of a controlled group within the meaning of Section 1563(a) except that 50 percent is substituted where 80 percent appears therein.

[21] Reg. 1.103–10(d)(3).

finance inventory.[22] Although the regulations do not define what is meant by "insubstantial," one of the examples indicates that the use of $95,000 out of $1,000,000 of proceeds for working capital would not prevent an issue from being tax-exempt.[23]

Small Issues—the $5,000,000 Exemption

In lieu of the $1,000,000 limitation on industrial development bonds, an issuer may elect to have a $5,000,000 limitation apply provided certain requirements are met.[24]

As with the $1,000,000 exemption, prior issues must be taken into consideration in determining whether the $5,000,000 limitation has been exceeded. The rules for taking into account prior issues are the same for the $5,000,000 limitation as for the $1,000,000 exemption.[25]

Also, as with the $1,000,000 exemption, the proceeds of the issue must be used for the acquisition, construction, or improvement of land or property of a character subject to the allowance for depreciation under Section 167, or to redeem all or part of a prior issue utilized for such purposes or a prior refunding issue. In addition to these requirements, however, in computing the $5,000,000 limitation, certain capital expenditures paid or incurred during the six-year period beginning three years before the date of the issue in question and ending three years after such date must also be taken into consideration. The capital expenditures which must be taken into consideration are facilities—

1. Located in the same incorporated municipality or located in the same county (but not in any incorporated municipality), and

2. The principal user of which is or will be the same person or two or more related persons, and

3. Which were not financed out of prior small issues.

For purposes of (1), the determination of whether or not facilities are located in the same governmental unit is to be made as of the date of issue of the issue in question.[26]

> *Example:* A, a corporation, wishes to build a $4,000,000 plant in city X borrowing the necessary funds from city X, an incorporated municipality. X obtains the funds by issuing $4,000,000 in bonds on January 1, 1974, and makes an election to have the $5,000,000 limitation apply. If A has not made any capital expenditures in city X during the three years prior to January 1, 1974, and does not make any in the three years following, the $5,000,000 limitation will apply and the bonds will be tax exempt. If, however, A had constructed a $3,000,000 factory in city X in 1972, the $5,000,000 exemption would not

---

[22] Reg. 1.103–10(b)(1)(ii).
[23] Reg. 1.103–10(f), Example (6).
[24] Sec. 103(c)(6)(D).
[25] Reg. 1.103–10(d).
[26] Sec. 103(c)(6)(D) and (E).

apply since the total of the prior capital expenditures and the issue in question would exceed $5,000,000.

The only capital expenditures which are not required to be taken into account are those:

1. To replace property destroyed or damaged by fire, storm, or other casualty, to the extent of the fair market value of the property replaced,

2. Required by a change made after the date of issue of the issue in question in a Federal or State law or local ordinance of general application or required by a change made after such date in rules and regulations of general application issued under such a law or ordinance, or

3. Required by circumstances which could not be reasonably foreseen on such date of issue or arising out of a mistake of law or fact (but the aggregate amount of expenditures not taken into account under this clause with respect to any issue shall not exceed $1,000,000).[27]

One problem associated with the $5,000,000 limitation is that since expenditures within the three-year period following the date of issue are taken into consideration, an issue which was exempt may become taxable. Although the loss of tax exemption is not retroactive, i.e., it begins only with the date on which the capital expenditures in question are paid or incurred, the fact remains that a person who bought a tax-free obligation may suddenly find himself holding a bond which is no longer tax-free. One way of avoiding this problem, to some extent, is either to require the user of the facility to provide the funds necessary for redemption of the issue in the event subsequent capital expenditures disqualify the issue, or to provide for an increased rental which will allow an increase in the interest rate sufficient to overcome the loss of the tax exemption. There should be no difficulty with such provisions, as the following example, which is taken from the regulations[28] indicates:

> *Example:* City C and corporation Y enter into an arrangement under which C will provide a factory that Y will lease for 25 years. The arrangement provides (1) that C will issue $4 million of bonds on March 1, 1969, after making the election under Section 103(c)(6)(D) and paragraph (b)(2) of Reg. 1.103–10, (2) that the proceeds of the bond issue will be used to acquire land in the city and to construct and equip a factory on such land in accordance with Y's specifications, (3) that Y will rent the facilities for 25 years at an annual rental equal to the amount necessary to amortize the principal and pay the interest on the outstanding bonds, (4) that such payments by Y and the facility itself shall be the security for the bonds, and (5) that, if corporation Y pays or incurs capital expenditures in excess of $1 million within 3 years from the date of issue which disqualify the bonds as an exempt small issue under Section 103(c)(6)(D), it will either furnish funds to C to redeem such bonds at

---

[27] Sec. 103(c)(6)(F).
[28] Reg. 1.103–10(f), Example (9).

par or at a premium, or increase the rental payments to C in an amount sufficient to pay a premium interest rate. Although the bonds issued are industrial development bonds, they are an exempt small issue under Section 103(c)(6)(A) by reason of the election under Section 103(c)(6)(D) and paragraph (b)(2) of this section, since the aggregate authorized face amount of the bond issue is $5 million or less and all of the proceeds of the bond issue are to be used to acquire and improve land and acquire and construct depreciable property. The provisions for redemption of the bonds or an increase in rental if the bonds are disqualified as an exempt small issue under Section 103(c)(6)(A) will not disqualify an otherwise valid election under Section 103(c)(6)(D) and paragraph (b)(2) of this section.

BONDS HELD BY SUBSTANTIAL USERS

It is important to realize that the exemptions under Section 103(c)(4)(5) and (6) for exempt facilities and small issues do not apply with respect to an obligation during any period during which it is held either by a person who is a substantial user of the facilities for which the proceeds of the obligation were used or by a related person within the meaning of Section 103(c)(6)(C).[29] In general, a substantial user of a facility includes any nonexempt person who regularly uses a part of such facility in his trade or business. However, unless a facility, or a part thereof, is constructed, reconstructed, or acquired specifically for a nonexempt person or persons, such a nonexempt person shall be considered to be a substantial user of a facility only if (1) the gross revenue derived by such user with respect to such facility is more than 5 percent of the total revenue derived by all users of such facility, or (2) the amount of area of the facility occupied by such user is more than 5 percent of the entire usable area of the facility.[30]

> *Example:*[31] City D issues $25 million of its revenue bonds and will use $10 million of the proceeds to finance construction of a sports facility which qualifies as an exempt facility under Section 103(c)(4)(B) and paragraph (c) of §1.103–8; $8 million to acquire and develop land as the site for an industrial park within the meaning of Section 103(c)(5) and §1.103–9; and $7 million to finance the construction of an office building to be used exclusively by the city, an exempt person. The revenues from the sports facility and the industrial park and all the facilities themselves will be the security for the bonds. The sports facility and the industrial park sites will be used in the trades or businesses of nonexempt persons. The bonds are industrial development bonds, but under the provisions of paragraph (a)(1) of §1.103–8 and paragraph (a) of §1.103–9, the interest on the $25 million issue will not be includable in gross income. However, the interest on bonds held shall be includable in the gross income of a substantial user of either the sports facility or the industrial park if such substantial user holds any of the obligations of the $25 million issue. The 5-percent limitations of paragraph (b) of Reg. 1.103–11 are applied separately with respect to each facility.

---

[29] Reg. 1.103–11(a).
[30] Reg. 1.103–11(b).
[31] Reg. 1.103–11(c), Example (5).

SUBJECT INDEX

INDEX OF CASES